STOCK
TRADER'S
ALMANAC
2 O O 5

D1608574

Yale Hirsch & Jeffrey A. Hirsch

WILEY

John Wiley & Sons, Inc.

The Hirsch Organization Inc. ♦ 184 Central Avenue ♦ Old Tappan NJ 07675
www.hirschorg.com

Published by John Wiley & Sons, Inc., Hoboken, New Jersey
Published simultaneously in Canada

Editor in Chief	Jeffrey A. Hirsch
Editor at Large	Yale Hirsch
Vice President	J. Taylor Brown
Associate Editor	Robert Cardwell
Data Coordinator	Christopher Mistal
Web Development	Nexgen (nexgenus.com)
Graphic Design	Darlene Dion Design

For general information on our other products and services, or technical support, please contact our Customer Care Department within the United States at 800-762-2974, outside the United States at 317-572-3993 or fax 317-572-4002.

Wiley also publishes its books in a variety of electronic formats. Some content that appears in print may not be available in electronic books.

For more information about Wiley products, visit our Web site at www.wiley.com.

ISBN: 0-471-64936-8

Printed in the United States of America

10 9 8 7 6 5 4 3 2 1

This Thirty-Eighth Edition is respectfully dedicated to:

Bob Pisani

A CNBC On-Air Stocks Editor since 1990, who reports on the Markets from the floor of the New York Stock Exchange. Nominated twice for a CableACE Award, in 1993 and 1995, he is a voice of reason during turbulent markets, providing excellent insight to viewers while conveying market seasonality and recurring patterns with unmatched clarity.

The *Stock Trader's Almanac®* is an organizer. Its wealth of information is presented on a calendar basis. The Almanac puts investing in a business framework and makes investing easier because it:

- updates investment knowledge and informs you of new techniques and tools.
- is a monthly reminder and refresher course.
- alerts you to both seasonal opportunities and dangers.
- furnishes an historical viewpoint by providing pertinent statistics on past market performance.
- supplies forms necessary for portfolio planning, record keeping and tax preparation.

We are constantly searching for new insights and nuances about the stock market and welcome any suggestions from our readers.

Have a healthy and prosperous 2005!

 Signifies THIRD FRIDAY OF THE MONTH on calendar pages and alerts you to extraordinary volatility due to expiration of equity and index options and index futures contracts. Triple-witching days appear during March, June, September and December.

 The BULL SYMBOL on calendar pages signifies very favorable trading days based on the S&P 500 rising 60% or more of the time on a particular trading day during the 21-year period January 1983 to December 2003 (see <u>Recent</u> S&P 500 Market Probability Calendar 2005, page 123). Market Probability Calendars for the NASDAQ, Dow and S&P for other time periods appear on pages 120-122. Other seasonalities near the ends, beginnings and middles of months; options expirations; around holidays; and other times are noted for *Almanac* investors' convenience on the weekly planner pages.

INTRODUCTION TO THE THIRTY-EIGHTH EDITION

We are pleased and proud to introduce the Thirty-Eighth Edition of the *Stock Trader's Almanac*. The Almanac provides you with the necessary tools to invest successfully in the twenty-first century.

J.P. Morgan's classic retort "Stocks will fluctuate" is often quoted with a wink-of-the-eye implication that the only prediction one can make about the stock market is that it will go up, down, or sideways. Many investors agree that no one ever really knows which way the market will move. Nothing could be further from the truth. We discovered that while stocks do indeed fluctuate, they do so in well-defined, often predictable, patterns. These patterns recur too frequently to be the result of chance or coincidence. How else do we explain that since 1950 practically all the gains in the market were made during November through April compared to almost nothing May through October? (See page 50.)

The Almanac is a practical investment tool. Its wealth of information is organized on a calendar basis. It alerts you to those little-known market patterns and tendencies on which shrewd professionals enhance profit potential.

You will be able to forecast market trends with accuracy and confidence when you use the Almanac to help you understand:

• How our presidential elections affect the economy and the stock market — just as the moon affects the tides. Many investors have made fortunes following the political cycle. You can be sure that money managers who control billions of millions of dollars are also political cycle watchers. Astute people do not ignore a pattern that has been working effectively throughout most of our economic history.

• How the passage of the Twentieth Amendment to the Constitution fathered the January Barometer. This barometer has an outstanding record for predicting the general course of the stock market each year with only five major errors since 1950 for a 90.7% accuracy ratio.

• Why there is a significant market bias at certain times of the day, week, month and year.

Even if you are an investor who pays scant attention to cycles, indicators and patterns, your investment survival could hinge on your interpretation of one of the recurring patterns found within these pages. One of the most intriguing and important patterns is the symbiotic relationship between Washington and Wall Street. Aside from the potential profitability in seasonal patterns, there's the pure joy of seeing the market very often do just what you expected.

There has never been a losing "fifth" year since 1885 (page 126). Years ending in five have the best record, as the strongest bull markets tend to favor the middle years of decades. But 2005 is a Post-Election year and investors have often "paid the piper" (page 36) the first year of a President's term. In addition the struggling economy, swelling federal deficit, high oil and commodity prices, inflation and interest rates are likely to weigh heavily on stock prices.

We are observing the potential formation of an ominous pattern — Three Peaks and Domed House. Developed by the late George Lindsay, this pattern, one of the most extraordinary in history, has occurred at almost every major market top as it did in 2000. Presently, the major averages have traced out the Three Peaks half of the pattern with tops in February (January for NASDAQ), April and June — the crucial separating decline section is now potentially underway. That could put the Domed House top sometime in the first half of 2005. We'll be monitoring to see if this pattern pans out in our *Almanac Investor* newsletter and at *stocktradersalmanac.com*.

Barring an unforeseen exogenous event that causes the market to collapse in the rest of 2004, by mid-2005 the bull cycle in play since the October 2002 bottom will likely be wearing thin and Wall Street as well as Washington will be wrestling with a host of economic and geopolitical hurdles, making the prospects for 2005 flat to down.

— Jeffrey A. Hirsch, August 9, 2004

THE 2005 STOCK TRADER'S ALMANAC

CONTENTS

DIRECTORY OF TRADING PATTERNS & DATABANK

STRATEGY PLANNING & RECORD SECTION

2005 STRATEGY CALENDAR
(Option expiration dates encircled)

	MONDAY	TUESDAY	WEDNESDAY	THURSDAY	FRIDAY	SATURDAY	SUNDAY
JANUARY	27	28	29	30	31	1 JANUARY New Year's Day	2
	3	4	5	6	7	8	9
	10	11	12	13	14	15	16
	17 Martin Luther King Day	18	19	20	(21)	22	23
	24	25	26	27	28	29	30
FEBRUARY	31	1 FEBRUARY	2	3	4	5	6
	7	8	9 Ash Wednesday	10	11	12	13
	14 ♥	15	16	17	(18)	19	20
	21 Presidents' Day	22	23	24	25	26	27
MARCH	28	1 MARCH	2	3	4	5	6
	7	8	9	10	11	12	13
	14	15	16	17 ♣ St. Patrick's Day	(18)	19	20
	21	22	23	24	25 Good Friday	26	27 Easter
APRIL	28	29	30	31	1 APRIL	2	3 Daylight Saving Time Begins
	4	5	6	7	8	9	10
	11	12	13	14	(15)	16	17
	18	19	20	21	22	23	24 Passover
	25	26	27	28	29	30	1 MAY
MAY	2	3	4	5	6	7	8 Mother's Day
	9	10	11	12	13	14	15
	16	17	18	19	(20)	21	22
	23	24	25	26	27	28	29
JUNE	30 Memorial Day	31	1 JUNE	2	3	4	5
	6	7	8	9	10	11	12
	13	14	15	16	(17)	18	19 Father's Day
	20	21	22	23	24	25	26

Market closed on shaded weekdays; closes early when half-shaded.

2005 STRATEGY CALENDAR
(Option expiration dates encircled)

MONDAY	TUESDAY	WEDNESDAY	THURSDAY	FRIDAY	SATURDAY	SUNDAY	
27	28	29	30	1 JULY	2	3	
4 Independence Day	5	6	7	8	9	10	JULY
11	12	13	14	(15)	16	17	
18	19	20	21	22	23	24	
25	26	27	28	29	30	31	
1 AUGUST	2	3	4	5	6	7	
8	9	10	11	12	13	14	AUGUST
15	16	17	18	(19)	20	21	
22	23	24	25	26	27	28	
29	30	31	1 SEPTEMBER	2	3	4	
5 Labor Day	6	7	8	9	10	11	SEPTEMBER
12	13	14	15	(16)	17	18	
19	20	21	22	23	24	25	
26	27	28	29	30	1 OCTOBER	2	
3	4 Rosh Hashanah	5	6	7	8	9	OCTOBER
10 Columbus Day	11	12	13 Yom Kippur	14	15	16	
17	18	19	20	(21)	22	23	
24	25	26	27	28	29	30 Daylight Saving Time Ends	
31 🎃	1 NOVEMBER	2	3	4	5	6	NOVEMBER
7	8 Election Day	9	10	11 Veterans' Day	12	13	
14	15	16	17	(18)	19	20	
21	22	23	24 Thanksgiving	25	26	27	
28	29	30	1 DECEMBER	2	3	4	DECEMBER
5	6	7	8	9	10	11	
12	13	14	15	(16)	17	18	
19	20	21	22	23	24	25 Christmas	
26 Chanukah	27	28	29	30	31		

PROGNOSTICATING TOOLS AND PATTERNS FOR 2005

For 38 years, Almanac readers have profited from being able to predict the timing of the Political Market Cycle. To help you gain perspective in 2005, a Post-Presidential Election year, a valuable array of tables, charts and pertinent information can be found on the pages noted.

THE FIFTH YEAR OF DECADES

No losers in 120 years. In every "fifth" year since 1885 the market has advanced. Bull markets have favored the middle of decades, giving years ending in five the best record. *Page 26.*

MARKET CHARTS OF POST-PRESIDENTIAL ELECTION YEARS

Individual charts for each of the last 21 Post-Presidential Election years, including winners. *Page 28.*

MARKET BEHAVIOR WHEN WHITE HOUSE CHANGES HANDS

Democrats ousting Republicans have fared better in Post-Election years than when the reverse occurred. The market will have challenges in 2005 as either party deals with the recovery and security. *Page 34.*

POST-ELECTION YEARS: PAYING THE PIPER

Graphic presentation of the four-year cycle with Post-Election years highlighted, along with capsule comments on the record since 1913. *Page 36.*

UNDER DEMOCRATS $10,000 GROWS TO $279,705
BUT ONLY TO $78,699 UNDER THE REPUBLICANS

Democrats scored greater gains the first half of the 20th century. The parties were more evenly matched in the second half. Republicans were less inflationary as most major wars (which produce inflation) began under the Democrats. *Page 42.*

GRIDLOCK ON CAPITOL HILL IS BEST FOR THE MARKETS

Of all the possible combinations in Washington the market has performed best with a Democratic President and a Republican Congress. *Page 68.*

POLITICS AND STOCK MARKETS, THE 171-YEAR
SAGA CONTINUES

Stock prices have been impacted by presidential elections for 171 years, gaining 742.8% in second halves of terms vs. 227.6% in first halves. *Page 127.*

DECEMBER 2004

MONDAY

20

There has never been a commercial technology like this (Internet)
in the history of the world, whereby the minute you adopt it,
it forces you to think and act globally.
— Robert Hormats (Goldman, Sachs)

TUESDAY

21

Prosperity is a great teacher; adversity a greater.
— William Hazlitt (English essayist, 1778-1830)

Watch for Santa Claus Rally (page 116)   **WEDNESDAY**

 # 22

I invest in people, not ideas;
I want to see fire in the belly and intellect.
— Arthur Rock

Trading day before Christmas Dow up 8 of last 13,   **THURSDAY**
but last 3 weak (pages 86 & 110)   # 23

In nature there are no rewards or punishments;
there are consequences.
— Horace Annesley Vachell (*The Face of Clay*, 1861-1955)

(Market Closed)   **FRIDAY**

24

Successful innovation is not a feat of intellect, but of will.
— Joseph A. Schumpeter (Austrian-American economist,
Theory of Economic Development, 1883-1950)

Christmas Day   **SATURDAY**

25

SUNDAY

26

JANUARY ALMANAC

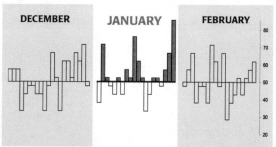

JANUARY						
S	M	T	W	T	F	S
						1
2	3	4	5	6	7	8
9	10	11	12	13	14	15
16	17	18	19	20	21	22
23	24	25	26	27	28	29
30	31					

FEBRUARY						
S	M	T	W	T	F	S
		1	2	3	4	5
6	7	8	9	10	11	12
13	14	15	16	17	18	19
20	21	22	23	24	25	26
27	28					

Market Probability Chart above is a graphic representation of the Market Probability Calendar on page 123.

◆ January Barometer's perfect record in odd-numbered years derailed by 2001 (2 Jan rate cuts and 9/11) and 2003 (down ahead of Iraq war) ◆ Excluding 2001, last 13 Post-Election years followed January's direction ◆ Every down January on the S&P since 1950, *without exception*, preceded a new or extended bear market, or a flat market (page 44), including six down Post-Election Year Januarys ◆ January's first five days tend to decline in a bear market and have a better record forecasting Post-Election years (page 14) ◆ November, December and January constitute the year's best three-month span, a 4.9% S&P gain, 21.1% annualized (page 48) ◆ At this rate, $1000 since 1950 grew to over $35 million ◆ January NASDAQ powerful 3.9% since 1971 (page 54) ◆ "January Effect" now starts in mid-December and favors small-cap stocks (pages 106, 114).

JANUARY DAILY POINT CHANGES DOW JONES INDUSTRIALS

Previous Month	1995	1996	1997	1998	1999	2000	2001	2002	2003	2004
Close	3834.44	5117.12	6448.27	7908.25	9181.43	11497.12	10786.85	10021.50	8341.63	10453.92
1	H	H	H	H	H	H	H	H	H	H
2	Closed	60.33	− 5.78	56.79	−	−	− 140.70	51.90	265.89	− 44.07
3	4.04	16.62	101.60	−	−	− 139.61	299.60	98.74	− 5.83	−
4	19.17	− 20.23	−	−	2.84	− 359.58	− 33.34	87.60	−	−
5	− 6.73	7.59	−	13.95	126.92	124.72	− 250.40	−	−	134.22
6	16.49	−	23.09	− 72.74	233.78	130.61	−	−	171.88	− 5.41
7	−	−	33.48	− 3.98	− 7.21	269.30	−	− 62.69	− 32.98	− 9.63
8	−	16.25	− 51.18	− 99.65	105.56	−	− 40.66	− 46.50	− 145.28	63.41
9	− 6.06	− 67.55	76.19	− 222.20	−	−	− 48.80	− 56.46	180.87	− 133.55
10	5.39	− 97.19	78.12	−	−	49.64	31.72	− 26.23	8.71	−
11	− 4.71	32.16	−	−	− 23.43	− 61.12	5.28	− 80.33	−	−
12	− 3.03	− 3.98	−	66.76	− 145.21	40.02	− 84.17	−	−	26.29
13	49.46	−	5.39	84.95	− 125.12	31.33	−	−	1.09	− 58.00
14	−	−	53.11	52.56	− 228.63	140.55	−	− 96.11	56.64	111.19
15	−	− 17.34	− 35.41	− 92.92	219.62	−	H	32.73	− 119.44	15.48
16	23.88	44.44	38.49	61.78	−	−	127.28	− 211.88	− 25.31	46.66
17	− 1.68	− 21.32	67.73	−	−	H	− 68.32	137.77	− 111.13	−
18	− 1.68	57.45	−	−	H	− 162.26	93.94	− 78.19	−	−
19	− 46.77	60.33	−	H	14.67	− 71.36	− 90.69	−	−	H
20	− 12.78	−	10.77	119.57	− 19.31	− 138.06	−	−	H	− 71.85
21	−	−	40.03	− 78.72	− 71.83	− 99.59	−	H	− 143.84	94.96
22	−	34.68	− 33.87	− 63.52	− 143.41	−	− 9.35	− 58.05	− 124.17	− 0.44
23	− 2.02	− 27.09	− 94.28	− 30.14	−	−	71.57	17.16	50.74	− 54.89
24	− 4.71	50.57	− 59.27	−	−	− 243.54	− 2.84	65.11	− 238.46	−
25	8.75	− 26.01	−	−	82.65	21.72	82.55	44.01	−	−
26	− 1.01	54.92	−	12.20	121.26	3.10	− 69.54	−	−	134.22
27	− 12.45	−	− 35.79	102.14	− 124.35	− 4.97	−	−	− 141.45	− 92.59
28	−	−	− 4.61	100.39	81.10	− 289.15	−	25.67	99.28	− 141.55
29	−	33.23	84.66	57.55	77.50	−	42.21	− 247.51	21.87	41.92
30	− 25.91	76.23	83.12	− 66.52	−	−	179.01	144.62	− 165.58	− 22.22
31	11.78	14.09	− 10.77	−	−	201.66	6.16	157.14	108.68	−
Close	3843.86	5395.30	6813.09	7906.50	9358.83	10940.53	10887.36	9920.00	8053.81	10488.07
Change	9.42	278.18	364.82	− 1.75	177.40	− 556.59	100.51	− 101.50	− 287.82	34.15

20th Amendment made "Lame Ducks" disappear
Now, "As January goes, so goes the odd-numbered year"

DECEMBER 2004/JANUARY 2005

MONDAY
27

First trading day after Christmas
Dow up 11 of last 13

TUESDAY
 ## 28

New Lows perform better when selected last
settlement day of year (page 112)

WEDNESDAY
 ## 29

Almanac Investor FREE LUNCH Menu of New
Lows served to subscribers,
visit stocktradersalmanac.com for details

THURSDAY
 ## 30

FRIDAY
31

(Shortened Trading Day)
Last day of year NASDAQ up 29 of 33, but down last 4
Dow down 5 of last 8, with some big losers

SATURDAY
1

New Year's Day

SUNDAY
2

January Sector Seasonalities:
Bullish: Banking, Semiconductor;
Bearish: Natural Gas, Utilities (page 118)

JANUARY'S FIRST FIVE DAYS AN "EARLY WARNING" SYSTEM

Of the 34 up First Five Days since 1950, 29 were followed by full-year gains for an 85.3% accuracy ratio and a 13.8% average gain in those 34 years. Of the five exceptions, 1994 was a flat year and four were war-related: Vietnam military spending delayed start of 1966 bear market; ceasefire imminence in early 1973 raised stocks temporarily; Saddam Hussein turned 1990 into a bear; and the war on terrorism, instability in the Near and Middle East and corporate malfeasance shaped 2002 into one of the worst years on record. The 20 down First Five Days were followed by 10 up years and 10 down (50% accurate).

In 8 of the last 13 Post-Election Years the S&P 500 posted a loss for January's First Five Days. Six were followed by full-year losses averaging -11.1%. 1993 rebounded 7.1% after the sluggish 1992 economy that factored into Bush Senior's ouster and 1985 followed the trend of no losing "5" years *(see page 126)*. Five Post-Election First Five Days showed gains and only one subsequent full year, 1973, was a loser. This was the start of the previous major bear — caused by Vietnam, Watergate and OPEC. The other four years gained 22.6% on average.

THE FIRST-FIVE-DAYS-IN-JANUARY INDICATOR

	Chronological Data				Ranked By Performance		
	Previous Year's Close	January 5th Day	5-Day Change	Year Change	Rank		5-Day Change	Year Change
1950	16.76	17.09	2.0%	21.8%	1	1987	6.2%	2.0%
1951	20.41	20.88	2.3	16.5	2	1976	4.9	19.1
1952	23.77	23.91	0.6	11.8	3	1999	3.7	19.5
1953	26.57	26.33	−0.9	− 6.6	4	2003	3.4	26.4
1954	24.81	24.93	0.5	45.0	5	1983	3.3	17.3
1955	35.98	35.33	−1.8	26.4	6	1967	3.1	20.1
1956	45.48	44.51	−2.1	2.6	7	1979	2.8	12.3
1957	46.67	46.25	−0.9	−14.3	8	1963	2.6	18.9
1958	39.99	40.99	2.5	38.1	9	1958	2.5	38.1
1959	55.21	55.40	0.3	8.5	10	1984	2.4	1.4
1960	59.89	59.50	−0.7	− 3.0	11	1951	2.3	16.5
1961	58.11	58.81	1.2	23.1	12	1975	2.2	31.5
1962	71.55	69.12	−3.4	−11.8	13	1950	2.0	21.8
1963	63.10	64.74	2.6	18.9	14	2004	1.8	??
1964	75.02	76.00	1.3	13.0	15	1973	1.5	−17.4
1965	84.75	85.37	0.7	9.1	16	1972	1.4	15.6
1966	92.43	93.14	0.8	−13.1	17	1964	1.3	13.0
1967	80.33	82.81	3.1	20.1	18	1961	1.2	23.1
1968	96.47	96.62	0.2	7.7	19	1989	1.2	27.3
1969	103.86	100.80	−2.9	−11.4	20	2002	1.1	−23.4
1970	92.06	92.68	0.7	0.1	21	1997	1.0	31.0
1971	92.15	92.19	0.04	10.8	22	1980	0.9	25.8
1972	102.09	103.47	1.4	15.6	23	1966	0.8	−13.1
1973	118.05	119.85	1.5	−17.4	24	1994	0.7	− 1.5
1974	97.55	96.12	−1.5	−29.7	25	1965	0.7	9.1
1975	68.56	70.04	2.2	31.5	26	1970	0.7	0.1
1976	90.19	94.58	4.9	19.1	27	1952	0.6	11.8
1977	107.46	105.01	−2.3	−11.5	28	1954	0.5	45.0
1978	95.10	90.64	−4.7	1.1	29	1996	0.4	20.3
1979	96.11	98.80	2.8	12.3	30	1959	0.3	8.5
1980	107.94	108.95	0.9	25.8	31	1995	0.3	34.1
1981	135.76	133.06	−2.0	− 9.7	32	1992	0.2	4.5
1982	122.55	119.55	−2.4	14.8	33	1968	0.2	7.7
1983	140.64	145.23	3.3	17.3	34	1990	0.1	− 6.6
1984	164.93	168.90	2.4	1.4	35	1971	0.04	10.8
1985	167.24	163.99	−1.9	26.3	36	1960	−0.7	− 3.0
1986	211.28	207.97	−1.6	14.6	37	1957	−0.9	−14.3
1987	242.17	257.28	6.2	2.0	38	1953	−0.9	− 6.6
1988	247.08	243.40	−1.5	12.4	39	1974	−1.5	−29.7
1989	277.72	280.98	1.2	27.3	40	1998	−1.5	26.7
1990	353.40	353.79	0.1	− 6.6	41	1988	−1.5	12.4
1991	330.22	314.90	−4.6	26.3	42	1993	−1.5	7.1
1992	417.09	418.10	0.2	4.5	43	1986	−1.6	14.6
1993	435.71	429.05	−1.5	7.1	44	2001	−1.8	−13.0
1994	466.45	469.90	0.7	− 1.5	45	1955	−1.8	26.4
1995	459.27	460.83	0.3	34.1	46	2000	−1.9	−10.1
1996	615.93	618.46	0.4	20.3	47	1985	−1.9	26.3
1997	740.74	748.41	1.0	31.0	48	1981	−2.0	− 9.7
1998	970.43	956.04	−1.5	26.7	49	1956	−2.1	2.6
1999	1229.23	1275.09	3.7	19.5	50	1977	−2.3	−11.5
2000	1469.25	1441.46	−1.9	−10.1	51	1982	−2.4	14.8
2001	1320.28	1295.86	−1.8	−13.0	52	1969	−2.9	−11.4
2002	1148.08	1160.71	1.1	−23.4	53	1962	−3.4	−11.8
2003	879.82	909.93	3.4	26.4	54	1991	−4.6	26.3
2004	1111.92	1131.91	1.8	??	55	1978	−4.7	1.1

Based on S&P 500

JANUARY

January first trading day Dow up 10 of last 15 **MONDAY**

3

A good new chairman of the
Federal Reserve Bank is worth a $10 billion tax cut.
— Paul H. Douglas (U.S. Senator, 1949-1967)

Second trading day Dow up 10 of last 15 **TUESDAY**
often with larger gains than first trading day

 4

Brazil is the country of the future and always will be.
— Brazilian joke

Average January gains last 34 years **WEDNESDAY**
NAS 3.9%   Dow 2.0%   S&P 1.9%
Up 24 Down 10   Up 23 Down 11   Up 22 Down 12
Rank # 1   Rank #2   Rank #1

5

Excellent firms don't believe in excellence — only in constant
improvement and constant change.
— Tom Peters (*In Search of Excellence*)

THURSDAY

6

If you are not willing to study, if you are not sufficiently
interested to investigate and analyze the stock market yourself,
then I beg of you to become an outright long-pull investor,
to buy good stocks, and hold on to them; for otherwise
your chances of success as a trader will be nil.
— Humphrey B. Neill (*Tape Reading and Market Tactics*, 1931)

January's First Five Days, an "Early Warning" System (page 14) **FRIDAY**

7

When I have to depend upon hope in a trade, I get out of it.
— Jesse Livermore

SATURDAY

8

SUNDAY

9

THE INCREDIBLE JANUARY BAROMETER (DEVISED 1972) ONLY FIVE SIGNIFICANT ERRORS IN 54 YEARS

Our January Barometer, devised by Yale Hirsch in 1972, states that as the S&P goes in January, the year follows suit. The indicator has registered **only five major errors since 1950 for a 90.7% accuracy ratio**. Vietnam affected 1966 and 1968; 1982 saw the start of a major bull market in August; two January rate cuts and 9/11 affected 2001; and the market in January 2003 was held down by the anticipation of military action in Iraq. (*Almanac Investor* newsletter subscribers were warned at the time not to heed the January Barometer's negative reading as it was being influenced by Iraqi concerns.)

Including the six flat years yields a 79.6% accuracy ratio. A full comparison of all monthly barometers for the Dow, S&P and NASDAQ at *http://www.hirschorg.com/2005p016* details January's market forecasting prowess. Bear markets began or continued when Januarys suffered a loss *(see page 44)*. Excluding 2001, **full years followed January's direction in the last thirteen Post-Election years**. *See pages 18, 22 and 24 for more January Barometer items.*

AS JANUARY GOES, SO GOES THE YEAR

Market Performance In January

	Previous Year's Close	January Close	January Change	Year Change
1950	16.76	17.05	1.7%	21.8%
1951	20.41	21.66	6.1	16.5
1952	23.77	24.14	1.6	11.8
1953	26.57	26.38	−0.7	− 6.6
1954	24.81	26.08	5.1	45.0
1955	35.98	36.63	1.8	26.4
1956	45.48	43.82	−3.6	2.6
1957	46.67	44.72	−4.2	−14.3
1958	39.99	41.70	4.3	38.1
1959	55.21	55.42	0.4	8.5
1960	59.89	55.61	−7.1	− 3.0
1961	58.11	61.78	6.3	23.1
1962	71.55	68.84	−3.8	−11.8
1963	63.10	66.20	4.9	18.9
1964	75.02	77.04	2.7	13.0
1965	84.75	87.56	3.3	9.1
1966	92.43	92.88	0.5	−13.1 X
1967	80.33	86.61	7.8	20.1
1968	96.47	92.24	−4.4	7.7 X
1969	103.86	103.01	−0.8	−11.4
1970	92.06	85.02	−7.6	0.1
1971	92.15	95.88	4.0	10.8
1972	102.09	103.94	1.8	15.6
1973	118.05	116.03	−1.7	−17.4
1974	97.55	96.57	−1.0	−29.7
1975	68.56	76.98	12.3	31.5
1976	90.19	100.86	11.8	19.1
1977	107.46	102.03	−5.1	−11.5
1978	95.10	89.25	−6.2	1.1
1979	96.11	99.93	4.0	12.3
1980	107.94	114.16	5.8	25.8
1981	135.76	129.55	−4.6	− 9.7
1982	122.55	120.40	−1.8	14.8 X
1983	140.64	145.30	3.3	17.3
1984	164.93	163.41	−0.9	1.4
1985	167.24	179.63	7.4	26.3
1986	211.28	211.78	0.2	14.6
1987	242.17	274.08	13.2	2.0
1988	247.08	257.07	4.0	12.4
1989	277.72	297.47	7.1	27.3
1990	353.40	329.08	−6.9	− 6.6
1991	330.22	343.93	4.2	26.3
1992	417.09	408.79	−2.0	4.5
1993	435.71	438.78	0.7	7.1
1994	466.45	481.61	3.3	− 1.5
1995	459.27	470.42	2.4	34.1
1996	615.93	636.02	3.3	20.3
1997	740.74	786.16	6.1	31.0
1998	970.43	980.28	1.0	26.7
1999	1229.23	1279.64	4.1	19.5
2000	1469.25	1394.46	−5.1	−10.1
2001	1320.28	1366.01	3.5	−13.0 X
2002	1148.08	1130.20	−1.6	−23.4
2003	879.82	855.70	−2.7	26.4 X
2004	1111.92	1131.13	1.7	??

Ranked By Performance

Rank	Year	January Change	Year Change
1	1987	13.2%	2.0%
2	1975	12.3	31.5
3	1976	11.8	19.1
4	1967	7.8	20.1
5	1985	7.4	26.3
6	1989	7.1	27.3
7	1961	6.3	23.1
8	1997	6.1	31.0
9	1951	6.1	16.5
10	1980	5.8	25.8
11	1954	5.1	45.0
12	1963	4.9	18.9
13	1958	4.3	38.1
14	1991	4.2	26.3
15	1999	4.1	19.5
16	1971	4.0	10.8
17	1988	4.0	12.4
18	1979	4.0	12.3
19	2001	3.5	−13.0 X
20	1965	3.3	9.1
21	1983	3.3	17.3
22	1996	3.3	20.3
23	1994	3.3	− 1.5 flat
24	1964	2.7	13.0
25	1995	2.4	34.1
26	1972	1.8	15.6
27	1955	1.8	26.4
28	1950	1.7	21.8
29	2004	1.7	??
30	1952	1.6	11.8
31	1998	1.0	26.7
32	1993	0.7	7.1
33	1966	0.5	−13.1 X
34	1959	0.4	8.5
35	1986	0.2	14.6
36	1953	−0.7	− 6.6
37	1969	−0.8	−11.4
38	1984	−0.9	1.4 flat
39	1974	−1.0	−29.7
40	2002	−1.6	−23.4
41	1973	−1.7	−17.4
42	1982	−1.8	14.8 X
43	1992	−2.0	4.5 flat
44	2003	−2.7	26.4 X
45	1956	−3.6	2.6 flat
46	1962	−3.8	−11.8
47	1957	−4.2	−14.3
48	1968	−4.4	7.7 X
49	1981	−4.6	− 9.7
50	1977	−5.1	−11.5
51	2000	−5.1	−10.1
52	1978	−6.2	1.1 flat
53	1990	−6.9	− 6.6
54	1960	−7.1	− 3.0
55	1970	−7.6	0.1 flat

X = 5 major errors   *Based on S&P 500*

JANUARY

MONDAY
10

To affect the quality of the day, that is the highest of the arts.
— Henry David Thoreau

TUESDAY
11

When everybody starts looking really smart,
and not realizing that a lot of it was luck, I get scared.
— Raphael Yavneh (*Forbes*)

WEDNESDAY
12

Things may come to those who wait,
but only the things.left by those who hustle.
— Abraham Lincoln (16th U.S. President, 1809-1865)

THURSDAY
13

Mate selection is usually a far greater determinant
of individual well-being than stock selection.
— Ross Miller (President, Miller Risk Advisors,
Paving Wall Street: Experimental Economics
and the Quest for the Perfect Market, December 2001)

FRIDAY
 # 14

There is only one corner of the universe
you can be certain of improving, and that's yourself.
— Aldous Huxley (English author, *Brave New World*, 1894-1963)

SATURDAY
15

SUNDAY
16

JANUARY BAROMETER IN GRAPHIC FORM SINCE 1950

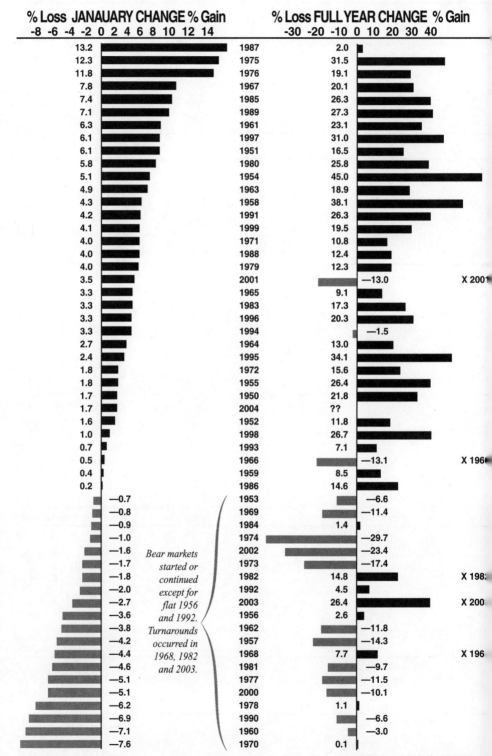

% Loss	JANUARY CHANGE	% Gain	Year	% Loss	FULL YEAR CHANGE	% Gain	
	-8 -6 -4 -2 0 2 4 6 8 10 12 14				-30 -20 -10 0 10 20 30 40		
13.2			1987	2.0			
12.3			1975	31.5			
11.8			1976	19.1			
7.8			1967	20.1			
7.4			1985	26.3			
7.1			1989	27.3			
6.3			1961	23.1			
6.1			1997	31.0			
6.1			1951	16.5			
5.8			1980	25.8			
5.1			1954	45.0			
4.9			1963	18.9			
4.3			1958	38.1			
4.2			1991	26.3			
4.1			1999	19.5			
4.0			1971	10.8			
4.0			1988	12.4			
4.0			1979	12.3			
3.5			2001	—13.0			X 2001
3.3			1965	9.1			
3.3			1983	17.3			
3.3			1996	20.3			
3.3			1994	—1.5			
2.7			1964	13.0			
2.4			1995	34.1			
1.8			1972	15.6			
1.8			1955	26.4			
1.7			1950	21.8			
1.7			2004	??			
1.6			1952	11.8			
1.0			1998	26.7			
0.7			1993	7.1			
0.5			1966	—13.1			X 1966
0.4			1959	8.5			
0.2			1986	14.6			
—0.7			1953	—6.6			
—0.8			1969	—11.4			
—0.9			1984	1.4			
—1.0			1974	—29.7			
—1.6			2002	—23.4			
—1.7			1973	—17.4			
—1.8			1982	14.8			X 1982
—2.0			1992	4.5			
—2.7			2003	26.4			X 2003
—3.6			1956	2.6			
—3.8			1962	—11.8			
—4.2			1957	—14.3			
—4.4			1968	7.7			X 1968
—4.6			1981	—9.7			
—5.1			1977	—11.5			
—5.1			2000	—10.1			
—6.2			1978	1.1			
—6.9			1990	—6.6			
—7.1			1960	—3.0			
—7.6			1970	0.1			

Bear markets started or continued except for flat 1956 and 1992. Turnarounds occurred in 1968, 1982 and 2003.

X = 5 major errors   *Based on S&P 500*

JANUARY

Martin Luther King Jr. Day (Market Closed)

MONDAY

17

*Never will a man penetrate deeper into error than
when he is continuing on a road that has led him to great success.*
— Friedrich von Hayek (*Counterrevolution of Science*)

First trading day of expiration week Dow up 6 of last 8 **TUESDAY**

18

*The only thing that saves us from the bureaucracy
is its inefficiency.*
— Eugene McCarthy

WEDNESDAY

19

Financial genius is a rising stock market.
— John Kenneth Galbraith

THURSDAY

20

*Marketing is our No. 1 priority...
A marketing campaign isn't worth doing unless it serves three purposes.
It must grow the business, create news, and enhance our image.*
— James Robinson III (American Express)

Expiration day Dow down 5 of last 6, 2004 broke a 5-year dog run **FRIDAY**

21

*While markets often make double bottoms,
three pushes to a high is the most common topping pattern.*
— John Bollinger (Bollinger Capital Management, created Bollinger
Bands, *Capital Growth Letter, Bollinger on Bollinger Bands*)

SATURDAY

22

SUNDAY

23

FEBRUARY ALMANAC

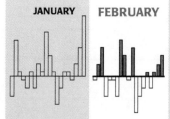

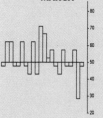

Market Probability Chart above is a graphic representation of the Market Probability Calendar on page 123.

◆ Sharp January moves usually correct or consolidate in February ◆ Compare January and February performance on page 140 ◆ Tends to follow current market trend ◆ RECORD: S&P 29 up, 26 down, average change –0.1% for 55 years; recent 15 years 0.1% ◆ Worst NASDAQ month in Post-Election Years (page 150) average –4.6% loss, up 2, down 6, off over 1% in S&P and Dow ◆ Day before Presidents' Day weekend S&P and NASDAQ down 12 of 13, Dow 11 of 13; day after improving lately, up 7 of 10 (see below and page 86) ◆ Many technicians modify market predictions based on January's market.

FEBRUARY DAILY POINT CHANGES DOW JONES INDUSTRIALS

Previous Month	1995	1996	1997	1998	1999	2000	2001	2002	2003	2004
Close	3843.86	5395.30	6813.09	7906.50	9358.83	10940.53	10887.36	9920.00	8053.81	10488.07
1	3.70	9.76	—	—	– 13.13	100.52	96.27	– 12.74	—	—
2	23.21	– 31.07	—	201.28	– 71.58	– 37.85	– 119.53	—	—	11.11
3	57.87	—	– 6.93	52.57	92.69	10.24	—	—	56.01	6.00
4	—	—	27.32	– 30.64	– 62.31	49.64	—	– 220.17	– 96.53	– 34.44
5	—	33.60	– 86.58	– 12.46	– 0.26	—	101.75	– 1.66	– 28.11	24.81
6	9.09	52.02	26.16	72.24	—	—	– 8.43	– 32.04	– 55.88	97.48
7	– 0.34	32.51	82.74	—	—	58.01	– 10.70	– 27.95	– 65.07	—
8	– 2.02	47.33	—	—	– 13.13	51.81	– 66.17	118.80	—	—
9	– 2.69	2.17	—	– 8.97	– 158.08	– 258.44	– 99.10	—	—	– 14.00
10	6.39	—	– 49.26	115.09	44.28	– 55.53	—	—	55.88	34.82
11	—	—	51.57	18.94	186.15	– 218.42	—	140.54	– 77.00	123.85
12	—	58.53	103.52	55.05	– 88.57	—	165.32	– 21.04	– 84.94	– 43.63
13	15.14	1.08	60.81	0.50	—	—	– 43.45	125.93	– 8.30	– 66.22
14	4.04	– 21.68	– 33.48	—	—	94.63	– 107.91	12.32	158.93	—
15	27.92	– 28.18	—	—	H	198.25	95.61	– 98.95	—	—
16	1.35	– 48.05	—	H	22.14	– 156.68	– 91.20	—	—	H
17	– 33.98	—	H	28.40	– 101.56	– 46.84	—	—	H	87.03
18	—	—	78.50	52.56	103.16	– 295.05	—	H	132.35	– 42.89
19	—	H	– 47.33	– 75.48	41.32	—	H	– 157.90	– 40.55	– 7.26
20	H	– 44.79	– 92.75	38.36	—	—	– 68.94	196.03	– 85.64	– 45.70
21	10.43	57.44	4.24	—	—	H	– 204.30	– 106.49	103.15	—
22	9.08	92.49	—	—	212.73	85.32	0.23	133.47	—	—
23	30.28	22.03	—	– 3.74	– 8.26	– 79.11	– 84.91	—	—	– 9.41
24	8.41	—	76.58	– 40.10	– 144.75	133.10	—	—	– 159.87	– 43.25
25	—	—	30.01	87.68	– 33.33	230.51	—	177.56	51.26	35.25
26	—	– 65.39	– 55.03	32.89	– 59.76	—	200.63	– 30.45	– 102.52	– 21.48
27	– 23.17	– 15.89	– 58.11	55.05	—	—	– 5.65	12.32	78.01	3.78
28	22.48	– 43.00	– 47.33	—	—	176.53	– 141.60	– 21.45	6.09	—
29		– 20.59			89.66					
Close	4011.05	5485.62	6877.74	8545.72	9306.58	10128.31	10495.28	10106.13	7891.08	10583.92
Change	167.19	90.32	64.65	639.22	– 52.25	– 812.22	– 392.08	186.13	– 162.73	95.85

Either go short, or stay away
The day before Presidents' Day

JANUARY

MONDAY
24

A good trader has to have three things:
a chronic inability to accept things at face value,
to feel continuously unsettled, and to have humility.
— Michael Steinhardt

TUESDAY
25

A.I. (artificial intelligence) is the science of how to get machines
to do the things they do in the movies.
— Professor Astro Teller (Carnegie Mellon University)

WEDNESDAY
26

We go to the movies to be entertained, not see rape,
ransacking, pillage and looting. We can get all that in the stock market.
— Kennedy Gammage (*The Richland Report*)

THURSDAY
27

It isn't as important to buy as cheap as possible
as it is to buy at the right time.
— Jesse Livermore

FRIDAY
28

A bull market tends to bail you out of all your mistakes.
Conversely, bear markets make you PAY for your mistakes.
— Richard Russell (*Dow Theory Letters*)

SATURDAY
29

February Sector Seasonalities:
Bullish: Natural Gas; Bearish: Internet (page 118)

SUNDAY
30

HOT JANUARY INDUSTRIES BEAT S&P NEXT 11 MONTHS

Just as January tends to predict the market's direction for the year, we thought perhaps the best performing stocks and industries in January could be the top performers for the year.

Our friend Sam Stovall, Chief Investment Strategist at S&P, crunched the numbers and proved the hypothesis. Since 1970 a portfolio of the top ten S&P Industries during January has beaten the S&P 500 itself — and performed even better in years when January was up. He dubbed it the January Barometer Portfolio or JBP.

The JBP went on to outperform the S&P 500 during the remaining 11 months of the year 74% of the time, 16.3% to 6.9%, on average. When the S&P 500 is up in January, a top-10 industries portfolio increases the average portfolio gain to 22.0% for the last 11 months of the year vs. 13.0% for the S&P.

For more check Sam's Sector Watch at *businessweek.com* or our March 2004 *Almanac Investor* newsletter in the archives at *stocktradersalmanac.com*. Also highlighted are Sam's selected stocks from within the top ten sectors.

AS JANUARY GOES, SO GOES THE YEAR
FOR TOP PERFORMING INDUSTRIES
January's Top 10 Industries vs. S&P 500 Next 11 Months

	11 Month % Change		S&P Jan	After S&P Up in January		After S&P Down in January	
	Portfolio	S&P	%	Portfolio	S&P	Portfolio	S&P
1970	− 4.7	− 0.3	− 7.6			− 4.7	− 0.3
1971	23.5	6.1	4.0	23.5	6.1		
1972	19.7	13.7	1.8	19.7	13.7		
1973	5.2	− 20.0	− 1.7			5.2	− 20.0
1974	− 29.2	− 30.2	− 1.0			− 29.2	− 30.2
1975	57.3	22.2	12.3	57.3	22.2		
1976	16.3	8.1	11.8	16.3	8.1		
1977	− 9.1	− 9.6	− 5.1			− 9.1	− 9.6
1978	7.3	6.5	− 6.2			7.3	6.5
1979	21.7	8.1	4.0	21.7	8.1		
1980	38.3	20.4	5.8	38.3	20.4		
1981	5.0	− 6.9	− 4.6			5.0	− 6.9
1982	37.2	18.8	− 1.8			37.2	18.8
1983	17.2	13.9	3.3	17.2	13.9		
1984	− 5.0	− 1.1	− 0.9			− 5.0	− 1.1
1985	28.2	20.8	7.4	28.2	20.8		
1986	18.1	19.4	0.2	18.1	19.4		
1987	− 1.5	− 8.9	13.2	− 1.5	− 8.9		
1988	18.4	10.4	4.0	18.4	10.4		
1989	16.1	22.1	7.1	16.1	22.1		
1990	− 4.4	− 3.3	− 6.9			− 4.4	− 3.3
1991	35.7	19.4	4.2	35.7	19.4		
1992	14.6	4.7	− 2.0			14.6	4.7
1993	23.7	7.2	0.7	23.7	7.2		
1994	− 7.1	− 4.6	3.3	− 7.1	− 4.6		
1995	25.6	30.9	2.4	25.6	30.9		
1996	5.4	16.5	3.3	5.4	16.5		
1997	4.7	23.4	6.1	4.7	23.4		
1998	45.2	25.4	1.0	45.2	25.4		
1999	67.9	14.8	4.1	67.9	14.8		
2000	23.6	− 5.3	− 5.1			23.6	− 5.3
2001	− 13.1	− 16.0	3.5	− 13.1	− 16.0		
2002	− 16.2	− 22.2	− 1.6			− 16.2	− 22.2
2003	69.3	29.9	− 2.7			69.3	29.9
2004			1.7				
Averages	16.3%	6.9%		22.0%	13.0%	7.2%	-3.0%

JANUARY/FEBRUARY

Historically one of two (July 14) best trading days of the year (page 123)
"January Barometer" 90.7% accurate (page 16)
Only two errors in odd-numbered years since 1937 (page 24)
Almanac Investor subscribers emailed official final results,
visit stocktradersalmanac.com for details

MONDAY

31

*I believe in the exceptional man —
the entrepreneur who is
always out of money,
not the bureaucrat who
generates cash flow and pays dividends.*
— Armand Erpf

FOMC Meeting (2 days)
"Best Three-Month Span" normally ends here (pages 48, 54, 138 and 139)

TUESDAY

1

*One of the more prolonged and extreme periods favoring
large-cap stocks was 1994-1999. The tide turned in 2000.
A cycle has begun of investors favoring small-cap stocks,
which is likely to continue through the next several years.*
— Jim Oberweis (The Oberweis Report, February 2001)

Average February gains last 34 years
NAS 0.6%   Dow 0.4%   S&P 0.1%
Up 19 Down 15   Up 19 Down 15   Up 18 Down 16
Rank #7   Rank #9   Rank #9

WEDNESDAY

2

*All free governments are managed by
the combined wisdom and folly of the people.*
— James A. Garfield (20th U.S. President, 1831-1881)

THURSDAY

3

*If a battered stock refuses to sink any lower
no matter how many negative articles appear in the papers,
that stock is worth a closer look.*
— James L. Fraser (Contrary Investor)

FRIDAY

4

*There have been three great inventions since the beginning of time:
fire, the wheel, and central banking.*
— Will Rogers

SATURDAY

5

SUNDAY

6

1933 "LAME DUCK" AMENDMENT REASON JANUARY BAROMETER WORKS

There would be no January Barometer without the passage in 1933 of the Twentieth "Lame Duck" Amendment to the Constitution. Since then it has essentially been "As January goes, so goes the year." January's direction has correctly forecasted the major trend for the market in most of the subsequent years.

Prior to 1934, newly elected Senators and Representatives did not take office until December of the following year, 13 months later (except when new Presidents were inaugurated). Defeated Congressmen stayed in Congress for all of the following session. They were known as "lame ducks."

Since 1934, Congress convenes in the first week of January and includes those members newly elected the previous November. Inauguration Day was also moved up from March 4 to January 20. As a result several events have been squeezed into January, which affect our economy and our stock market and quite possibly those of many nations of the world.

The basis for January's predictive capacity comes from the fact that so many important events occur in the month: new Congresses convene; the President gives the State of the Union message, presents the annual budget and sets national goals and priorities. Switch these events to any other month and chances are the January Barometer would become a memory.

The table shows the January Barometer in odd years. In 1935 and 1937, the Democrats already had the most lopsided Congressional margins in history, so when these two Congresses convened it was anticlimactic.

The JB in subsequent odd-numbered years had compiled a perfect record until two January interest rate cuts and 9/11 affected 2001 and the anticipation of military action in Iraq held the market down in January 2003.

See January Barometer compared to prior "New Congress Barometers" at *www.hirschorg.com/2005p024.*

JANUARY BAROMETER (ODD YEARS)

January % Change	12 Month % Change	Same	Opposite
− 4.2%	41.2%		1935
3.8	− 38.6		1937
− 6.9	− 5.4	1939	
− 4.8	− 17.9	1941	
7.2	19.4	1943	
1.4	30.7	1945	
2.4	N/C	1947	
0.1	10.3	1949	
6.1	16.5	1951	
− 0.7	− 6.6	1953	
1.8	26.4	1955	
− 4.2	− 14.3	1957	
0.4	8.5	1959	
6.3	23.1	1961	
4.9	18.9	1963	
3.3	9.1	1965	
7.8	20.1	1967	
− 0.8	− 11.4	1969	
4.0	10.8	1971	
− 1.7	− 17.4	1973	
12.3	31.5	1975	
− 5.1	− 11.5	1977	
4.0	12.3	1979	
− 4.6	− 9.7	1981	
3.3	17.3	1983	
7.4	26.3	1985	
13.2	2.0	1987	
7.1	27.3	1989	
4.1	26.3	1991	
0.7	7.1	1993	
2.4	34.1	1995	
6.1	31.0	1997	
4.1	19.5	1999	
3.5	− 13.0		2001
− 2.7	26.4		2003

12 month's % change includes January's % change
Based on S&P 500

FEBRUARY

MONDAY
7

If you don't profit from your investment mistakes,
someone else will.
— Yale Hirsch

TUESDAY
8

I want the whole of Europe to have one currency;
it will make trading much easier.
— Napoleon Bonaparte (Emperor of France 1804-1815, 1769-1821)

Ash Wednesday
WEDNESDAY
9

Fortune favors the brave.
— Virgil (Roman poet, *Aeneid*, 70-19 B.C.)

THURSDAY
 # 10

If the models are telling you to sell, sell, sell,
but only buyers are out there, don't be a jerk. Buy!
— William Silber, Ph.D. (N.Y.U., *Newsweek*, 1986)

FRIDAY
 # 11

Let us have the courage to stop borrowing
to meet the continuing deficits. Stop the deficits.
— Franklin D. Roosevelt (1932)

SATURDAY
12

SUNDAY
13

THE FIFTH YEAR OF DECADES –
NO LOSERS IN 120 YEARS

There has not been one losing "five" year in twelve decades. But 2005 is a post-election year, the weakest of that more influential four-year cycle. Depending on the strength of election year 2004, we'd be more cautious in 2005.

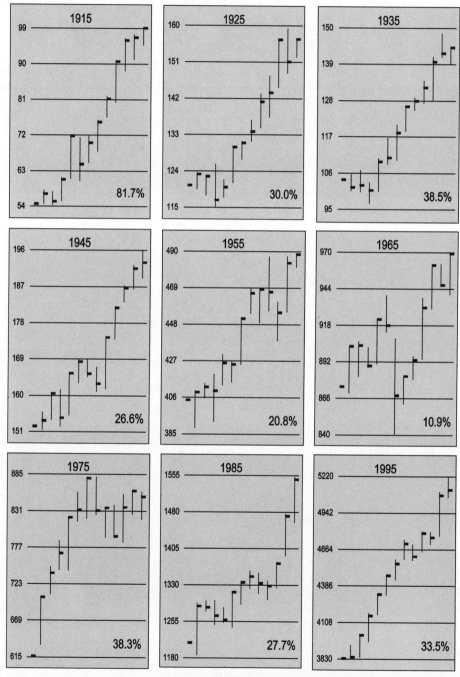

Based on Dow Jones Industrial Average monthly ranges and closing prices

FEBRUARY

Valentine's Day
Monday before expiration Dow up 11 straight

MONDAY
14

*When you loved me I gave you the whole sun and stars to play with.
I gave you eternity in a single moment, strength of the mountains in one clasp of
your arms, and the volume of all the seas in one impulse of your soul.*
— George Bernard Shaw (Irish dramatist, *Getting Married*, 1856-1950)

TUESDAY
15

*Small business has been the first rung on the ladder upward
for every minority group in the nation's history.*
— S. I. Hayakawa (1947)

WEDNESDAY
16

*Liberal institutions straightaway cease from being liberal
the moment they are firmly established.*
— Friedrich Nietzsche (German philosopher, 1844-1900)

THURSDAY
17

*Industrial capitalism has generated the greatest productive power
in human history. To date, no other socioeconomic system
has been able to generate comparable productive power.*
— Peter L. Berger (*The Capitalist Revolution*)

*Dow down 11 of 13 day before Presidents' Day weekend
S&P and NAS down 12 of 13 (pages 20 and 86)
Expiration day Dow down big 4 of last 5*

FRIDAY
18

*Don't fritter away your time. Create, act,
take a place wherever you are and be somebody.*
— Theodore Roosevelt

SATURDAY
19

SUNDAY
20

MARKET CHARTS OF POST-PRESIDENTIAL ELECTION YEARS

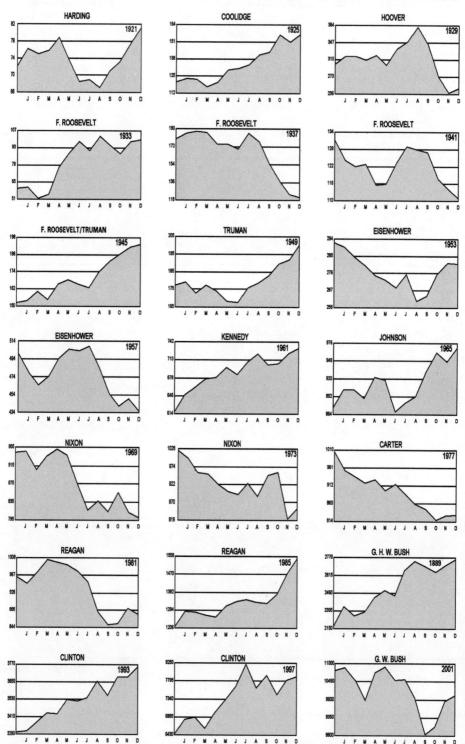

Based on Dow Jones Industrial Average monthly closing prices

FEBRUARY

Presidents' Day
(Market Closed)

MONDAY

21

A man isn't a man until he has to meet a payroll.
— Ivan Shaffer (The Stock Promotion Game)

Day after Presidents' Day Dow up 7 of last 10

TUESDAY

22

In every generation there has to be some fool
who will speak the truth as he sees it.
— Boris Pasternak (Russian writer and poet,
1958 Nobel Laureate in Literature, Doctor Zhivago, 1890-1960)

WEDNESDAY

23

The task of leadership is not to put greatness into humanity,
but to elicit it, for the greatness is already there.
— Sir John Buchan (Former Governor-General of Canada)

THURSDAY

24

Don't confuse brains with a bull market.
— Humphrey Neill

FRIDAY

25

It is the growth of total government spending
as a percentage of gross national product —
not the way it is financed — that crowds out the private sector.
— Paul Craig Roberts (Business Week, 1984)

SATURDAY

26

March Sector Seasonalities:
Bullish: Airline, Oil, Broker/Dealers;
Bearish: Biotech (page 118)

SUNDAY

27

MARCH ALMANAC

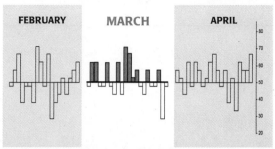

FEBRUARY MARCH APRIL

Market Probability Chart above is a graphic representation of the Market Probability Calendar on page 123.

◆ Early and mid-month strength and late-month weakness are most evident above ◆ RECORD: S&P 36 up, 19 down, average gain 1.0%, fifth best ◆ Rather stormy in recent years with wild fluctuations and large gains and losses ◆ March has been taking some mean end-of-quarter hits — revealed below, down 1469 Dow points March 9-22, 2001 ◆ Last three or four days a net loser eleven out of last thirteen years ◆ NASDAQ hard hit in 2001, down 14.5% after 22.4% drop in February ◆ Market much luckier the day before St. Patrick's Day ◆ Post-Election Year Marchs weak Dow and S&P off fractionally, NASDAQ average drop –1.9%, up 3, down 5 ◆ Last day of March Dow down 8 of 10, average –0.7%.

MARCH DAILY POINT CHANGES DOW JONES INDUSTRIALS

	1995	1996	1997	1998	1999	2000	2001	2002	2003	2004
Previous Month Close	4011.05	5485.62	6877.74	8545.72	9306.58	10128.31	10495.2	10106.13	7891.08	10583.92
1	− 16.25	50.94	—	—	18.20	9.62	− 45.14	262.73	—	94.22
2	− 14.87	—	—	4.73	− 27.17	26.99	16.17	—	—	− 86.66
3	9.68	—	41.18	34.38	− 21.73	202.28	—	—	− 53.22	1.63
4	—	63.59	− 66.20	− 45.59	191.52	—	—	217.96	− 132.99	− 5.11
5	—	42.27	93.13	− 94.91	268.68	—	95.99	− 153.41	70.73	7.55
6	7.95	− 12.65	− 1.15	125.06	—	− 196.70	28.92	140.88	− 101.61	—
7	− 34.93	11.92	56.19	—	—	− 374.47	138.38	− 48.92	66.04	—
8	16.60	− 171.24	—	—	− 8.47	60.50	128.65	47.12	—	− 66.07
9	4.16	—	—	− 2.25	− 33.85	154.20	− 213.63	—	—	− 72.52
10	52.22	—	78.50	75.98	79.08	− 81.91	—	—	− 171.85	− 160.07
11	—	110.55	5.77	32.63	124.60	—	—	38.75	− 44.12	− 168.51
12	—	2.89	− 45.79	− 16.19	− 21.09	—	− 436.37	21.11	28.01	111.70
13	− 10.38	− 15.17	− 160.48	− 57.04	—	18.31	82.55	− 130.50	269.68	—
14	23.52	17.34	56.57	—	—	− 135.89	− 317.34	15.29	37.96	—
15	− 10.38	− 1.09	—	—	82.42	320.17	57.82	90.09	—	− 137.19
16	30.78	—	—	116.33	− 28.30	499.19	− 207.87	—	—	81.78
17	4.50	—	20.02	31.14	− 51.06	− 35.37	—	—	282.21	115.63
18	—	98.63	− 58.92	25.41	118.21	—	—	− 29.48	52.31	− 4.52
19	—	− 14.09	− 18.88	27.65	− 94.07	—	135.70	57.50	71.22	− 109.18
20	10.03	− 14.09	− 57.40	103.38	—	85.01	− 238.35	− 133.68	21.15	—
21	− 11.07	− 28.54	− 15.49	—	—	227.10	− 233.76	− 21.73	235.37	—
22	10.38	9.76	—	—	− 13.04	− 40.64	− 97.52	− 52.17	—	− 121.85
23	4.84	—	—	− 90.18	− 218.68	253.16	115.30	—	—	− 1.11
24	50.84	—	100.46	88.19	− 4.99	− 7.14	—	—	− 307.29	− 15.41
25	—	7.22	− 29.08	− 31.64	169.55	—	—	− 146.00	65.55	170.59
26	—	26.74	4.53	− 25.91	− 14.15	—	182.75	71.69	− 50.35	5.85
27	18.67	− 43.72	− 140.11	− 50.81	—	− 86.87	260.01	73.55	− 28.43	—
28	− 5.53	3.97	H	—	—	− 89.74	− 162.19	− 22.97	− 55.68	—
29	8.99	− 43.71	—	—	184.54	82.61	13.71	H	—	116.66
30	11.76	—	—	− 13.96	− 93.52	− 38.47	79.72	—	—	52.07
31	− 14.87	—	− 157.11	17.69	− 127.10	− 58.33	—	—	− 153.64	− 24.00
Close	4157.69	5587.14	6583.48	8799.81	9786.16	10921.92	9878.78	10403.94	7992.13	10357.70
Change	146.64	101.52	− 294.26	254.09	479.58	793.61	− 616.50	297.81	101.05	− 226.22

*March has Ides and St. Patrick's Day
Begins bullishly, then fades away*

MONDAY

28

*Companies which do well generally tend to report
(their quarterly earnings) earlier than those which do poorly.*
— Alan Abelson (*Barron's*)

March first trading day Dow up 7 of last 9   TUESDAY

1

Buy when you are scared to death; sell when you are tickled to death.
— Market Maxim (*The Cabot Market Letter*, April 12, 2001)

Average March gains last 34 years   WEDNESDAY
NAS 0.3%   Dow 0.9%   S&P 0.9%
Up 21 Down 13   Up 22 Down 12   Up 22 Down 12   2
Rank #9   Rank #5   Rank #6

When an old man dies, a library burns down.
— African proverb

THURSDAY

3

He who knows nothing is confident of everything.
— Anonymous

FRIDAY

4

*Marx's great achievement was to
place the system of capitalism on the defensive.*
— Charles A. Madison (1977)

SATURDAY

5

SUNDAY

6

PROFIT ON DAY BEFORE ST. PATRICK'S DAY

We first published St. Patrick's Day bullishness in the 1977 Almanac. Dan Turov, editor of *Turov On Timing*, notes gains the day before St. Patrick's Day have proved best, outperforming the days before many legal holidays for an average gain of 0.33% on the S&P. Irish luck, or coincidence?

During the past 52 years, St. Patrick's Day itself has posted just a wee gain of 0.14%. St. Pat's 2004 landed on Wednesday in the middle of Triple-Witching Week. Both St. Pat's and the day before gained ground, but the rest of the week was off (likely due to the Madrid train bombing a few days earlier) as the first correction of the year-plus bull market took hold.

St. Patrick's Day 2005 falls on Thursday making Wednesday, March 16th, a potential up day. But with the first Triple-Witching Week of the year tending towards weakness of late, we would exercise caution and perhaps jump in only for a quick trade on a selloff Tuesday, March 15th — depending on market conditions.

Perhaps it's the anticipation of the patron saint's holiday that boosts the market and the distraction of the parade down Fifth Avenue that holds the market back — or is it the absent, and then hungover, traders? Or maybe it's the fact that Saint Pat's usually falls in Triple-Witching Week.

ST. PATRICK'S DAY TRADING RECORD (DAYS BEFORE AND AFTER)

Year	St. Pat's Day	% Change 2 Days Prior	% Change 1 Day Prior	S&P 500 St. Pat's Day or Next *	% Change St. Pat's Day *	% Change Day After
1953	Tue	0.19%	0.15%	26.33	0.42%	− 0.34%
1954	Wed	− 0.45	− 0.04	26.62	0.23	0.41
1955	Thu	2.15	0.76	36.12	0.39	0.17
1956	Sat	0.97	0.31	48.59	0.93	0.58
1957	Sun	0.07	− 0.05	43.85	− 0.45	0.43
1958	Mon	0.12	− 0.31	42.04	− 0.69	− 0.36
1959	Tue	0.12	− 1.08	56.52	0.82	− 0.23
1960	Thu	0.77	0.55	54.96	− 0.15	0.09
1961	Fri	0.30	1.01	64.60	0.61	0.40
1962	Sat	0.21	− 0.17	70.85	− 0.13	− 0.27
1963	Sun	− 0.47	0.50	65.61	− 0.49	− 0.21
1964	Tue	0.08	0.00	79.32	0.23	0.08
1965	Wed	0.03	− 0.13	87.02	− 0.13	− 0.24
1966	Thu	− 0.57	0.58	88.17	0.35	0.41
1967	Fri	0.95	1.01	90.25	0.18	− 0.06
1968	Sun	− 1.90	0.88	89.59	0.55	− 0.67
1969	Mon	− 0.67	− 0.40	98.25	0.26	0.24
1970	Tue	− 0.53	− 1.08	87.29	0.44	0.29
1971	Wed	1.14	0.50	101.12	− 0.09	0.07
1972	Fri	0.13	− 0.23	107.92	0.39	− 0.31
1973	Sat	− 0.75	− 0.51	112.17	− 1.21	− 0.20
1974	Sun	− 0.09	− 0.37	98.05	− 1.24	− 0.84
1975	Mon	0.18	1.22	86.01	1.47	− 1.02
1976	Wed	− 1.05	1.12	100.86	− 0.06	− 0.41
1977	Thu	0.55	0.19	102.08	− 0.09	− 0.22
1978	Fri	− 0.26	0.44	90.20	0.77	0.69
1979	Sat	0.15	0.83	101.06	0.37	− 0.55
1980	Mon	− 1.17	− 0.18	102.26	− 3.01	1.80
1981	Tue	− 0.06	1.18	133.92	− 0.56	0.22
1982	Wed	0.77	− 0.16	109.08	− 0.18	1.12
1983	Thu	0.35	− 1.03	149.59	− 0.14	0.21
1984	Sat	0.41	1.18	157.78	− 0.94	0.68
1985	Sun	− 0.20	− 0.74	176.88	0.20	1.50
1986	Mon	0.28	1.44	234.67	− 0.79	0.47
1987	Tue	− 0.46	− 0.57	292.47	1.47	0.11
1988	Thu	− 0.09	0.95	271.22	0.96	− 0.04
1989	Fri	0.52	0.93	292.69	− 2.25	− 0.95
1990	Sat	0.36	1.14	343.53	0.47	− 0.57
1991	Sun	− 0.29	0.02	372.11	− 0.40	− 1.48
1992	Tue	0.48	0.14	409.58	0.78	− 0.10
1993	Wed	0.36	− 0.01	448.31	− 0.68	0.80
1994	Thu	− 0.08	0.52	470.89	0.31	0.04
1995	Fri	− 0.20	0.72	495.52	0.02	0.13
1996	Sun	0.37	0.09	652.65	1.75	− 0.15
1997	Mon	− 1.83	0.46	795.71	0.32	− 0.76
1998	Tue	− 0.13	1.00	1080.45	0.11	0.47
1999	Wed	0.98	− 0.07	1297.82	− 0.65	1.44
2000	Fri	2.43	4.76	1464.47	0.41	− 0.54
2001	Sat	0.59	− 1.96	1170.81	1.76	− 2.41
2002	Sun	− 0.09	1.14	1165.55	− 0.05	− 0.41
2003	Mon	3.45	0.16	862.79	3.54	0.42
2004	Wed	− 1.43	0.56	1123.75	1.17	− 0.13
Average		**0.13%**	**0.33%**		**0.14%**	**0.01%**

When St. Patrick's Day falls on Saturday or Sunday, the following trading day is used. Based on S&P 500

MARCH

MONDAY
7

An entrepreneur tends to lie some of the time.
An entrepreneur in trouble tends to lie most of the time.
— Anonymous

TUESDAY
 ### 8

The commodity futures game is a money game —
not a game involving the supply-demand
of the actual commodity as commonly depicted.
— R. Earl Hadady

WEDNESDAY
9

An inventor fails 999 times, and if he succeeds once, he's in.
He treats his failures simply as practice shots.
— Charles Kettering (Inventor of electric ignition,
founded Delco in 1909, 1876-1958)

THURSDAY
10

I really do inhabit a system in which
words are capable of shaking the entire structure of government,
where words can prove mightier than ten military divisions.
— Vaclav Havel (Czech dramatist, essayist,
political leader and president, b.1936)

FRIDAY
 ### 11

History is replete with episodes in which the real patriots were the
ones who defied their governments.
— Jim Rogers (Financier, *Adventure Capitalist*, b. 1942)

SATURDAY
12

SUNDAY
13

MARKET BEHAVIOR WHEN
WHITE HOUSE CHANGES HANDS

For 38 annual editions of this *Almanac* we have had to look ahead six to eighteen months and try to anticipate what the stock market will do in the year to come. It was not too difficult many times because quadrennial Presidential and biennial Congressional elections had predictable effects on the economy and stock market. Also, bear markets lasted six to ten months and tended to begin in the first year of Republican and second of Democratic terms.

Prognosticating was tougher in the 1990s during the greatest bull cycle in history. Being bullish and staying bullish was the best course, as bear markets were few and far between. And when they did come, they were swift and over in a couple of months. Market timers and fundamentalists, as a result, did not keep pace with the momentum players. With the market back to earth we expect many of these patterns to reemerge.

POST-ELECTION MARKETS WHEN PARTY IN POWER IS OUSTED

New Democrats		Dow %	New Republicans		Dow %
Wilson	1913	− 10.3%	Harding	1921	12.7%
Roosevelt	1933	66.7	Eisenhower	1953	− 3.8
Kennedy	1961	18.7	Nixon	1969	− 15.2
Carter	1977	− 17.3	Reagan	1981	− 9.2
Clinton	1993	13.7	G.W. Bush	2001	− 7.1

Looking at the past you can see that when Democrats ousted Republican White House occupants the market fared better in post-election years than when the reverse occurred. In the past Democrats came to power over domestic issues and Republicans won the White House on foreign shores.

Wilson won after the Republican Party split in two, and Carter after the Watergate scandal. Roosevelt, Kennedy and Clinton won elections during bad economies. The Republicans took over after major wars were begun under Democrats, benefiting Harding, Eisenhower and Nixon.

The Iranians made Jimmy Carter appear helpless, which favored Reagan. With no recession and no embarrassing foreign entanglement, the major advantage for Bush was the Clinton scandal.

In 2004 the first Presidential election of the new millennium presents an entirely different set of circumstances. A struggling economy, the dilemma in Iraq and terrorism have put Bush's reelection prospects in question, creating a statistical dead heat between himself and Kerry, the Democratic Presidential nominee.

Prospects for the stock market in 2005 look thin. Although we have never had a losing "fifth" year of a decade (page 126), the economy is still floundering, the national debt continues to balloon and higher oil and commodity prices and interest rates loom large. The bull-run off the October 2002 bottom is also getting long in the tooth.

After a final push in the fall of 2004 and early 2005, we would become cautious as the stock market will likely stand aside while either resident of Pennsylvania Avenue deals with the plethora of domestic and international matters at hand.

MARCH

*Dow down up 7 of 9 Mondays before Triple Witching,
but walloped 436 points in 2001 and 137 in 2004*

MONDAY

14

*The greatest good you can do for another
is not just to share your riches, but to reveal to him his own.*
— Benjamin Disraeli (British prime minister, 1804-1881)

TUESDAY

15

640K ought to be enough for anybody.
— William H. Gates (Microsoft founder, 1981,
Try running Microsoft XP on less than 256 megs)

Market much luckier day before St. Patrick's Day (page 32)

WEDNESDAY

16

*Averaging down in a bear market is tantamount to
taking a seat on the down escalator at Macy's.*
— Richard Russell (*Dow Theory Letters*, 1984)

St. Patrick's Day

THURSDAY

**17**

*Try to surround yourself with people
who can give you a little happiness,
because you can only pass through this life once, Jack.
You don't come back for an encore.*
— Elvis Presley (1935-1977)

FRIDAY

Triple-Witching Day Dow down 6 of last 9

18

I do not rule Russia; ten thousand clerks do.
— Nicholas I (1795-1855)

SATURDAY

19

SUNDAY

20

POST-ELECTION YEARS: PAYING THE PIPER

Politics being what it is, incumbent administrations during election years try to make the economy look good to impress the electorate and tend to put off unpopular decisions until the votes are counted. This produces an American phenomenon—the Post-Election Year Syndrome. The year begins with an Inaugural Ball, after which the piper must be paid, and we Americans have often paid dearly in the past 91 years.

Victorious candidates rarely succeed in fulfilling campaign promises of "peace and prosperity." In the past 23 post-election years, three major wars began: World War I (1917), World War II (1941), and Vietnam (1965); four drastic bear markets started in 1929, 1937, 1969, and 1973; 9/11, a recession and a continuing bear market (2001); and less severe bear markets occurred or were in progress in 1913, 1917, 1921, 1941, 1949, 1953, 1957, 1977, and 1981. Only in 1925, 1989, 1993, and 1997 were Americans blessed with peace and prosperity.

THE RECORD SINCE 1913

1913 Wilson (D)	Minor bear market.
1917 Wilson (D)	World War I and a bear market.
1921 Harding (R)	Post-war depression and bear market.
1925 Coolidge (R)	Peace and prosperity. Hallelujah!
1929 Hoover (R)	Worst market crash in history until 1987.
1933 Roosevelt (D)	Devaluation, bank failures, depression still on but market strong.
1937 Roosevelt (D)	Another crash, 20% unemployment rate.
1941 Roosevelt (D)	World War II and a continuing bear.
1945 Roosevelt (D)	Post-war industrial contraction, strong market precedes 1946 crash.
1949 Truman (D)	Minor bear market.
1953 Eisenhower (R)	Minor post-war (Korea) bear market.
1957 Eisenhower (R)	Major bear market.
1961 Kennedy (D)	Bay of Pigs fiasco, strong market precedes 1962 crash.
1965 Johnson (D)	Vietnam escalation. Bear came in 1966.
1969 Nixon (R)	Start of worst bear market since 1937.
1973 Nixon, Ford (R)	Start of worst bear market since 1929.
1977 Carter (D)	Bear market in blue chip stocks.
1981 Reagan (R)	Bear strikes again.
1985 Reagan (R)	No bear in sight.
1989 Bush (R)	Effect of 1987 crash wears off.
1993 Clinton (D)	S&P up 7.1%, next year off 1.5%.
1997 Clinton (D)	S&P up 31.0%, next year up 26.7%.
2001 Bush, GW (R)	9/11, recession, worst bear market since 1929 takes hold.

Republicans took back the White House following foreign involvements under the Democrats in 1921 (World War I), 1953 (Korea), 1969 (Vietnam), and 1981 (Iran); and a scandal (2001). Bear markets occurred during all or part of these post-election years.

Democrats recaptured power after domestic problems under the Republicans: in 1913 (GOP split in two), 1933 (crash and depression), 1961 (recession), 1977 (Watergate), and 1993 (sluggish economy). Democratic post-election years after resuming power were bearish following a Republican Party squabble or scandal and bullish following bad economic times.

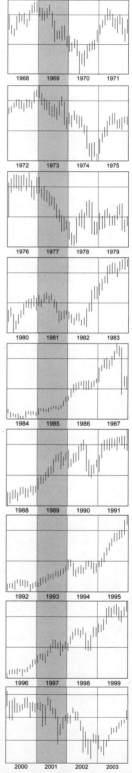

Graph shows Post-Election years screened
Based on Dow Jones industrial average monthly ranges

MARCH

MONDAY

21

A leader has the ability to create infectious enthusiasm.
— Ted Turner (Billionaire, *New Yorker Magazine*, April 23, 2001)

FOMC Meeting

TUESDAY

22

In democracies, nothing is more great or brilliant than commerce;
it attracts the attention of the public and fills the imagination of the multitude;
all passions of energy are directed towards it.
— Alexis de Tocqueville (Author, *Democracy in America* 1840, 1805-1859)

WEDNESDAY

23

When a falling stock becomes a screaming buy
because it cannot conceivably drop further, try to buy it 30 percent lower.
— Al Rizzo (1986)

THURSDAY

24

Charts not only tell what was, they tell what is;
and a trend from was to is (projected linearly into the will be)
contains better percentages than clumsy guessing.
— R. A. Levy

Good Friday
(Market Closed)

FRIDAY

25

The fear of capitalism has compelled socialism to widen freedom, and
the fear of socialism has compelled capitalism to increase equality.
— Will and Ariel Durant

SATURDAY

26

Easter Sunday
Bullish April Sector Seasonalities:
Biotech, Internet, Semiconductor, Utilities (page 118)

SUNDAY

27

APRIL ALMANAC

APRIL							MAY						
S	M	T	W	T	F	S	S	M	T	W	T	F	S
					1	2		1	2	3	4	5	6	7
3	4	5	6	7	8	9	8	9	10	11	12	13	14
10	11	12	13	14	15	16	15	16	17	18	19	20	21
17	18	19	20	21	22	23	22	23	24	25	26	27	28
24	25	26	27	28	29	30	29	30	31				

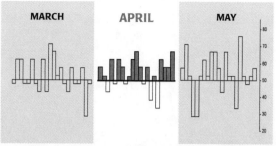

Market Probability Chart above is a graphic representation of the Market Probability Calendar on page 123.

◆ April is still the best Dow month (average 1.9%) since 1950 (page 48) ◆ April 1999 first month ever to gain 1000 Dow points, 856 in 2001, knocked off its high horse in 2002 down 458, 2003 up 488 ◆ Prone to weakness after mid-month tax deadline ◆ Stocks anticipate great first quarter earnings by rising sharply before earnings are reported, rather than after ◆ Rarely a dangerous month except in big bear markets (like 2002) ◆ "Best Six Months" of the year end with April (page 50) ◆ NASDAQ post-election years up 6, down 2, average 2.0% ◆ Post-election Dow & S&P Aprils better after reelection ◆ End of April NASDAQ strength (page 120)

APRIL DAILY POINT CHANGES DOW JONES INDUSTRIALS

Previous Month Close	1995	1996	1997	1998	1999	2000	2001	2002	2003	2004
	4157.69	5587.14	6583.48	8799.81	9786.16	10921.92	9878.78	10403.94	7992.13	10357.70
1	—	50.58	27.57	68.51	46.35	—	—	− 41.24	77.73	15.63
2	—	33.96	− 94.04	118.32	H	—	− 100.85	− 48.99	215.20	97.26
3	10.72	18.06	− 39.66	− 3.23	—	300.01	− 292.22	− 115.42	− 44.68	—
4	33.20	− 6.86	48.72	—	—	− 57.09	29.71	36.88	36.77	—
5	− 1.04	H	—	—	174.82	− 130.92	402.63	36.47	—	87.78
6	4.84	—	—	49.82	− 43.84	80.35	− 126.96	—	—	12.44
7	− 12.79	—	29.84	− 76.73	121.82	− 2.79	—	—	23.26	− 90.66
8	—	− 88.51	53.25	− 65.02	112.39	—	—	− 22.56	− 1.49	− 38.12
9	—	− 33.96	− 45.32	103.38	− 23.86	—	54.06	− 40.41	− 100.98	H
10	5.53	− 74.43	− 23.79	H	—	75.08	257.59	173.06	23.39	—
11	− 11.07	1.09	− 148.36	—	—	100.52	− 89.27	− 205.65	− 17.92	—
12	10.73	45.52	—	—	165.67	− 161.95	113.47	14.74	—	73.53
13	10.37	—	—	17.44	55.50	− 201.58	H	—	—	− 134.28
14	H	—	60.21	97.90	16.65	− 617.78	—	—	147.69	− 3.33
15	—	60.33	135.26	52.07	51.06	—	—	− 97.15	51.26	19.51
16	—	27.10	92.71	− 85.70	31.17	—	31.62	207.65	− 144.75	54.51
17	− 12.80	− 70.09	− 21.27	90.93	—	276.74	58.17	− 80.54	80.04	—
18	− 16.25	1.81	44.95	—	—	184.91	399.10	− 15.50	H	—
19	28.36	− 16.26	—	—	− 53.36	− 92.46	77.88	51.83	—	− 14.12
20	23.17	—	—	− 25.66	8.02	169.09	− 113.86	—	—	− 123.35
21	39.43	—	− 43.34	43.10	132.87	H	—	—	− 8.75	2.77
22	—	29.26	173.38	− 8.22	145.76	—	—	− 120.68	156.09	143.93
23	—	23.85	− 20.87	− 33.39	− 37.51	—	− 47.62	− 47.19	30.67	11.64
24	33.89	− 34.69	− 20.47	− 78.71	—	62.05	− 77.89	− 58.81	− 75.62	—
25	− 3.81	13.01	− 53.38	—	—	218.72	170.86	4.63	− 133.69	—
26	− 0.34	1.08	—	—	28.92	− 179.32	67.15	− 124.34	—	− 28.11
27	14.87	—	—	− 146.98	113.12	− 57.40	117.70	—	—	33.43
28	6.57	—	44.15	− 18.68	13.74	− 154.19	—	—	165.26	− 135.56
29	—	5.42	179.01	52.56	32.93	—	—	− 90.85	31.38	− 70.33
30	—	− 4.33	46.96	111.85	− 89.34	—	− 75.08	126.35	− 22.90	− 46.70
Close	4321.27	5569.08	7008.99	9063.37	10789.04	10733.91	10734.97	9946.22	8480.09	10225.57
Change	163.58	− 18.06	425.51	263.56	1002.88	− 188.01	856.19	− 457.72	487.96	− 132.13

April "Best Month" for Dow since 1950
Day-before-Good Friday gains are nifty

MARCH/APRIL

End of March terrible lately

MONDAY

28

*In the course of evolution and a higher civilization
we might be able to get along comfortably without Congress,
but without Wall Street, never.*
— Henry Clews (1900)

TUESDAY

29

*Nothing gives one person so much advantage over another
as to remain always cool and unruffled under all circumstances.*
— Thomas Jefferson

WEDNESDAY

30

Capitalism without bankruptcy is like Christianity without hell.
— Frank Borman (CEO Eastern Airlines, April 1986)

Last day of March Dow down 8 of last 10, average –0.7%

THURSDAY

31

*The secret to business
is to know something that nobody else knows.*
— Aristotle Onassis (Greek shipping billionaire)

April first trading day Dow up 8 of last 10

FRIDAY

1

Victory goes to the player who makes the next-to-last mistake.
— Savielly Grigorievitch Tartakower (Chess master, 1887-1956)

SATURDAY

2

Daylight Saving Time begins

SUNDAY

3

THE DECEMBER LOW INDICATOR: A USEFUL PROGNOSTICATING TOOL

The December Low Indicator was brought to our attention a few years ago by Jeffrey Saut, managing director of investment strategy at Raymond James. Basically, if the Dow closes below its December closing low in the first quarter, it is a warning sign. The original analysis is credited to Lucien Hooper, a *Forbes* columnist and Wall Street analyst back in the 1970s. Hooper dismissed the importance of January and January's first week as reliable indicators. He noted that the trend could be random or even manipulated during a holiday-shortened week. Instead, said Hooper, "Pay much more attention to the December low. If that low is violated during the first quarter of the New Year, watch out!"

Twelve of the 26 occurrences were followed by gains for the rest of the year — and full-year gains — after the low for the year was reached. For perspective we've included the January Barometer readings for the selected years. Hooper's "Watch Out" warning was absolutely correct, though. All but one of the instances since 1952 experienced further declines, as the Dow fell an additional 10.7% on average when December's low was breached in Q1.

Only three significant drops occurred (not shown) when December's low was not breached in Q1 (1974, 1981 and 1987). Both indicators were wrong only three times and three years ended flat. If the December low is not crossed, turn to our January Barometer for guidance. It has been virtually perfect, right nearly 100% of these times (view the complete results at *http://www.hirschorg.com/2005p040*).

YEARS DOW FELL BELOW DECEMBER LOW IN FIRST QUARTER

Year	Previous Dec Low	Date Crossed	Crossing Price	Subseq. Low	% Change Cross-Low	Rest of Year % Change	Full Year % Change	Jan Bar
1952	262.29	2/19/52	261.37	256.35	− 1.9%	11.7%	8.4%	1.6%²
1953	281.63	2/11/53	281.57	255.49	− 9.3	− 0.2	− 3.8	− 0.7
1956	480.72	1/9/56	479.74	462.35	− 3.6	4.1	2.3	− 3.6²³
1957	480.61	1/18/57	477.46	419.79	− 12.1	− 8.7	− 12.8	− 4.2
1960	661.29	1/12/60	660.43	566.05	− 14.3	− 6.7	− 9.3	− 7.1
1962	720.10	1/5/62	714.84	535.76	− 25.1	− 8.8	− 10.8	− 3.8
1966	939.53	3/1/66	938.19	744.32	− 20.7	− 16.3	− 18.9	0.5¹
1968	879.16	1/22/68	871.71	825.13	− 5.3	8.3	4.3	− 4.4¹²
1969	943.75	1/6/69	936.66	769.93	− 17.8	− 14.6	− 15.2	− 0.8
1970	769.93	1/26/70	768.88	631.16	− 17.9	9.1	4.8	− 7.6²³
1973	1000.00	1/29/73	996.46	788.31	− 20.9	− 14.6	− 16.6	− 1.7
1977	946.64	2/7/77	946.31	800.85	− 15.4	− 12.2	− 17.3	− 5.1
1978	806.22	1/5/78	804.92	742.12	− 7.8	0.0	− 3.1	− 6.2
1980	819.62	3/10/80	818.94	759.13	− 7.3	17.7	14.9	5.8²
1982	868.25	1/5/82	865.30	776.92	− 10.2	20.9	19.6	− 1.8¹²
1984	1236.79	1/25/84	1231.89	1086.57	− 11.8	− 1.6	− 3.7	− 0.9³
1990	2687.93	1/15/90	2669.37	2365.10	− 11.4	− 1.3	− 4.3	− 6.9
1991	2565.59	1/7/91	2522.77	2470.30	− 2.1	25.6	20.3	4.2²
1993	3255.18	1/8/93	3251.67	3241.95	− 0.3	15.5	13.7	0.7²
1994	3697.08	3/30/94	3626.75	3593.35	− 0.9	5.7	2.1	3.3²³
1996	5059.32	1/10/96	5032.94	5032.94	0.0	28.1	26.0	3.3²
1998	7660.13	1/9/98	7580.42	7539.07	− 0.5	21.1	16.1	1.0²
2000	10998.39	1/4/00	10997.93	9796.03	− 10.9	− 1.9	− 6.2	− 5.1
2001	10318.93	3/12/01	10208.25	8235.81	− 19.3	− 1.8	− 7.1	3.5¹
2002	9763.96	1/16/02	9712.27	7286.27	− 25.0	− 14.1	− 16.8	− 1.6
2003	8303.78	1/24/03	8131.01	7524.06	− 7.5	28.6	25.3	− 2.7¹²
			Average Drop		**− 10.7%**			

¹ *January Barometer wrong* ² *December Low Indicator wrong* ³ *Year Flat*

APRIL

Average April gains last 34 years

NAS 1.2%	*Dow 2.1%*	*S&P 1.3%*
Up 22 Down 12	*Up 19 Down 15*	*Up 22 Down 12*
Rank #5	*Rank #1*	*Rank #4*

MONDAY
4

> *Those who are of the opinion that money will do everything*
> *may very well be suspected to do everything for money.*
> — Sir George Savile

TUESDAY
5

Start looking for Dow and S&P MACD seasonal SELL Signal (page 52)
Almanac Investor subscribers will be emailed the alert when it triggers
visit stocktradersalmanac.com for details

> *If you develop the absolute sense of certainty that powerful beliefs provide,*
> *then you can get yourself to accomplish virtually anything,*
> *including those things that other people are certain are impossible.*
> — Anthony Robbins (Motivator, advisor, consultant,
> author, entrepreneur, philanthropist, b. 1960)

WEDNESDAY
 # 6

> *Short-term volatility is greatest at*
> *turning points and diminishes as a trend becomes established.*
> — George Soros (Financier, philanthropist,
> political activist, author and philosopher, b. 1930)

THURSDAY
7

> *Institutions tend to dump stock in a single transaction and buy,*
> *if possible, in smaller lots, gradually accumulating a position.*
> *Therefore, many more big blocks are traded on downticks*
> *than on upticks.*
> — Justin Mamis

FRIDAY
 # 8

> *If you destroy a free market you create a black market.*
> *If you have ten thousand regulations*
> *you destroy all respect for the law.*
> — Winston Churchill (British statesman, 1874-1965)

SATURDAY
9

SUNDAY
10

UNDER DEMOCRATS $10,000 GROWS TO $279,705, BUT ONLY TO $78,699 UNDER THE REPUBLICANS

Does the market perform better under Republicans or Democrats? The market surge under Reagan and Bush after Vietnam, OPEC and Iran inflation almost helped Republicans even up the score in the 20th century vs. the Democrats, who benefited when Roosevelt came in following an 89.2% drop by the Dow. However, under Clinton, the Democrats took the lead again. Both parties were more evenly matched in the last half of the century.

THE STOCK MARKET UNDER REPUBLICANS AND DEMOCRATS

Republican Eras		% Change	Democratic Eras		% Change
1901-1912	12 Years	48.3%	1913-1920	8 Years	29.2%
1921-1932	12 Years	− 24.5%	1933-1952	20 Years	318.4%
1953-1960	8 Years	121.2%	1961-1968	8 Years	58.3%
1969-1976	8 Years	2.1%	1977-1980	4 Years	− 3.0%
1981-1992	12 Years	247.0%	1993-2000	8 Years	236.7%
2001-2004*	4 Years	− 10.4%			
Totals	**56* Years**	**383.7%**	**Totals**	**48 Years**	**639.6%**
Average Annual Change 6.9%			**Average Annual Change 13.3%**		

Based on Dow Jones Industrial Average on previous year's Election Day or day before when closed
*Through August 6, 2004

. A $10,000 investment compounded during Democratic eras would have grown to $279,705 in 48 years. The same investment during 56* Republican years would have appreciated to $78,699. After lagging for many years, performance under the Republicans improved under Reagan and Bush. But under Clinton, Democratic performance surged way ahead.

DECLINE OF THE DOLLAR UNDER REPUBLICANS AND DEMOCRATS

Republican Eras		Loss in Purch. Power	Value of Dollar	Democratic Eras		Loss in Purch. Power	Value of Dollar
1901-1912	12 Years	− 23.6%	$0.76	1913-1920	8 Years	− 51.4%	$0.49
1921-1932	12 Years	+ 46.9%	$1.12	1933-1952	20 Years	− 48.6%	$0.25
1953-1960	8 Years	− 10.2%	$1.01	1961-1968	8 Years	− 15.0%	$0.21
1969-1976	8 Years	− 38.9%	$0.62	1977-1980	4 Years	− 30.9%	$0.15
1981-1992	12 Years	− 41.3%	$0.36	1993-2000	8 Years	− 18.5%	$0.12
2001-2004**	4 Years	− 8.2%	$0.33				

The Republican Dollar declined to $0.33 in 56 years.   **The Democratic Dollar declined to $0.12 in 48 years.**

Based on average annual Consumer Price Index 1982-1984 = 100
** Through June 30, 2004

Adjusting stock market performance for loss of purchasing power reduced the Democrats' $279,705 to $33,426 and the Republicans' $78,699 to $26,145. Republicans may point out that all four major wars of the 20th century began while the Democrats were in power. Democrats can counter that the 46.7 percent increase in purchasing power occurred during the Depression and was not very meaningful to the 25 percent who were unemployed.

For the record, there have been 14 recessions and 14 bear markets under the Republicans and 7 recessions and 10 bear markets under the Democrats.

Monday before expiration Dow up 8 of last 9 (2002 lone loser) **MONDAY**

11

A statistician is someone who can draw a straight line
from an unwarranted assumption to a foregone conclusion.
— Anonymous

TUESDAY

12

There is one thing stronger than all the armies in the world,
and this is an idea whose time has come.
— Victor Hugo (French novelist, playwright,
Hunchback of Notre Dame and *Les Misérables*, 1802-1885)

WEDNESDAY

13

Live beyond your means; then you're forced to work hard,
you have to succeed.
— Edward G. Robinson (American actor)

THURSDAY

 # 14

A man will fight harder for his interests than his rights.
— Napoleon Bonaparte
(Emperor of France 1804-1815, 1769-1821)

Income Tax Deadline **FRIDAY**
Expiration day Dow up 7 of last 8 (2001 lone loser)  # 15

The monuments of wit survive the monuments of power.
— Francis Bacon (English philosopher,
essayist, statesman, 1561-1626)

SATURDAY

16

SUNDAY

17

DOWN JANUARYS: A REMARKABLE RECORD

In the first third of the 20th century there was no correlation between January markets and the year as a whole (page 24). Then in 1972 we discovered that the 1933 "Lame Duck" Amendment to the Constitution changed the political calendar and the January Barometer was born. And its record has been magnificent. But to those who would like bull and bear markets to begin on January First and end on the last day of December, sorry, we can't oblige.

Down Januarys are harbingers of trouble ahead, in the economic, political, or military arenas. Eisenhower's heart attack in 1955 cast doubt on whether he could run in 1956, a flat year. Two other election years were also flat. Eleven bear markets began with poor Januarys and four of them continued into second years. 1968 started down as we were mired in Vietnam, but Johnson's "bombing halt" changed the climate. Affected by uncertainty regarding pending military action in Iraq, January 2003 closed down and the market triple-bottomed in March just before U.S. led forces began their blitz to Baghdad. Once the doubt about the first phase in Iraq was removed, the market put three years of the bear behind it. Pre-election and recovery forces turned 2003 into a banner year.

Excluding 1956, down Januarys were followed by substantial declines averaging *minus* 13.0%, providing excellent buying opportunities later in most years.

FROM DOWN JANUARY S&P CLOSES TO LOW AND NEXT 11 MONTHS

Year	January Close	% Change	11-Month Low	Date of Low	Jan Close to Low %	% Feb to Dec	Year % Change	
1953	26.38	− 0.7	22.71	14-Sep	− 13.9%	− 6.0%	− 6.6	bear
1956	43.82	− 3.6	44.10	28-May	0.9	6.5	2.6	FLAT
1957	44.72	− 4.2	38.98	22-Oct	− 12.8	− 10.6	− 14.3	bear
1960	55.61	− 7.1	52.30	25-Oct	− 6.0	4.5	− 3.0	bear
1962	68.84	− 3.8	52.32	26-Jun	− 24.0	− 8.3	− 11.8	bear
1968	92.24	− 4.4	87.72	5-Mar	− 4.9	12.6	7.7	Cont. bear
1969	103.01	− 0.8	89.20	17-Dec	− 13.4	− 10.6	− 11.4	bear
1970	85.02	− 7.6	69.20	26-May	− 18.6	8.4	0.1	Cont. bear
1973	116.03	− 1.7	92.16	5-Dec	− 20.6	− 15.9	− 17.4	bear
1974	96.57	− 1.0	62.28	3-Oct	− 35.5	− 29.0	− 29.7	bear
1977	102.03	− 5.1	90.71	2-Nov	− 11.1	− 6.8	− 11.5	bear
1978	89.25	− 6.2	86.90	6-Mar	− 2.6	7.7	1.1	Cont. bear
1981	129.55	− 4.6	112.77	25-Sep	− 13.0	− 5.4	− 9.7	bear
1982	120.40	− 1.8	102.42	12-Aug	− 14.9	16.8	14.8	Cont. bear
1984	163.42	− 0.9	147.82	24-Jul	− 9.5	2.3	1.4	FLAT
1990	329.07	− 6.9	295.46	11-Oct	− 10.2	0.4	− 6.6	bear
1992	408.79	− 2.0	394.50	8-Apr	− 3.5	6.6	4.5	FLAT
2000	1394.46	− 5.1	1264.74	20-Dec	− 9.3	− 5.3	− 10.1	bear
2002	1130.20	− 1.6	776.76	9-Oct	− 31.3	− 22.2	− 23.4	Cont. bear
2003	855.70	− 2.7	800.73	11-Mar	− 6.4	29.9	26.4	Cont. bear
				Totals	− 260.6%	− 24.4%	− 97.0%	
				Average	− 13.0%	− 1.2%	− 4.9%	

APRIL

MONDAY
18

*The pursuit of gain is the only way in which people can serve
the needs of others whom they do not know.*
— Friedrich von Hayek (*Counterrevolution of Science*)

TUESDAY
19

*Almost any insider purchase is worth investigating
for a possible lead to a superior speculation.
But very few insider sales justify concern.*
— William Chidester

WEDNESDAY
20

*Spend at least as much time researching a stock
as you would choosing a refrigerator.*
— Peter Lynch

THURSDAY
21

*A loss never bothers me after I take it. I forget it overnight.
But being wrong — not taking the loss —
that is what does damage to the pocketbook and to the soul.*
— Jesse Livermore

FRIDAY
22

*Those who cast the votes decide nothing.
Those who count the votes decide everything.*
— Joseph Stalin

SATURDAY
23

Passover

SUNDAY
24

MAY ALMANAC

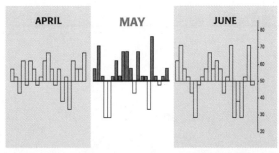

Market Probability Chart above is a graphic representation of the Market Probability Calendar on page 123.

◆ "May/June disaster area" between 1965 and 1984 with 15 out of 20 down Mays ◆ Between 1985 and 1997 May was the best month, gaining 3.3% per year on average ◆ Recent record four of last seven Mays down after 13 straight gains in S&P ◆ Still sports a 1.9% average in last 15 years ◆ Worst six months of the year begin with May (page 50) ◆ A $10,000 investment compounded to $492,060 for November-April in 54 years compared to $318 loss for May-October ◆ Memorial Day week record: up 12 years in a row (1984-1995), down five of the last nine years; up 240 Dow points in 1999, 495 points in 2000 and 249 in 2003 ◆ Post-Election Year Mays rank #2 on S&P (1.3%, up 7, down 6) and NASDAQ (2.9% up 6, down 8), #5 for the Dow (1.0%, up 7, down 6).

MAY DAILY POINT CHANGES DOW JONES INDUSTRIALS

Previous Month	1995	1996	1997	1998	1999	2000	2001	2002	2003	2004
Close	4321.27	5569.08	7008.99	9063.37	10789.04	10733.91	10734.97	9946.22	8480.09	10225.57
1	− 5.19	6.14	− 32.51	83.70	—	77.87	163.37	113.41	− 25.84	—
2	12.80	− 76.95	94.72	—	—	− 80.66	− 21.66	32.24	128.43	—
3	44.27	− 20.24	—	—	225.65	− 250.99	− 80.03	− 85.24	—	88.43
4	− 13.49	—	—	45.59	− 128.58	− 67.64	154.59	—	—	3.20
5	− 16.26	—	143.29	− 45.09	69.30	165.37	—	—	− 51.11	− 6.25
6	—	− 13.72	10.83	− 92.92	− 8.59	—	—	− 198.59	56.79	− 69.69
7	—	− 43.36	− 139.67	− 77.97	84.77	—	− 16.07	28.51	− 27.73	− 123.92
8	40.47	53.11	50.97	78.47	—	25.77	− 51.66	305.28	− 69.41	—
9	6.91	1.08	32.91	—	—	− 66.88	− 16.53	− 104.41	113.38	—
10	13.84	43.00	—	—	− 24.34	− 168.97	43.46	− 97.50	—	− 127.32
11	6.57	—	—	36.37	18.90	178.19	− 89.13	—	—	29.45
12	19.37	—	123.22	70.25	− 25.78	63.40	—	—	122.13	25.69
13	—	64.46	− 18.54	50.07	106.82	—	—	169.74	− 47.48	− 34.42
14	—	42.11	11.95	− 39.61	− 193.87	—	56.02	188.48	− 31.43	2.13
15	6.91	0.73	47.39	− 76.23	—	198.41	− 4.36	− 54.46	65.32	—
16	− 2.42	9.61	− 138.88	—	—	126.79	342.95	45.53	− 34.17	—
17	− 12.45	52.45	—	—	− 59.85	− 164.83	32.66	63.87	—	− 105.96
18	− 81.96	—	—	− 45.09	− 16.52	7.54	53.16	—	—	61.60
19	0.69	—	34.21	3.74	50.44	− 150.43	—	—	− 185.58	− 30.80
20	—	61.32	74.58	116.83	− 20.65	—	—	− 123.58	− 2.03	− 0.07
21	—	− 12.56	12.77	− 39.11	− 37.46	—	36.18	− 123.79	25.07	29.10
22	54.30	41.74	− 32.56	− 17.93	—	− 84.30	− 80.68	52.17	77.59	—
23	40.81	− 15.88	87.78	—	—	− 120.28	− 151.73	58.20	7.36	—
24	1.72	0.74	—	—	− 174.61	113.08	16.91	− 111.82	—	− 8.31
25	− 25.93	—	—	H	− 123.58	− 211.43	− 117.05	—	—	159.19
26	− 43.23	—	H	− 150.71	171.07	− 24.68	—	—	H	− 7.73
27	—	H	37.50	− 27.16	− 235.23	—	—	H	179.97	95.31
28	—	− 53.19	− 26.18	33.63	92.81	—	H	− 122.68	11.77	16.75
29	H	− 35.84	− 27.05	− 70.25	—	H	33.77	− 58.54	− 81.94	—
30	9.68	19.58	0.86	—	—	227.89	− 166.50	− 11.35	139.08	—
31	86.46	− 50.23	—	—	H	− 4.80	39.30	13.56	—	H
Close	4465.14	5643.18	7331.04	8899.95	10559.74	10522.33	10911.94	9925.25	8850.26	10188.45
Change	143.87	74.10	322.05	− 163.42	− 229.30	− 211.58	176.97	− 20.97	370.17	− 37.12

Was Number One month for nine straight years
But five out of the last seven have caused May tears

APRIL/MAY

MONDAY
25

*In an uptrend, if a higher high is made but fails to carry through,
and prices dip below the previous high, the trend is apt to reverse.
The converse is true for downtrends.*
— Victor Sperandeo
(*Trader Vic — Methods of a Wall Street Master*)

TUESDAY
 ## 26

*Investors operate with limited funds and limited intelligence,
they don't need to know everything. As long as they understand
something better than others, they have an edge.*
— George Soros (Financier, philanthropist,
political activist, author and philosopher, b. 1930)

WEDNESDAY
27

*Resentment is like taking poison
and waiting for the other person to die.*
— Malachy McCourt (*A Monk Swimming: A Memoir*)

THURSDAY
28

*Small volume is usually accompanied by a fall in price;
large volume by a rise in price.*
— Charles C. Ying (Computer Study)

End of "Best Six Months" of the Year (page 50)   **FRIDAY**
 ## 29

*One machine can do the work of fifty ordinary men.
No machine can do the work of one extraordinary man.*
— Elbert Hubbard
(American author, *A Message To Garcia*, 1856-1915)

SATURDAY
30

Bearish May Sector Seasonalities: Semiconductors (page 118)   **SUNDAY**
1

TOP PERFORMING MONTHS PAST 54½ YEARS
STANDARD & POOR'S 500 & DOW JONES INDUSTRIALS

Monthly performance of the S&P and the Dow are ranked over the past 54½ years. NASDAQ monthly performance is shown on page 54.

January, April, November and December still hold the top four positions in both the Dow and S&P. This led to our discovery in 1986 of the market's best-kept secret. You can divide the year into two sections and have practically all the gains in one six-month section and very little in the other. (See "Best Six Months" on page 50.) September has been the worst month on both lists.

MONTHLY % CHANGES (JANUARY 1950 – JUNE 2004)

Standard & Poor's 500					Dow Jones Industrials				
Month	Total % Change	Avg. % Change	# Up	# Down	Month	Total % Change	Avg. % Change	# Up	# Down
Jan	80.0%	1.5	35	20	Jan	77.5%	1.4%	37	18
Feb	— 2.9	— 0.1	29	26	Feb	8.7	0.2	31	24
Mar	57.3	1.0	36	19	Mar	52.7	1.0	35	20
Apr	73.8	1.3	37	18	Apr	102.1	1.9	34	21
May	14.2	0.3	31	24	May	2.9	0.1	28	27
Jun	13.5	0.2	30	25	Jun	— 3.4	— 0.1	28	27
Jul	49.1	0.9	29	25	Jul	58.7	1.1	33	21
Aug	0.8	0.02	29	25	Aug	— 3.0	— 0.1	30	24
Sep*	— 39.2	— 0.7	21	32	Sep	— 57.5	— 1.1	19	35
Oct	49.4	0.9	32	22	Oct	32.0	0.6	32	22
Nov	91.5	1.7	36	18	Nov	87.7	1.6	36	18
Dec	92.5	1.7	41	13	Dec	95.5	1.8	39	15
% Rank					**% Rank**				
Dec	92.5%	1.7%	41	13	Apr	102.1%	1.9%	34	21
Nov	91.5	1.7	36	18	Dec	95.5	1.8	39	15
Jan	80.0	1.5	35	20	Nov	87.7	1.6	36	18
Apr	73.8	1.3	37	18	Jan	77.5	1.4	37	18
Mar	57.3	1.0	36	19	Jul	58.7	1.1	33	21
Oct	49.4	0.9	32	22	Mar	52.7	1.0	35	20
Jul	49.1	0.9	29	25	Oct	32.0	0.6	32	22
May	14.2	0.3	31	24	Feb	8.7	0.2	31	24
Jun	13.5	0.2	30	25	May	2.9	0.1	28	27
Aug	0.8	0.02	29	25	Aug	— 3.0	— 0.1	30	24
Feb	— 2.9	— 0.1	29	26	Jun	— 3.4	— 0.1	28	27
Sep*	— 39.2	— 0.7	21	32	Sep	— 57.5	— 1.1	19	35
Totals	**480.0%**	**8.7%**			**Totals**	**453.9%**	**8.4%**		
Average		**0.73%**			**Average**		**0.70%**		

*No change 1979

Anticipators, shifts in cultural behavior and faster information flow have altered seasonality in recent years. Here is how the months ranked over the past 15 years (180 months) using total percentage gains on the Dow: November 36.4, October 34.1, April 32.8, December 31.6, May 28.0, July 23.6, March 13.4, January 11.2, February 10.5, June –6.0, August –22.4, September –30.3.

During the last 15 years, notice how anticipators of our Best Six Months may have helped push October into the number-two spot. July and May have also edged out January and March. The October 1987 crash month that was down 23.2% is no longer in the most recent 15 years and we've seen some sizeable turnarounds in "bear killing" October the last six years. Big losses in the period were: August 1990 (Kuwait), off 10.0%; August 1998 (SE Asia crisis), off 15.1%; September 2001 (9/11 attack) off 11.1%; September 2002 (Iraq war drums) off 12.4%.

MAY

May first trading day Dow up 6 of last 7

MONDAY

2

Become more humble as the market goes your way.
— Bernard Baruch

FOMC Meeting

TUESDAY

 3

*Securities pricing is, in every sense, a psychological phenomenon
that arises from the interaction of human beings with fear.
Why not greed and fear as the equation is usually stated?
Because greed is simply fear of not having enough.*
— John Bollinger (Bollinger Capital Management, created Bollinger
Bands, *Capital Growth Letter, Bollinger on Bollinger Bands*)

Average May gains last 34 years

WEDNESDAY

NAS 1.0%	Dow 0.5%	S&P 0.8%
Up 20 Down 14	Up 18 Down 16	Up 20 Down 14
Rank #6	Rank #7	Rank #8

4

*Liberals have practiced tax and tax, spend and spend,
elect and elect but conservatives have perfected borrow and
borrow, spend and spend, elect and elect.*
— George Will (*Newsweek*, 1989)

THURSDAY

5

*Give me a stock clerk with a goal
and I will give you a man who will make history.
Give me a man without a goal, and I will give you a stock clerk.*
— James Cash Penney (J.C. Penney founder)

Day before Mother's Day Dow up 7 of last 10

FRIDAY

6

*I had an unshakable faith. I had it in my head that if I had to,
I'd crawl over broken glass. I'd live in a tent —
it was gonna happen. And I think when you have
that kind of steely determination…people get out of the way.*
— Rick Newcombe (Syndicator, *Investor's Business Daily*)

SATURDAY

7

Mother's Day

SUNDAY

8

"BEST SIX MONTHS" STILL AN EYE-POPPING STRATEGY

Our Best Six Months Switching Strategy (discovered in 1986) consistently delivers. Investing in the Dow Jones industrial average between November 1st and April 30th each year and then switching into fixed income for the other six months has produced reliable returns with reduced risk since 1950.

The chart on page 138 shows November, December, January, March and April to be the top months since 1950. Add February, and an excellent strategy is born! These six consecutive months gained 10599.68 Dow points in 54 years, while the remaining May through October months *lost* 588.44 points. The S&P gained 1089.23 points in the same best six months and just 62.09 points in the worst six.

Percentage changes for the Dow during each six-month period since 1950 are shown along with a compounding $10,000 investment.

The November-April $482,060 gain overshadows the May-October $318 loss. (S&P results were $349,165 to $7,102.) Just two November-April losses were double-digit and were due to our April 1970 Cambodian invasion and the fall 1973 OPEC oil embargo.

An exogenous event, such as war, could affect the seasonality as it did in 1970 and 2003.

When we discovered this strategy in 1986, November-April outperformed May-October by $88,163 to minus $1,522. Results improved substantially these past 18 years, $393,897 to $1,204. As sensational as these results are, they are nearly tripled with a simple timing indicator, see page 52.

SIX-MONTH SWITCHING STRATEGY

	DJIA % Change May 1-Oct 31	Investing $10,000	DJIA % Change Nov 1-Apr 30	Investing $10,000
1950	5.0%	$10,500	15.2%	$11,520
1951	1.2	10,626	− 1.8	11,313
1952	4.5	11,104	2.1	11,551
1953	0.4	11,148	15.8	13,376
1954	10.3	12,296	20.9	16,172
1955	6.9	13,144	13.5	18,355
1956	− 7.0	12,224	3.0	18,906
1957	− 10.8	10,904	3.4	19,549
1958	19.2	12,998	14.8	22,442
1959	3.7	13,479	− 6.9	20,894
1960	− 3.5	13,007	16.9	24,425
1961	3.7	13,488	− 5.5	23,082
1962	− 11.4	11,950	21.7	28,091
1963	5.2	12,571	7.4	30,170
1964	7.7	13,539	5.6	31,860
1965	4.2	14,108	− 2.8	30,968
1966	− 13.6	12,189	11.1	34,405
1967	− 1.9	11,957	3.7	35,678
1968	4.4	12,483	− 0.2	35,607
1969	− 9.9	11,247	− 14.0	30,622
1970	2.7	11,551	24.6	38,155
1971	− 10.9	10,292	13.7	43,382
1972	0.1	10,302	− 3.6	41,820
1973	3.8	10,693	− 12.5	36,593
1974	− 20.5	8,501	23.4	45,156
1975	1.8	8,654	19.2	53,826
1976	− 3.2	8,377	− 3.9	51,727
1977	− 11.7	7,397	2.3	52,917
1978	− 5.4	6,998	7.9	57,097
1979	− 4.6	6,676	0.2	57,211
1980	13.1	7,551	7.9	61,731
1981	− 14.6	6,449	− 0.5	61,422
1982	16.9	7,539	23.6	75,918
1983	− 0.1	7,531	− 4.4	72,578
1984	3.1	7,764	4.2	75,626
1985	9.2	8,478	29.8	98,163
1986	5.3	8,927	21.8	119,563
1987	− 12.8	7,784	1.9	121,835
1988	5.7	8,228	12.6	137,186
1989	9.4	9,001	0.4	137,735
1990	− 8.1	8,272	18.2	162,803
1991	6.3	8,793	9.4	178,106
1992	− 4.0	8,441	6.2	189,149
1993	7.4	9,066	0.03	189,206
1994	6.2	9,628	10.6	209,262
1995	10.0	10,591	17.1	245,046
1996	8.3	11,470	16.2	284,743
1997	6.2	12,181	21.8	346,817
1998	− 5.2	11,548	25.6	435,602
1999	− 0.5	11,490	0.04	435,776
2000	2.2	11,743	− 2.2	426,189
2001	− 15.5	9,923	9.6	467,103
2002	− 15.6	8,375	1.0	471,774
2003	15.6	9,682	4.3	492,060
54-Year Gain (Loss)		**($318)**		**$482,060**

Day after Mother's Day Dow up 12 of last 15

MONDAY
9

Whom the gods would destroy,
they first put on the cover of Business Week.
— Paul Krugman (*Economist*, referring to CEO of Enron,
New York Times Op-Ed August 17, 2001,
On cover 2/12, gets pie in the face 6/23, and quits 8/16)

TUESDAY
 # 10

All a parent can give a child is roots and wings.
— Chinese proverb

WEDNESDAY
11

Bankruptcy was designed to forgive stupidity,
not reward criminality.
— William P. Barr (Verizon executive VP and General Counsel,
after calling for government liquidation
of MCI-WorldCom in Chap. 7, April 14, 2003)

THURSDAY
 # 12

When I talk to a company that tells me the last analyst showed up
three years ago, I can hardly contain my enthusiasm.
— Peter Lynch

FRIDAY
13

Why is it right-wing [conservatives] always stand
shoulder to shoulder in solidarity,
while liberals always fall out among themselves?
— Yevgeny Yevtushenko (Russian poet, Babi Yar,
quoted in London *Observer* December 15, 1991, b. 1933)

SATURDAY
14

SUNDAY
15

MACD-TIMING TRIPLES "BEST SIX MONTHS" RESULTS

Using the simple MACD (Moving Average Convergence Divergence) indicator developed by our friend Gerald Appel to better time entries and exits into and out of the Best Six Months period nearly triples the results.

In his book, *Riding the Bear, Street Smart Report,* writer Sy Harding revealed the benefits of trading our November–through–April Best Six Months Switching Strategy (page 50) with MACD triggers, and termed it the "best mechanical system ever."

We have implemented the system for a number of years in our *Almanac Investor Newsletter* and *Platform* with quite a degree of success. Starting October 1 we look to catch the market's first hint of an uptrend after the summer doldrums, and beginning April 1 we prepare to exit these seasonal positions as soon as the market falters.

In up-trending markets MACD signals get you in earlier and keep you in longer. But if the market is trending down, entries are delayed until the market turns up and exit points can come a month earlier. Thus, our "Best Six Months" could be lengthened or shortened a month or so.

The results are astounding applying the simple MACD signals. Instead of $10,000 gaining $482,060 over the 54 recent years when invested only during the Best Six Months (page 50), the gain nearly tripled to $1,411,142. The $318 loss during the worst six months expanded to a loss of $6,598.

Impressive results for being invested during only 6 1/2 months of the year on average! For the rest of the year you could park in a money market fund, or if a long-term holder, you could write options on your positions (sell call options).

Updated signals are emailed to our monthly newsletter subscribers as soon as they are triggered. For further information on how the MACD indicator is calculated, dates when signals were given, or for a FREE 1-month trial to our *Almanac Investor Platform*, visit **http:// www.hirschorg.com/2005p052**.

SIX-MONTH SWITCHING STRATEGY+TIMING

	DJIA % Change May 1-Oct 31*	Investing $10,000	DJIA % Change Nov 1-Apr 30*	Investing $10,000
1950	7.3%	$10,730	13.3%	$11,330
1951	0.1	10,741	1.9	11,545
1952	1.4	10,891	2.1	11,787
1953	0.2	10,913	17.1	13,803
1954	13.5	12,386	16.3	16,053
1955	7.7	13,340	13.1	18,156
1956	− 6.8	12,433	2.8	18,664
1957	−12.3	10,904	4.9	19,579
1958	17.3	12,790	16.7	22,849
1959	1.6	12,995	−3.1	22,141
1960	− 4.9	12,358	16.9	25,883
1961	2.9	12,716	−1.5	25,495
1962	−15.3	10,770	22.4	31,206
1963	4.3	11,233	9.6	34,202
1964	6.7	11,986	6.2	36,323
1965	2.6	12,298	−2.5	35,415
1966	−16.4	10,281	14.3	40,479
1967	− 2.1	10,065	5.5	42,705
1968	3.4	10,407	0.2	42,790
1969	−11.9	9,169	−6.7	39,923
1970	− 1.4	9,041	20.8	48,227
1971	−11.0	8,046	15.4	55,654
1972	− 0.6	7,998	−1.4	54,875
1973	−11.0	7,118	0.1	54,930
1974	−22.4	5,524	28.2	70,420
1975	0.1	5,530	18.5	83,448
1976	− 3.4	5,342	−3.0	80,945
1977	−11.4	4,733	0.5	81,350
1978	− 4.5	4,520	9.3	88,916
1979	− 5.3	4,280	7.0	95,140
1980	9.3	4,678	4.7	99,612
1981	−14.6	3,995	0.4	100,010
1982	15.5	4,614	23.5	123,512
1983	2.5	4,729	−7.3	114,496
1984	3.3	4,885	3.9	118,961
1985	7.0	5,227	38.1	164,285
1986	− 2.8	5,081	28.2	210,613
1987	−14.9	4,324	3.0	216,931
1988	6.1	4,588	11.8	242,529
1989	9.8	5,038	3.3	250,532
1990	− 6.7	4,700	15.8	290,116
1991	4.8	4,926	11.3	322,899
1992	− 6.2	4,621	6.6	344,210
1993	5.5	4,875	5.6	363,486
1994	3.7	5,055	13.1	411,103
1995	7.2	5,419	16.7	479,757
1996	9.2	5,918	21.9	584,824
1997	3.6	6,131	18.5	693,016
1998	−12.4	5,371	39.9	969,529
1999	− 6.4	5,027	5.1	1,018,975
2000	− 6.0	4,725	5.4	1,074,000
2001	−17.3	3,908	15.8	1,243,692
2002	−25.2	2,923	6.0	1,318,314
2003	16.4	3,402	7.8	1,421,142
54-Year Gain (Loss)		**(6,598)**		**$1,411,142**

*MACD generated entry and exit points (earlier or later) can lengthen or shorten six-month periods

Monday before expiration Dow up 15 of 17

MONDAY

16

*In the stock market those who expect history to repeat itself
exactly are doomed to failure.*
— Yale Hirsch

TUESDAY

17

*It's a buy when the 10-week moving average
crosses the 30-week moving average
and the slope of both averages is up.*
— Victor Sperandeo
(*Trader Vic—Methods of a Wall Street Master*)

WEDNESDAY

 # 18

Life is an illusion. You are what you think you are.
— Yale Hirsch

THURSDAY

19

It is impossible to please all the world and one's father.
— Jean de La Fontaine (French poet, 1621-1695)

Expiration day Dow down 10 of 17, but up 3 of last 4

FRIDAY

 # 20

*The market is a voting machine,
whereon countless individuals register choices
which are the product partly of reason and partly of emotion.*
— Graham & Dodd

SATURDAY

21

SUNDAY

22

TOP PERFORMING NASDAQ MONTHS PAST 33½ YEARS

NASDAQ stocks continue to run away during three consecutive months, November, December and January, with an average gain of 7.9% despite the slaughter of November 2000, down 22.9%, December 2001, up only 1.0%, January 2002, –0.8%, and December 2002, –9.7% during the three-year bear that shrank the tech-dominated index by 77.9%.

You can see the months graphically on page 139. January by itself is impressive, up 3.9% on average. April, May and June also shine, creating our NASDAQ Best Eight Months strategy. What appears as a Death Valley abyss occurs during NASDAQ's bleakest four months: July, August, September and October. NASDAQ's Best Eight Months seasonal strategy using MACD timing is displayed on page 58.

MONTHLY CHANGES (JANUARY 1971 — JUNE 2004)

NASDAQ Composite*

Month	Total % Change	Avg. % Change	# Up	# Down
Jan	134.0%	3.9%	24	10
Feb	21.7	0.6	19	15
Mar	11.9	0.3	21	13
Apr	40.7	1.2	22	12
May	34.7	1.0	20	14
Jun	43.8	1.3	22	12
Jul	— 7.2	— 0.2	16	17
Aug	10.1	0.3	18	15
Sep	— 37.9	— 1.1	17	16
Oct	15.7	0.5	17	16
Nov	63.7	1.9	22	11
Dec	68.1	2.1	20	13

% Rank				
Jan	134.0%	3.9%	24	10
Dec	68.1	2.1	20	13
Nov	63.7	1.9	22	11
Jun	43.8	1.3	22	12
Apr	40.7	1.2	22	12
May	34.7	1.0	20	14
Feb	21.7	0.6	19	15
Oct	15.7	0.5	17	16
Mar	11.9	0.3	21	13
Aug	10.1	0.3	18	15
Jul	— 7.2	— 0.2	16	17
Sep	— 37.9	— 1.1	17	16
Totals	**399.3%**	**11.8%**		
Average		**0.98%**		

Dow Jones Industrials

Month	Total % Change	Avg. % Change	# Up	# Down
Jan	67.6%	2.0%	23	11
Feb	14.3	0.4	19	15
Mar	31.6	0.9	22	12
Apr	71.1	2.1	19	15
May	16.3	0.5	18	16
Jun	13.7	0.4	20	14
Jul	15.4	0.5	17	16
Aug	— 5.7	— 0.2	18	15
Sep	— 53.6	— 1.6	9	24
Oct	20.7	0.6	20	13
Nov	43.6	1.3	22	11
Dec	59.1	1.8	24	9

% Rank				
Apr	71.1%	2.1%	19	15
Jan	67.6	2.0	23	11
Dec	59.1	1.8	24	9
Nov	43.6	1.3	22	11
Mar	31.6	0.9	22	12
Oct	20.7	0.6	20	13
May	16.3	0.5	18	16
Jul	15.4	0.5	17	16
Feb	14.3	0.4	19	15
Jun	13.7	0.4	20	14
Aug	— 5.7	— 0.2	18	15
Sep	— 53.6	— 1.6	9	24
Totals	**294.1%**	**8.7%**		
Average		**0.73%**		

For comparison, Dow figures are shown. During this period NASDAQ averaged a 0.98% gain per month, 34 percent more than the Dow's 0.73% per month. Between January 1971 and January 1982 NASDAQ's composite index doubled in the twelve years, while the Dow stayed flat. But while NASDAQ plummeted 77.9% from its 2000 highs to the 2002 bottom, the Dow only lost 37.8%.

*Based on NASDAQ composite, prior to February 5, 1971, based on National Quotation Bureau indices

MAY

MONDAY

23

I've never been poor, only broke. Being poor is a frame of mind.
Being broke is only a temporary situation.
— Mike Todd (Movie producer, 1903-1958)

TUESDAY

 ## 24

I'm a great believer in luck,
and I find the harder I work the more I have of it.
— Thomas Jefferson

WEDNESDAY

25

Love your enemies, for they tell you your faults.
— Benjamin Franklin

THURSDAY

26

Behold, my son, with what little wisdom the world is ruled.
— Count Axel Gustafsson Oxenstierna
(1648 letter to his son at conclusion of Thirty Years War, 1583-1654)

FRIDAY

27

Every truth passes through three stages before it is recognized.
In the first it is ridiculed; in the second it is opposed;
in the third it is regarded as self evident.
— Arthur Schopenhauer (German philosopher, 1788-1860)

SATURDAY

28

Bearish June Sector Seasonalities: Natural Gas (page 118)

SUNDAY

29

JUNE ALMANAC

S	M	T	W	T	F	S
				1	2	3	4
5	6	7	8	9	10	11
12	13	14	15	16	17	18
19	20	21	22	23	24	25
26	27	28	29	30		

JULY

S	M	T	W	T	F	S
					1	2
3	4	5	6	7	8	9
10	11	12	13	14	15	16
17	18	19	20	21	22	23
24	25	26	27	28	29	30
31						

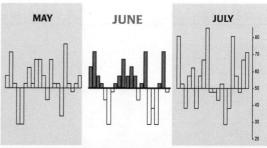

Market Probability Chart above is a graphic representation of the Market Probability Calendar on page 123.

◆ The "summer rally" in most years is the weakest rally of all four seasons (page 70) ◆ Week after June Triple-Witching Day in last 15 years was up in 1995 and 1998 and down all other thirteen times (page 76) ◆ RECORD: S&P up 30, down 25; Dow 28/27; NAS 22/12 ◆ Average gain a mere 0.2% on the S&P, –0.1% on the Dow but a surprisingly strong 1.3% for NASDAQ ◆ June ranks near the bottom on the Dow along with August and September since 1950 (see page 48) ◆ Watch out for end-of-quarter "portfolio pumping" on last day of June, Dow down 10 of last 14, S&P down 9 of last 14, but surprise NASDAQ up 12 of last 14 ◆ Post-Election Year Junes much weaker: Dow –1.2%, S&P –0.8%, NAS 0.6% ◆ June ends NASDAQ's Best Eight Months.

JUNE DAILY POINT CHANGES DOW JONES INDUSTRIALS

Previous Month	1995	1996	1997	1998	1999	2000	2001	2002	2003	2004
Close	4465.14	5643.18	7331.04	8899.95	10559.74	10522.33	10911.94	9925.25	8850.26	10188.45
1	7.61	—	—	22.42	36.52	129.87	78.47	—	—	14.20
2	– 28.36	—	– 41.64	– 31.13	– 18.37	142.56	—	—	47.55	60.32
3	—	– 18.47	22.75	– 87.44	85.80	—	—	– 215.46	25.14	– 67.06
4	—	41.00	– 42.49	66.76	136.15	—	71.11	– 21.95	116.03	46.91
5	32.16	31.77	35.63	167.15	—	20.54	114.32	108.96	2.32	—
6	8.65	– 30.29	130.49	—	— – 79.73	– 105.60	– 172.16	21.49	—
7	– 23.17	29.92	—	—	109.54	77.29	20.50	– 34.97	—	148.26
8	– 3.46	—	—	31.89	– 143.74	– 144.14	– 113.74	—	—	41.44
9	– 34.58	—	42.72	– 19.68	– 75.35	– 54.66	—	—	– 82.79	– 64.08
10	—	– 9.24	60.77	– 78.22	– 69.02	—	—	55.73	74.89	41.66
11	—	– 19.21	36.56	– 159.93	– 130.76	—	– 54.91	– 128.14	128.33	Closed*
12	22.47	– 0.37	135.64	23.17	—	– 49.85	26.29	100.45	13.33	—
13	38.05	– 10.34	70.57	—	—	57.63	– 76.76	– 114.91	– 79.43	—
14	6.57	– 8.50	—	—	72.82	66.11	– 181.49	– 28.59	—	– 75.37
15	5.19	—	—	– 207.01	31.66	26.87	– 66.49	—	—	45.70
16	14.52	—	– 9.95	37.36	189.96	– 265.52	—	—	201.84	– 0.85
17	—	3.33	– 11.31	164.17	56.68	—	—	213.21	4.06	– 2.06
18	—	– 24.75	– 42.07	– 16.45	13.93	—	21.74	18.70	– 29.22	38.89
19	42.89	20.32	58.35	– 100.14	—	108.54	– 48.71	– 144.55	– 114.27	—
20	– 3.12	11.08	19.45	—	—	– 122.68	50.66	– 129.80	21.22	—
21	– 3.46	45.80	—	—	– 39.58	62.58	68.10	– 177.98	—	– 44.94
22	42.54	—	—	– 1.74	– 94.35	– 121.62	– 110.84	—	—	23.60
23	– 3.80	—	– 192.25	117.33	– 54.77	28.63	—	—	– 127.80	84.50
24	—	12.56	153.80	95.41	– 132.03	—	—	28.03	36.90	– 35.76
25	—	1.48	– 68.08	11.71	17.73	—	– 100.37	– 155.00	– 98.32	– 71.97
26	– 34.59	– 36.57	– 35.73	8.96	—	138.24	– 31.74	– 6.71	67.51	—
27	– 8.64	– 5.17	33.47	—	— – 38.53	– 37.64	149.81	– 89.99	—
28	14.18	– 22.90	—	—	102.59	23.33	131.37	– 26.66	—	– 14.75
29	– 6.23	—	—	52.82	160.20	– 129.75	– 63.81	—	—	56.34
30	5.54	—	– 14.93	– 45.34	155.45	49.85	—	—	– 3.61	22.05
Close	4556.10	5654.63	7672.79	8952.02	10970.80	10447.89	10502.40	9243.26	8985.44	10435.48
Change	90.96	11.45	341.75	52.07	411.06	– 74.44	– 409.54	– 681.99	135.18	247.03

*Reagan funeral

*Last Day of June not hot for the Dow
But for stocks on NASDAQ, WOW!*

MAY/JUNE

MONDAY

30

Memorial Day
(Market Closed)

*Every time everyone's talking about something,
that's the time to sell.*
— George Lindemann (Billionaire, *Forbes*)

TUESDAY

31

*Memorial Day week Dow down 5 of last 9,
up 240 Dow points 1999, 495 points 2000, 249 points 2003*

*I have learned as a composer chiefly through my mistakes
and pursuits of false assumptions,
not by my exposure to founts of wisdom and knowledge.*
— Igor Stravinsky (Russian composer)

WEDNESDAY

 1

June first trading day Dow up 6 of last 7

*There is always plenty of capital for those
who can create practical plans for using it.*
— Napoleon Hill (Author, *Think and Grow Rich*, 1883-1970)

THURSDAY

 2

Average June gains last 34 years

NAS 1.3%	Dow 0.4%	S&P 0.8%
Up 22 Down 12	*Up 20 Down 14*	*Up 21 Down 13*
Rank #4	*Rank #10*	*Rank #7*

*When a company reports higher earnings for its first quarter
(over its previous year's first quarter), chances are almost
five to one it will also have increased earnings in its second quarter.*
— Niederhoffer, Cross & Zeckhauser

FRIDAY

3

*Whenever you see a successful business,
someone once made a courageous decision.*
— Peter Drucker (Management Consultant, "The man who
invented the corporate society," born in Austria 1909)

SATURDAY

4

SUNDAY

5

GET MORE OUT OF NASDAQ'S "BEST EIGHT MONTHS" WITH MACD TIMING

NASDAQ's amazing eight-month run from November through June is hard to miss on pages 54 and 139. A $10,000 investment in these eight months since 1971 gained $310,082 versus a loss of $4,066 during the void that is the four-month period July-October. Notice how October has moved up in the ranks, though.

Using the same MACD timing indicators on the NASDAQ as is done for the Dow (page 52) has enabled us to capture much of October's improved performance, pumping up NASDAQ's results considerably. Over the 33 years since NASDAQ began, the gain on the same $10,000 doubles to $632,746 and the loss during the four-month void increases to $7,198. Only four sizeable losses occur during the favorable period and the bulk of NASDAQ's bear markets were avoided including the worst of the 2000-2002 bear.

Updated signals are emailed to our monthly newsletter subscribers as soon as they are triggered. For further information on how the MACD indicator is calculated or for a FREE 1-month trial to our *Almanac Investor Platform*, visit **http://www.hirschorg.com/2005p058.**

BEST EIGHT MONTHS STRATEGY + TIMING

MACD Signal Date	Worst 4 Months July 1-Oct 31* NASDAQ	% Change	Investing $10,000	MACD Signal Date	Best 8 Months Nov 1-June 30* NASDAQ	% Change	Investing $10,000
22-Jul-71	109.54	− 3.6%	$9,640	4-Nov-71	105.56	24.1%	$12,410
7-Jun-72	131.00	− 1.8	9,466	23-Oct-72	128.66	− 22.7	9,593
25-Jun-73	99.43	− 7.2	8,784	7-Dec-73	92.32	− 20.2	7,655
3-Jul-74	73.66	− 23.2	6,746	7-Oct-74	56.57	47.8	11,314
11-Jun-75	83.60	− 9.2	6,125	7-Oct-75	75.88	20.8	13,667
22-Jul-76	91.66	− 2.4	5,978	19-Oct-76	89.45	13.2	15,471
27-Jul-77	101.25	− 4.0	5,739	4-Nov-77	97.21	26.6	19,586
7-Jun-78	123.10	− 6.5	5,366	6-Nov-78	115.08	19.1	23,327
3-Jul-79	137.03	− 1.1	5,307	30-Oct-79	135.48	15.5	26,943
20-Jun-80	156.51	26.2	6,697	9-Oct-80	197.53	11.2	29,961
4-Jun-81	219.68	− 17.6	5,518	1-Oct-81	181.09	− 4.0	28,763
7-Jun-82	173.84	12.5	6,208	7-Oct-82	195.59	57.4	45,273
1-Jun-83	307.95	− 10.7	5,544	3-Nov-83	274.86	− 14.2	38,844
1-Jun-84	235.90	5.0	5,821	15-Oct-84	247.67	17.3	45,564
3-Jun-85	290.59	− 3.0	5,646	1-Oct-85	281.77	39.4	63,516
10-Jun-86	392.83	− 10.3	5,064	1-Oct-86	352.34	20.5	76,537
30-Jun-87	424.67	− 22.7	3,914	2-Nov-87	328.33	20.1	91,921
8-Jul-88	394.33	− 6.6	3,656	29-Nov-88	368.15	22.4	112,511
13-Jun-89	450.73	0.7	3,682	9-Nov-89	454.07	1.9	114,649
11-Jun-90	462.79	− 23.0	2,835	2-Oct-90	356.39	39.3	159,706
11-Jun-91	496.62	6.4	3,016	1-Oct-91	528.51	7.4	171,524
11-Jun-92	567.68	1.5	3,061	14-Oct-92	576.22	20.5	206,686
7-Jun-93	694.61	9.9	3,364	1-Oct-93	763.23	− 4.4	197,592
17-Jun-94	729.35	5.0	3,532	11-Oct-94	765.57	13.5	224,267
1-Jun-95	868.82	17.2	4,140	13-Oct-95	1018.38	21.6	272,709
3-Jun-96	1238.73	1.0	4,181	7-Oct-96	1250.87	10.3	300,798
4-Jun-97	1379.67	24.4	5,201	3-Oct-97	1715.87	1.8	306,212
1-Jun-98	1746.82	− 7.8	4,795	15-Oct-98	1611.01	49.7	458,399
1-Jun-99	2412.03	18.5	5,682	6-Oct-99	2857.21	35.7	622,047
29-Jun-00	3877.23	− 18.2	4,648	18-Oct-00	3171.56	− 32.2	421,748
1-Jun-01	2149.44	− 31.1	3,202	1-Oct-01	1480.46	5.5	444,944
3-Jun-02	1562.56	− 24.0	2,434	2-Oct-02	1187.30	38.5	616,247
20-Jun-03	1644.72	15.1	2,802	6-Oct-03	1893.46	4.3	642,746
21-Jun-04	1974.38						
	33-Year Loss	**($7,198)**				**33-Year Gain**	**$632,746**

* MACD generated entry and exit points (earlier or later) can lengthen or shorten eight-month periods

JUNE

Start looking for NASDAQ MACD seasonal SELL Signal (page 58)
Almanac Investor subscribers will be emailed the alert when it triggers
visit stocktradersalmanac.com for details

MONDAY

6

*The dissenter (or "contrary investor") is every human
at those moments of his life when he resigns momentarily
from the herd and thinks for himself.*
— Archibald MacLeish
(American poet, writer and political activist, 1892-1982)

TUESDAY

7

*What is conservatism? Is it not adherence to the old and tried,
against the new and untried?*
— Abraham Lincoln (16th U.S. President, 1809-1865)

WEDNESDAY

8

*The measure of success is not whether you have a tough problem
to deal with, but whether it's the same problem you had last year.*
— John Foster Dulles
(Secretary of State under Eisenhower, 1888-1959)

THURSDAY

9

*First-rate people hire first-rate people;
second-rate people hire third-rate people.*
— Leo Rosten (American author, 1908-1997)

FRIDAY

10

*Friendship renders prosperity more brilliant, while it lightens
adversity by sharing it and making its burden common.*
— Marcus Tullius Cicero
(Great Roman orator, politician, 106-43 B.C.)

SATURDAY

11

SUNDAY

12

DOW GAINS MOST FIRST TWO DAYS OF WEEK

Except for 2001 and 2002, Monday* has been the most consistently bullish day of the week for the Dow, Friday** the most bearish since 1990, as traders have become reluctant to stay long going into the weekend. Since 1989 Mondays gained 6459.87 Dow points, while all four other days gained a total of 1069.47 points, Thursday and Friday combined for a total loss of 748.65 points. In past flat and bear market years Friday was the worst day of the week and Monday second worst. In bull years Monday is best and Friday number two. See pages 66 and 132-135 for more.

ANNUAL DOW POINT CHANGES FOR DAYS OF THE WEEK SINCE 1953

Year	Monday*	Tuesday	Wednesday	Thursday	Friday*	Year's DJIA Closing	Year's Point Change
1953	− 36.16	− 7.93	19.63	5.76	7.70	280.90	− 11.00
1954	15.68	3.27	24.31	33.96	46.27	404.39	123.49
1955	− 48.36	26.38	46.03	− 0.66	60.62	488.40	84.01
1956	− 24.79	− 19.36	− 15.41	8.43	64.56	499.47	11.07
1957	− 109.50	− 7.71	64.12	3.32	− 14.01	435.69	− 63.78
1958	17.50	23.59	29.10	22.67	61.44	583.65	147.96
1959	− 44.48	29.04	4.11	13.60	93.44	679.36	95.71
1960	− 111.04	− 3.75	− 5.62	6.74	50.20	615.89	− 63.47
1961	− 23.21	10.18	87.51	− 5.96	47.17	731.14	115.25
1962	− 101.60	26.19	9.97	− 7.70	− 5.90	652.10	− 79.04
1963	− 8.88	47.12	16.23	22.39	33.99	762.95	110.85
1964	− 0.29	− 17.94	39.84	5.52	84.05	874.13	111.18
1965	− 73.23	39.65	57.03	3.20	68.48	969.26	95.13
1966	− 153.24	− 27.73	56.13	− 46.19	− 12.54	785.69	− 183.57
1967	− 68.65	31.50	25.42	92.25	38.90	905.11	119.42
1968	6.41	34.94	25.16	− 72.06	50.86	943.75	38.64
1969	− 164.17	− 36.70	18.33	23.79	15.36	800.36	− 143.39
1970	− 100.05	− 46.09	116.07	− 3.48	72.11	838.92	38.56
1971	− 2.99	9.56	13.66	8.04	23.01	890.20	51.28
1972	− 87.40	− 1.23	65.24	8.46	144.75	1020.02	129.82
1973	− 174.11	10.52	− 5.94	36.67	− 36.30	850.86	− 169.16
1974	− 149.37	47.51	− 20.31	− 13.70	− 98.75	616.24	− 234.62
1975	39.46	− 109.62	56.93	124.00	125.40	852.41	236.17
1976	70.72	71.76	50.88	− 33.70	− 7.42	1004.65	152.24
1977	− 65.15	− 44.89	− 79.61	− 5.62	21.79	831.17	− 173.48
1978	− 31.29	− 70.84	71.33	− 64.67	69.31	805.01	− 26.16
1979	− 32.52	9.52	− 18.84	75.18	0.39	838.74	33.73
1980	− 86.51	135.13	137.67	− 122.00	60.96	963.99	125.25
1981	− 45.68	− 49.51	− 13.95	− 14.67	34.82	875.00	− 88.99
1982	5.71	86.20	28.37	− 1.47	52.73	1046.54	171.54
1983	30.51	− 30.92	149.68	61.16	1.67	1258.64	212.10
1984	− 73.80	78.02	− 139.24	92.79	− 4.84	1211.57	− 47.07
1985	80.36	52.70	51.26	46.32	104.46	1546.67	335.10
1986	− 39.94	97.63	178.65	29.31	83.63	1895.95	349.28
1987	− 559.15	235.83	392.03	139.73	− 165.56	1938.83	42.88
1988	268.12	166.44	− 60.48	− 230.84	86.50	2168.57	229.74
1989	− 53.31	143.33	233.25	90.25	171.11	2753.20	584.63
SubTotal	*−1934.40*	*941.79*	*1708.54*	*330.82*	*1430.36*		*2461.30*
1990	219.90	− 25.22	47.96	− 352.55	− 9.63	2633.66	− 119.54
1991	191.13	47.97	174.53	254.79	− 133.25	3168.83	535.17
1992	237.80	− 49.67	3.12	108.74	− 167.71	3301.11	132.28
1993	322.82	− 37.03	243.87	4.97	− 81.65	3754.09	452.98
1994	206.41	− 95.33	29.98	− 168.87	108.16	3834.44	80.35
1995	262.97	210.06	357.02	140.07	312.56	5117.12	1282.68
1996	626.41	155.55	− 34.24	268.52	314.91	6448.27	1331.15
1997	1136.04	1989.17	− 590.17	− 949.80	− 125.26	7908.25	1459.98
1998	649.10	679.95	591.63	−1579.43	931.93	9181.43	1273.18
1999	980.49	−1587.23	826.68	735.94	1359.81	11497.12	2315.69
2000	2265.45	306.47	−1978.34	238.21	−1542.06	10786.85	− 710.27
2001	− 389.33	336.86	− 396.53	976.41	−1293.10	10021.50	− 765.35
2002	−1404.94	− 823.76	1443.69	− 428.12	− 466.74	8341.63	−1679.87
2003	978.87	482.11	− 425.46	566.22	510.55	10453.92	2112.29
2004**	176.70	23.89	− 89.41	− 41.07	− 241.20	10282.83	− 171.09
SubTotal	*6459.82*	*1613.79*	*204.33*	*− 225.97*	*− 522.68*		*7529.63*
Totals	**4525.42**	**2555.58**	**1912.87**	**104.85**	**907.68**		**9990.93**

* On Monday holidays, the following Tuesday is included in the Monday figure
* On Friday holidays, the preceding Thursday is included in the Friday figure
** Partial year through July 2, 2004

JUNE

*Monday before Triple Witching Dow down 5 of last 8,
but back-to-back 200+ point gains in 2002 and 2003*

MONDAY

13

*When the S&P Index Future premium over "Cash" gets too high,
I sell the future and buy the stocks. If the premium disappears,
well, buy the future and sell the stocks.*
— Neil Elliott (Fahnestock)

TUESDAY

 # 14

*Of 120 companies from 1987 to 1992 that relied primarily on
cost cutting to improve the bottom line, 68 percent failed to
achieve profitable growth during the next five years.*
— Mercer Management Consulting
(*Smart Money Magazine*, August 2001)

WEDNESDAY

15

*The fewer analysts who follow a situation, the more pregnant its
possibilities...if Wall Street hates a stock, buy it.*
— Martin T. Sosnoff

THURSDAY

 # 16

*We pay the debts of the last generation
by issuing bonds payable by the next generation.*
— Lawrence J. Peter

Triple-Witching Day Dow up 9 of 15

FRIDAY

 # 17

*We are like tenant farmers chopping down the fence
around our house for fuel when we should be using
Nature's inexhaustible sources of energy — sun, wind and tide.
I'd put my money on the sun and solar energy. What a source of power!
I hope we don't have to wait until oil and coal run out before we tackle that.*
— Thomas Alva Edison (1847-1931)

SATURDAY

18

Father's Day

SUNDAY

19

FIRST-TRADING-DAY-OF-THE-MONTH PHENOMENON

First trading days of the month have an eye-popping history. While the Dow gained 2711.74 points between September 2, 1997 (7622.42) and July 1, 2004 (10334.16), it is incredible that 3559.06 points were gained on the first trading days of these 83 months. The remaining 1635 trading days combined saw the Dow lose 847.32 points during the period. This averages out to gains of 42.88 points on first days, in contrast to a 0.52-point loss on all others.

Note September 1997 through October 2000 racked up a total gain of 2639.32 Dow points on the first trading days of these 38 months (winners except for seven occasions). But between November 2000, when the recent bear trend really started to gnash its teeth, and September 2002, frightened investors switched from pouring money into the market on that day to pulling it out, fourteen months out of twenty-three, netting a 404.80 Dow point loss.

First days of August have performed miserably, falling five times out of six. In rising market trends first days perform much better as institutions are likely anticipating strong performance at each month's outset. With the current longer-term secular bear trend threatening to resume, first days of the month could be prone to weakness until and unless a bull market emerges. ·

DOW POINTS GAINED ON FIRST DAY OF MONTH
FROM SEPTEMBER 1997 TO JULY 1, 2004

	1997	1998	1999	2000	2001	2002	2003	2004	Totals
Jan		56.79	2.84	− 139.61	− 140.70	51.90	265.89	− 44.07	53.04
Feb		201.28	− 13.13	100.52	96.27	− 12.74	56.01	11.11	439.32
Mar		4.73	18.20	9.62	− 45.14	262.73	− 53.22	94.22	291.14
Apr		68.51	46.35	300.01	− 100.85	− 41.24	77.73	15.63	366.14
May		83.70	225.65	77.87	163.37	113.41	− 25.84	88.43	726.59
Jun		22.42	36.52	129.87	78.47	− 215.46	47.55	14.20	113.57
Jul		96.65	95.62	112.78	91.32	− 133.47	55.51	− 101.32	217.09
Aug		− 96.55	− 9.19	84.97	− 12.80	− 229.97	− 79.83		− 343.37
Sep	257.36	288.36	108.60	23.68	47.74	− 355.45	107.45		477.74
Oct	70.24	− 210.09	− 63.95	49.21	− 10.73	346.86	194.14		375.68
Nov	232.31	. 114.05	− 81.35	− 71.67	188.76	120.61	57.34		560.05
Dec	189.98	16.99	120.58	− 40.95	− 87.60	− 33.52	116.59		282.07
Totals	749.89	646.84	486.74	636.30	268.11	− 126.34	819.32	78.20	3559.06

SUMMARY FIRST DAYS VS. OTHER DAYS OF MONTH

	# of Days	Total Points Gained	Average Daily Point Gain
First days	83	3559.06	42.88
Other days	1635	—847.32	—0.52

JUNE

MONDAY
20

The generally accepted view is that markets are always right — that is,
market prices tend to discount future developments accurately even when it is
unclear what those developments are. I start with the opposite point of view. I believe
that market prices are always wrong in the sense that they present a biased view of the future.
— George Soros (1987, Financier, philanthropist, political activist, author and philosopher, b. 1930)

TUESDAY
21

If buying equities seems, the most hazardous and foolish thing
you could possibly do, then you are near the bottom
that will end the bear market.
— Joseph E. Granville

WEDNESDAY
 ## 22

It's no coincidence that three of the top five stock option traders
in a recent trading contest were all former Marines.
— Robert Prechter, Jr. (*Elliott Wave Theorist*)

THURSDAY
23

The job of central banks:
To take away the punch bowl just as the party is getting going.
— William McChesney Martin
(Federal Reserve Chairman 1951-1970, 1906-1998)

FRIDAY
24

Make it idiot-proof and someone will make a better idiot.
— Bumper sticker

SATURDAY
25

Bearish July Sector Seasonalities: Airline,
Internet, Russell 2000 (page 118)

SUNDAY
26

JULY ALMANAC

JULY							AUGUST					
S	M	T	W	T	F	S	S	M	T	W	T	F	S
					1	2							
3	4	5	6	7	8	9		1	2	3	4	5	6
10	11	12	13	14	15	16	7	8	9	10	11	12	13
17	18	19	20	21	22	23	14	15	16	17	18	19	20
24	25	26	27	28	29	30	21	22	23	24	25	26	27
31							28	29	30	31			

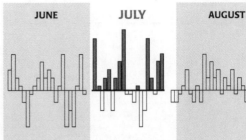

Market Probability Chart above is a graphic representation of the Market Probability Calendar on page 123.

◆ July is the best month of the third quarter (page 74) ◆ Start of 2nd half brings an inflow of retirement funds ◆ First trading day up 12 out of 15 times 1990-2004 ◆ S&P and NASDAQ down 6 of 7 1998-2004 ◆ Graph above shows strength through most of July except middle ◆ July closes well except if bear market in progress ◆ Average S&P move 0.9%, Dow 1.1%, NASDAQ –0.2% * RECORD: S&P up 29, down 25 ◆ Huge gain in July usually provides better buying opportunity over next 4 months ◆ Start of NASDAQ's worst four months of the year (page 54) ◆ Post-Election Julys #1 on S&P, 1.4%, up 7, down 6; #2 on Dow, 1.4%, up 10, down 3; #3 NASDAQ 2.1%, up 6 down 2.

JULY DAILY POINT CHANGES DOW JONES INDUSTRIALS

Previous Month	1994	1995	1996	1997	1998	1999	2000	2001	2002	2003
Close	3624.96	4556.10	5654.63	7672.79	8952.02	10970.80	10447.89	10502.40	9243.26	8985.44
1	21.69	—	75.35	49.54	96.65	95.62	—	—	– 133.47	55.51
2	—	—	– 9.60	73.05	– 23.41	72.82	—	91.32	– 102.04	101.89
3	—	29.05	– 17.36	100.43	Closed	—	112.78*	– 22.61*	47.22*	– 72.63
4	H	H	H	H	H	H	H	H	H	H
5	5.83	30.08	– 114.88	—	—	Closed	– 77.07	– 91.25	324.53	—
6	22.02	48.77	—	—	66.51	– 4.12	– 2.13	– 227.18	—	—
7	13.92	38.73	—	– 37.32	– 6.73	52.24	154.51	—	—	146.58
8	20.72	—	– 37.31	103.82	89.93	– 60.47	—	—	– 104.60	6.30
9	—	—	31.03	– 119.88	– 85.19	66.81	—	46.72	– 178.81	– 66.88
10	—	– 0.34	21.79	44.33	15.96	—	10.60	– 123.76	– 282.59	– 120.17
11	– 6.15	– 21.79	– 83.11	35.06	—	—	80.61	65.38	– 11.97	83.55
12	– 0.33	46.69	– 9.98	—	—	7.28	56.22	237.97	– 117.00	—
13	1.62	0.19	—	—	– 9.53	– 25.96	5.30	60.07	—	—
14	34.97	– 18.66	—	1.16	149.33	– 26.92	24.04	—	—	57.56
15	14.56	—	– 161.05	52.73	– 11.07	38.31	—	—	– 45.34	– 48.18
16	—	—	9.25	63.17	93.72	23.43	—	66.94	– 166.08	– 34.38
17	—	27.47	18.12	– 18.11	9.78	—	8.48	134.27	69.37	– 43.77
18	1.62	– 50.01	87.30	– 130.31	—	—	64.35	– 36.56	– 132.99	137.33
19	– 7.12	– 57.41	– 37.36	—	—	22.16	– 43.84	40.17	– 390.23	—
20	– 21.04	12.68	—	—	– 42.22	– 191.55	147.79	– 33.35	—	—
21	5.18	N/C	—	16.26	– 105.56	6.65	– 110.31	—	—	91.46
22	2.59	—	– 35.88	154.93	– 61.28	– 33.56	—	—	– 234.68	61.76
23	—	—	– 44.39	26.71	– 195.93	58.26	—	– 152.23	– 82.24	35.79
24	—	27.12	8.14	28.57	4.38	—	– 48.44	– 183.30	488.95	– 81.73
25	6.80	45.78	67.32	– 3.49	—	—	14.85	164.55	– 4.98	172.06
26	– 6.16	– 7.39	51.05	—	—	– 47.80	– 183.49	49.96	78.08	—
27	– 15.21	25.71	—	—	90.88	115.88	69.65	– 38.96	—	– 18.06
28	10.36	– 17.26	—	7.67	– 93.46	– 6.97	– 74.96	—	—	62.05
29	33.67	—	– 38.47	53.42	– 19.82	– 180.78	—	—	447.49	– 62.05
30	—	—	47.34	80.36	111.99	– 136.14	—	– 14.95	– 31.85	– 4.41
31	—	– 7.04	46.98	– 32.28	– 143.66	—	10.81	121.09	56.56	33.75
Close	3764.50	4708.47	5528.91	8222.61	8883.29	10655.15	10521.98	10522.81	8736.59	9233.80
Change	139.54	152.37	– 125.72	549.82	– 68.73	– 315.65	74.09	20.41	– 506.67	248.36

*Shortened trading day

When Dow and S&P in July are inferior
NASDAQ days tend to be even drearier

The Almanac Investor Platform
Almanac Investor Newsletter and Online Research Tool

Now you can update *Almanac* strategies, learn whether seasonal patterns are on course and be informed about upcoming favorable market periods.

Almanac Investor Platform includes:

Almanac Investor Newsletter: monthly issue provides market timing, seasonal strategies, unusual investing opportunities, exciting small-cap growth stocks and seasoned, undervalued equities, special situations hedging to preserve capital, safe, high-yield situations and investment strategies focusing on Exchange Traded Funds.

Online Almanac Research Tool: this product is designed to allow Almanac Investors to do their own historical research, update Almanac market indicators and strategies as well as create their own.

Almanac Investor Alerts: Subscribers receive important *Alerts* via email such as the January Barometer, MACD Seasonal Buy and Sell Signals, stock and strategy updates, the year-end FREE-LUNCH Menu, and more!

See page 104 for more information about getting inside the market with this tool. Then use the coupon below to try *Almanac Investor Newsletter* and the Research Tool risk free at 50% off…Or order from our website for an additional 20% discount off the prices below by using promotion code STA5.

Jeff Hirsch

Jeffrey A. Hirsch

PS: You can try the entire **Almanac Investor Platform** which includes *Almanac Investor Newsletter* and the **Online Research Tool** FREE for one month. Just go to our website *stocktradersalmanac.com* use promotion code TRIAL5.

Order online today or by calling **Toll-Free 800-477-3400, Ext. 21**, mailing the card below or **faxing it to 201-767-7337**.

Update Your Almanac
EVERY MONTH

Now you can find out what seasonal trends are on schedule and which are not...how to take advantage of them... what market-moving events are coming up... what the indicators say about the next move. All of the important *Almanac Investor Alerts* via email such as the MACD Seasonal Buy and Sell Signals, important updates, the year-end FREE-LUNCH Menu, and much more!

PLUS... Stock research focused on high-potential issues Wall Street hasn't yet discovered... Special situations with hidden value... Yield-enhancing strategies and more.

Place
Stamp
Here

The Hirsch Organization
184 Central Avenue
Old Tappan, NJ 07675

JUNE/JULY

June ends NASDAQ's "Best Eight Months" (page 54)

MONDAY

27

Show me a good phone receptionist
and I'll show you a good company.
— Harvey Mackay (*Pushing the Envelope*, 1999)

TUESDAY

28

One only gets to the top rung on the ladder by steadily climbing up
one at a time, and suddenly all sorts of powers,
all sorts of abilities, which you thought never belonged to you —
suddenly become within your own possibility....
— Margaret Thatcher (British Prime Minister 1979-1990)

FOMC Meeting (2 days)

WEDNESDAY

 # 29

The difference between great people and others is largely a habit
— a controlled habit of doing every task better,
faster and more efficiently.
— William Danforth (Ralston Purina founder)

Last day of second quarter Dow down 10 of last 14,
but NASDAQ up 12 of last 14

THURSDAY

30

Governments last as long as the under-taxed
can defend themselves against the over-taxed.
— Bernard Berenson (American art critic, 1865-1959)

July begins NASDAQ's worst 4 months of the year
July first trading day Dow up 12 of last 15

FRIDAY

 # 1

In investing, the return you want should depend
on whether you want to eat well or sleep well.
— J. Kenfield Morley

SATURDAY

2

SUNDAY

3

2003 DAILY DOW POINT CHANGES
(DOW JONES INDUSTRIAL AVERAGE)

Week #		Monday**	Tuesday	Wednesday	Thursday	Friday**	Weekly Dow Close	Net Point Change
						2002 Close	8341.63	
1				H	265.89	− 5.83	8601.69	260.06†
2	J	171.88	− 32.98	−145.28	180.87	8.71	8784.89	183.20
3	A	1.09	56.64	−119.44	− 25.31	−111.13	8586.74	−198.15
4	N	H	−143.84	−124.17	50.74	−238.46	8131.01	−455.73
5		−141.45	99.28	21.87	−165.58	108.68	8053.81	− 77.20
6	F	56.01	− 96.53	− 28.11	− 55.88	− 65.07	7864.23	−189.58
7	E	55.88	− 77.00	− 84.94	− 8.30	158.93	7908.80	44.57
8	B	H	132.35	− 40.55	− 85.64	103.15	8018.11	109.31
9		−159.87	51.26	−102.52	78.01	6.09	7891.08	−127.03
10	M	− 53.22	−132.99	70.73	−101.61	66.04	7740.03	−151.05
11	A	−171.85	− 44.12	28.01	269.68	37.96	7859.71	119.68
12	R	282.21	52.31	71.22	21.15	235.37	8521.97	662.26
13		−307.29	65.55	− 50.35	− 28.43	− 55.68	8145.77	−376.20
14		−153.64	77.73	215.20	− 44.68	36.77	8277.15	131.38
15	A	23.26	− 1.49	−100.98	23.39	− 17.92	8203.41	− 73.74
16	P	147.69	51.26	−144.75	80.04	H	8337.65	134.24
17	R	− 8.75	156.09	30.67	− 75.62	−133.69	8306.35	− 31.30
18		165.26	31.38	− 22.90	− 25.84	128.43	8582.68	276.33
19	M	− 51.11	56.79	− 27.73	− 69.41	113.38	8604.60	21.92
20	A	122.13	− 47.48	− 31.43	65.32	− 34.17	8678.97	74.37
21	Y	−185.58	− 2.03	25.07	77.59	7.36	8601.38	− 77.59
22		H	179.97	11.77	− 81.94	139.08	8850.26	248.88
23	J	47.55	25.14	116.03	2.32	21.49	9062.79	212.53
24	U	− 82.79	74.89	128.33	13.33	− 79.43	9117.12	54.33
25	N	201.84	4.06	− 29.22	−114.27	21.22	9200.75	83.63
26		−127.80	36.90	− 98.32	67.51	− 89.99	8989.05	−211.70
27		− 3.61	55.51	101.89	− 72.63	H	9070.21	81.16
28	J	146.58	6.30	− 66.88	−120.17	83.55	9119.59	49.38
29	U	57.56	− 48.18	− 34.38	− 43.77	137.33	9188.15	68.56
30	L	− 91.46	61.76	35.79	− 81.73	172.06	9284.57	96.42
31		− 18.06	− 62.05	− 4.41	33.75	− 79.83	9153.97	−130.60
32	A	32.07	−149.72	25.42	64.71	64.64	9191.09	37.12
33	U	26.26	92.71	− 38.30	38.80	11.13	9321.69	130.60
34	G	90.76	16.45	− 31.39	26.17	− 74.81	9348.87	27.18
35		− 31.23	22.81	− 6.66	40.42	41.61	9415.82	66.95
36	S	H	107.45	45.19	19.44	− 84.56	9503.34	87.52
37	E	82.95	− 79.09	− 86.74	39.30	11.79	9471.55	− 31.79
38	P	− 22.74	118.53	− 21.69	113.48	− 14.31	9644.82	173.27
39		−109.41	40.63	−150.53	− 81.55	− 30.88	9313.08	−331.74
40	O	67.16	−105.18	194.14	18.60	84.51	9572.31	259.23
41	C	22.67	59.63	− 23.71	49.11	− 5.33	9674.68	102.37
42	T	89.70	48.60	− 9.93	− 11.33	− 69.93	9721.79	47.11
43		56.15	− 30.30	−149.40	14.89	− 30.67	9582.46	−139.33
44		25.70	140.15	26.22	12.08	14.51	9801.12	218.66
45	N	57.34	− 19.63	− 18.00	36.14	− 47.18	9809.79	8.67
46	O	− 53.26	− 18.74	111.04	− 10.89	− 69.26	9768.68	− 41.11
47	V	− 57.85	− 86.67	66.30	− 71.04	9.11	9628.53	−140.15
48		119.26	16.15	15.63	H	2.89*	9782.46	153.93
49	D	116.59	− 45.41	19.78	57.40	− 68.14	9862.68	80.22
50	E	102.59	− 41.85	− 1.56	86.30	34.00	10042.16	179.48
51	C	− 19.34	106.74	15.70	102.82	30.14	10278.22	236.06
52		59.78	3.26	− 36.07	H	19.48*	10324.67	46.45
53		125.33	− 24.96	28.88	Year's Close		10453.92	129.25†
TOTALS		978.87**	482.11	−425.46	566.22	510.55**		2112.29

Bold Color: Down Friday, Down Monday   *Shortened trading days: Nov. 28, Dec. 26   †Partial week*

** On Monday holidays, the following Tuesday is included in the Monday total
** On Friday holidays, the preceding Thursday is included in the Friday total

66

JULY

MONDAY 4

Independence Day
(Market Closed)

*Wall Street's graveyards are filled with men
who were right too soon.*
— William Hamilton

TUESDAY 5

Average July gains last 33 years

NAS –0.2%	Dow 0.5%	S&P –0.04%
Up 16 Down 17	Up 17 Down 16	Up 13 Down 20
Rank #11	Rank #8	Rank #11

Eighty percent of success is showing up.
— Woody Allen

WEDNESDAY 6

*Stocks are super-attractive when
the Fed is loosening and interest rates are falling.
In sum: Don't fight the Fed!*
— Martin Zweig

THURSDAY 7

*Pullbacks near the 30-week moving average
are often good times to take action.*
— Michael Burke (*Investors Intelligence*)

FRIDAY 8

*I have a simple philosophy. Fill what's empty. Empty what's full.
And scratch where it itches.*
— Alice Roosevelt Longworth

SATURDAY 9

SUNDAY 10

GRIDLOCK ON CAPITOL HILL
IS BEST FOR THE MARKETS

There are six possible scenarios on Capitol Hill: Republican President with a Republican Congress, Republican President with a Democratic Congress, Republican President with a split Congress, Democratic President with a Democratic Congress, Democratic President with a Republican Congress, and a Democratic President with a split Congress.

First looking at just the historical performance of the Dow under the Democratic and Republican Presidents, we see a pattern that is contrary to popular belief. Under a Democrat, the Dow has performed much better than under a Republican. The Dow has historically returned 9.1% under the Democrats compared to only a 6.0% return under a Republican executive.

The results are the opposite with a Republican Congress, yielding an average 10.0% gain in the Dow compared to a 7.8% return when the Democrats have control of the Hill.

With total Republican control of Washington, the Dow has been up on average 9.3%. Democrats in power over the two branches have fared a bit worse with 8.4% gains. When power is split, with a Republican President and a Democratic Congress, the Dow has not done very well, averaging only a 6.8% gain. The best scenario for all investors is a Democrat in the White House and Republican control of Congress with average gains of 11.5%. The most of dire circumstance occurs with a Republican President and a split Congress, averaging a net loss of 1.2%. There has never been a Democratic President and a split Congress.

DOW JONES INDUSTRIALS AVERAGE PERCENT CHANGE SINCE 1901

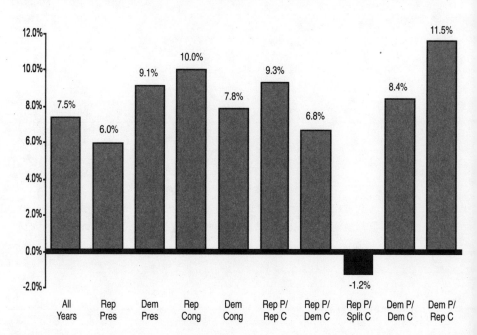

JULY

Monday before expiration Dow up 8 of last 15 in generally flat trading.

MONDAY

11

It's not the strongest of the species (think "traders") that survive,
nor the most intelligent, but the one most responsive to change.
— Charles Darwin

TUESDAY

12

Corporate guidance has become something of an art.
The CFO has refined and perfected his art,
gracefully leading on the bulls with the calculating grace
and cunning of a great matador.
— Joe Kalinowski (I/B/E/S)

WEDNESDAY

 # 13

The world has changed! You can't be an 800-pound gorilla;
you need to be an economic gazelle.
You've got to be able to change directions quickly.
— Mark Breier (*The 10-Second Internet Manager*)

Historically one of two (January 31) best trading
days of the year (page 123)

THURSDAY

 # 14

A small debt produces a debtor; a large one, an enemy.
— Publilius Syrus
(Syrian-born Roman mime and former slave, 83-43 B.C.)

Expiration day rough, Dow up only 4 of last 14,
off 390.23 points in 2002

FRIDAY

 # 15

It is tact that is golden, not silence.
— Samuel Butler (English writer, 1600-1680)

SATURDAY

16

SUNDAY

17

A RALLY FOR ALL SEASONS

Most years, especially when the market sells off mid-year, prospects for the perennial summer rally become the buzz on the street. Parameters for this "rally" were defined by the late Ralph Rotnem as the lowest close in the Dow Jones industrial average in May or June to the highest close in July, August, or September. Such a big deal is made of the "summer rally" that one might get the impression the market puts on its best performance in the summertime. Nothing could be further from the truth! Not only does the market "rally" in every season of the year, but it does so with more gusto in the winter, spring, and fall than in the summer.

Winters in 41 years averaged a 13.5% gain as measured from the low in November or December to the first quarter closing high. Spring was up 11.3% followed by fall with 10.9%. Last and least was the average 9.4% "summer rally." Even 2003's impressive 14.3% "summer rally" was outmatched by spring and fall. Nevertheless, no matter how thick the gloom or grim the outlook, don't despair! There's always a rally for all seasons, statistically.

SEASONAL GAINS IN DOW JONES INDUSTRIALS

	WINTER RALLY Nov/Dec Low to 1 Q. High	SPRING RALLY Feb/Mar Low to 2 Q. High	SUMMER RALLY May/Jun Low to 3 Q. High	FALL RALLY Aug/Sep Low to 4 Q. High
1964	15.3%	6.2%	9.4%	8.3%
1965	5.7	6.6	11.6	10.3
1966	5.9	4.8	3.5	7.0
1967	11.6	8.7	11.2	4.4
1968	7.0	11.5	5.2	13.3
1969	0.9	7.7	1.9	6.7
1970	5.4	6.2	22.5	19.0
1971	21.6	9.4	5.5	7.4
1972	19.1	7.7	5.2	11.4
1973	8.6	4.8	9.7	15.9
1974	13.1	8.2	1.4	11.0
1975	36.2	24.2	8.2	8.7
1976	23.3	6.4	5.9	4.6
1977	8.2	3.1	2.8	2.1
1978	2.1	16.8	11.8	5.2
1979	11.0	8.9	8.9	6.1
1980	13.5	16.8	21.0	8.5
1981	11.8	9.9	0.4	8.3
1982	4.6	9.3	18.5	37.8
1983	15.7	17.8	6.3	10.7
1984	5.9	4.6	14.1	9.7
1985	11.7	7.1	9.5	19.7
1986	31.1	18.8	9.2	11.4
1987	30.6	13.6	22.9	5.9
1988	18.1	13.5	11.2	9.8
1989	15.1	12.9	16.1	5.7
1990	8.8	14.5	12.4	8.6
1991	21.8	11.2	6.6	9.3
1992	14.9	6.4	3.7	3.3
1993	8.9	7.7	6.3	7.3
1994	9.7	5.2	9.1	5.0
1995	13.6	19.3	11.3	13.9
1996	19.2	7.5	8.7	17.3
1997	17.7	18.4	18.4	7.3
1998	20.3	13.6	7.2	24.3
1999	15.1	21.6	8.2	12.6
2000	10.8	15.2	9.8	3.5
2001	6.4	20.8	1.7	23.1
2002	14.8	7.9	2.8	17.6
2003	6.5	23.9	14.3	15.7
2004	11.6	5.2		
Totals	**553.2%**	**463.9%**	**374.4%**	**437.7%**
Average	**13.5%**	**11.1%**	**9.4%**	**10.9%**

JULY

MONDAY
18

In order to be a great writer (or "investor")
a person must have a built-in, shockproof crap detector.
— Ernest Hemingway

TUESDAY
19

The worst trades are generally when people freeze
and start to pray and hope rather than take some action.
— Robert Mnuchin (Goldman, Sachs)

WEDNESDAY
20

You know you're right when the other side starts to shout.
— I. A. O'Shaughnessy

THURSDAY
21

I don't know where speculation got such a bad name,
since I know of no forward leap which was not fathered by speculation.
— John Steinbeck

FRIDAY
22

The time to buy is when blood is running in the streets.
— Baron Nathan Rothschild (London financier, 1777-1836)

SATURDAY
23

SUNDAY
24

AUGUST ALMANAC

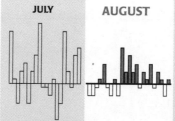

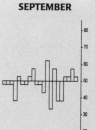

AUGUST						
S	M	T	W	T	F	S
		1	2	3	4	5
6	7	8	9	10	11	12

AUGUST
S M T W T F S
1 2 3 4 5 6
7 8 9 10 11 12 13
14 15 16 17 18 19 20
21 22 23 24 25 26 27
28 29 30 31

SEPTEMBER
S M T W T F S
1 2 3
4 5 6 7 8 9 10
11 12 13 14 15 16 17
18 19 20 21 22 23 24
25 26 27 28 29 30

Market Probability Chart above is a graphic representation of the Market Probability Calendar on page 123.

◆ Harvesting made August the best stock market month 1901-1951 ◆ Now that less than 2% farm, August has become the worst S&P month in the past 15 years, second worst Dow month and third worst NASDAQ month (though up 11.7% in 2000 but down 10.9% in 2001) ◆ Shortest bear in history (45 days) caused by turmoil in Russia ended here in 1998, with a record 1344.22 point drop in the Dow, off 15.1% ◆ Saddam Hussein triggered a 10.0% slide in 1990 ◆ Best Dow gains: 1982 (11.5%) and 1984 (9.8%) as bear markets ended ◆ End of August merciless 6 of the last 8 years average loss last 5 days Dow –3.4%, S&P –3.1%, NAS –2.7%.

AUGUST DAILY POINT CHANGES DOW JONES INDUSTRIALS

Previous Month	1994	1995	1996	1997	1998	1999	2000	2001	2002	2003
Close	3764.50	4708.47	5528.91	8222.61	8883.29	10655.15	10521.98	10522.81	8736.59	9233.80
1	33.67	– 8.10	65.84	– 28.57	—	—	84.97	– 12.80	– 229.97	– 79.83
2	– 1.95	– 10.22	85.08	—	—	– 9.19	80.58	41.17	– 193.49	—
3	– 3.56	11.27	—	—	– 96.55	31.35	19.05	– 38.40	—	—
4	– 26.87	– 17.96	—	4.41	– 299.43	– 2.54	61.17	—	—	32.07
5	– 18.77	—	– 5.55	– 10.91	59.47	119.05	—	—	– 269.50	– 149.72
6	—	—	21.83	71.77	30.90	– 79.79	—	– 111.47	230.46	25.42
7	—	9.86	22.56	– 71.31	20.34	—	99.26	57.43	182.06	64.71
8	6.79	N/C	– 5.18	– 156.78	—	—	109.88	– 165.24	255.87	64.64
9	1.95	– 21.83	– 32.18	—	—	6.33	– 71.06	5.06	33.43	—
10	11.00	– 27.83	—	—	– 23.17	– 52.55	2.93	117.69	—	—
11	– 15.86	– 25.36	—	30.89	– 112.00	132.65	119.04	—	—	26.26
12	17.81	—	23.67	– 101.27	90.11	1.59	—	—	– 56.56	92.71
13	—	—	– 57.70	– 32.52	– 93.46	184.26	—	0.34	– 206.50	– 38.30
14	—	41.56	19.60	13.71	– 34.50	—	148.34	– 3.74	260.92	38.80
15	– 8.42	– 19.02	– 1.10	– 247.37	—	—	– 109.14	– 66.22	74.83	11.13
16	24.28	– 1.76	23.67	—	—	73.14	– 58.61	46.57	– 40.08	—
17	– 8.09	– 8.45	—	—	149.85	70.29	47.25	– 151.74	—	—
18	– 21.05	– 13.03	—	108.70	139.80	– 125.70	– 9.16	—	—	90.76
19	– 0.32	—	9.99	114.74	– 21.37	– 27.54	—	—	212.73	16.45
20	—	—	21.82	103.13	– 81.87	136.77	—	79.29	– 118.72	31.39
21	—	– 2.82	– 31.44	– 127.28	– 77.76	—	33.33	– 145.93	85.16	26.17
22	– 3.89	5.64	43.65	6.04	—	199.15	59.34	102.76	96.41	– 74.81
23	24.61	– 35.57	– 10.73	—	—	199.15	5.50	– 47.75	– 180.68	—
24	70.90	– 4.23	—	—	32.96	– 16.46	38.09	194.02	—	—
25	– 16.84	20.78	—	– 28.34	36.04	42.74	9.89	—	—	– 31.23
26	51.16	—	– 28.85	– 77.35	– 79.30	– 127.59	—	—	46.05	22.81
27	—	—	17.38	5.11	– 357.36	– 108.28	—	– 40.82	– 94.60	6.66
28	—	– 7.40	1.11	– 92.90	– 114.31	—	60.21	– 160.32	– 130.32	40.42
29	17.80	14.44	– 64.73	– 72.01	—	—	– 37.74	– 131.13	– 23.10	41.61
30	18.45	– 3.87	– 31.44	—	—	– 176.04	– 112.09	– 171.32	– 7.49	—
31	– 3.88	5.99	—	—	– 512.61	– 84.85	112.09	30.17	—	—
Close	3913.42	4610.56	5616.21	7622.42	7539.07	10829.28	11215.10	9949.75	8663.50	9415.82
Change	148.92	– 97.91	87.30	– 600.19	– 1344.22	174.13	693.12	– 573.06	– 73.09	182.02

August's a good month to go on vacation
Trading stocks will likely lead to frustration

JULY

End of July closes well, EXCEPT if bear market in progress

MONDAY

 **25**

*The punishment of wise men who refuse to take part
in the affairs of government is to live under the government of unwise men.*
— Plato

TUESDAY

26

*Your emotions are often a reverse indicator
of what you ought to be doing.*
— John F. Hindelong (Dillon, Reed)

WEDNESDAY

27

Life is what happens, while you're busy making other plans.
— John Lennon (Beatle)

THURSDAY

 28

*Every great advance in natural knowledge
has involved the absolute rejection of authority.*
— Thomas H. Huxley (British scientist and humanist,
defender of Darwinism, 1825-1895)

FRIDAY

 29

*Make money and the whole nation
will conspire to call you a gentleman.*
— George Bernard Shaw

SATURDAY

30

*August Sector Seasonalities:
Bullish: Biotech; Gold/Silver Bearish: Cyclical (page 118)*

SUNDAY

31

FIRST MONTH OF QUARTERS IS THE MOST BULLISH

We have observed over the years that the investment calendar reflects the annual, semi-annual and quarterly operations of institutions during January, April and July. The opening month of the first three quarters produces the greatest gains in the Dow Jones industrials and the S&P 500. NASDAQ's record differs slightly.

The fourth quarter had behaved quite differently since it is affected by year-end portfolio adjustments and Presidential and Congressional elections in even-numbered years. But in recent years, with October 1987 not factored in, October has transformed into a bear-killing-turnaround month posting some mighty gains the last six years. (See pages 141, 145, 151.)

After experiencing the most powerful bull market of all time during the 1990s, followed by the down cycle of a generation (perhaps two), we divided the monthly average percent changes into two groups: before 1991 and after. Comparing the month-by-month quarterly behavior of the three major U.S. averages in the table, you'll see that first months of all quarters perform best overall. Nasty sell-offs in April 2000, 2002 and 2004 and July 2000-2002 hit the NASDAQ hardest. (See pages 141, 145, 151.)

Between 1950 and 1990, the S&P 500 gained 1.3% (Dow, 1.4%) on average in first months of the first three quarters. Second months barely eked out any gain, while third months, thanks to March, moved up 0.23% (Dow, 0.07%) on average. NASDAQ's first month of the first three quarters averages 1.67% from 1971-1990 with July being a negative drag.

The bear spread out much of its damage during 2000-2003 in the first three quarters staging turnarounds for the most part in October. The once-feared month has been the bulls' latter-day savior.

DOW JONES INDUSTRIALS, S&P 500 & NASDAQ
AVERAGE MONTHLY % CHANGES BY QUARTER

	DJIA 1950-1990			S&P 500 1950-1990			NASDAQ 1971-1990		
	1st Mo	2nd Mo	3rd Mo	1st Mo	2nd Mo	3rd Mo	1st Mo	2nd Mo	3rd Mo
1Q	1.5%	−0.01%	1.0%	1.5%	−0.1%	1.1%	3.8%	1.2%	0.9%
2Q	1.6	−0.4	0.1	1.3	−0.1	0.3	1.7	0.8	1.1
3Q	1.1	0.3	−0.9	1.1	0.3	−0.7	−0.5	0.1	−1.6
Tot	4.2%	−0.1%	0.2%	3.9%	0.1%	0.7%	5.0%	2.1%	0.4%
Avg	1.40%	−0.04%	0.07%	1.30%	0.03%	0.23%	1.67%	0.70%	0.13%
4Q	−0.1%	1.4%	1.7%	0.4%	1.7%	1.6%	−1.4%	1.6%	1.4%
	DJIA 1991-June 2004			S&P 500 1991-June 2004			NASDAQ 1991-June 2004		
1Q	1.2%	0.6%	0.7%	1.4%	0.04%	0.8%	4.2%	−0.2%	−0.4%
2Q	2.5	1.4	−0.4	1.5	1.3	0.2	0.5	1.3	1.6
3Q	1.1	−1.2	−1.7	0.3	−0.8	−1.0	0.3	0.6	−0.5
Tot	4.8%	0.8%	−1.4%	3.2%	0.5%	0.0%	5.0%	1.7%	0.7%
Avg	1.60%	0.27%	−0.47%	1.07%	0.18%	0.00%	1.67%	0.56%	0.23%
4Q	2.8%	2.2%	2.1%	2.6%	1.8%	2.1%	3.3%	2.5%	3.0%
	DJIA 1950-June 2004			S&P 500 1950-June 2004			NASDAQ 1971-June 2004		
1Q	1.4%	0.2%	1.0%	1.5%	−0.1%	1.0%	3.9%	0.6%	0.4%
2Q	1.9	0.1	−0.1	1.3	0.3	0.2	1.2	1.0	1.3
3Q	1.1	−0.05	−1.1	0.9	0.02	−0.7	−0.2	0.3	−1.1
Tot	4.4%	0.3%	−0.2%	3.7%	0.2%	0.5%	4.9%	1.9%	0.6%
Avg	1.47%	0.08%	−0.07%	1.23%	0.07%	0.17%	1.63%	0.64%	0.20%
4Q	0.6%	1.6%	1.8%	0.9%	1.7%	1.7%	0.5%	1.9%	2.1%

MONDAY

1

Average August gains last 33 years

NAS 0.3% Dow −0.2% S&P 0.1%
Up 18 Down 15 Up 18 Down 15 Up 18 Down 15
Rank #10 Rank #11 Rank #10

I keep hearing "Should I buy? Should I buy?"
When I start hearing "Should I sell?" that's the bottom.
— Nick Moore (Portfolio manager,
Jurika & Voyles, *TheStreet.com* Mar. 12, 2001)

TUESDAY

2

August worst S&P month last 15 years

New issues: The closest thing to a
"Sure Thing" Wall Street has to offer.
— Norm Fosback (*New Issues*)

WEDNESDAY

3

The world hates change,
but it is the only thing that has brought progress.
— Charles Kettering (Inventor of electric ignition,
founded Delco in 1909, 1876-1958)

THURSDAY

4

Stock prices tend to discount
what has been unanimously reported by the mass media.
— Louis Ehrenkrantz (Ehrenkrantz, Lyons & Ross)

FRIDAY

 5

I am glad that I paid so little attention to good advice;
had I abided by it I might have been saved from my most valuable mistakes.
— Gene Fowler (Journalist, screenwriter,
film director, biographer, 1890-1960)

SATURDAY

6

SUNDAY

7

AURA OF THE TRIPLE WITCH – QUARTERS 1 AND 4 BULLISH BUT DOWN WEEKS TRIGGER MORE WEAKNESS WEEK AFTER

Options expire the third Friday of every month but in March, June, September and December a powerful coven gathers. Since the S&P index futures began trading on April 21, 1982, stock options, index options as well as index futures all expire at the same time four times each year — known as Triple Witching. Traders have long sought to understand and master the magic of this quarterly phenomenon.

We have analyzed what the market does prior, during and following Triple Witching expirations in search of consistent trading patterns. This is never easy. For as soon as a pattern becomes obvious, the market almost always starts to anticipate it, and the pattern tends to shift. These are some of our findings of how the Dow Jones industrials perform around Triple-Witching Week (TWW).

- TWWs became more bullish since 1990, except in the second quarter.

- Following weeks became more bearish. (Prior to December 2003 seven in a row were down.)

- TWWs have tended to be down in flat periods and dramatically so during the 2000-2002 bear market.

- DOWN WEEKS TEND TO FOLLOW DOWN TWWs is a most interesting pattern. Since 1991, of 18 down TWWs, 14 following weeks were also down. This is surprising inasmuch as the previous decade had an exactly opposite pattern: There were 13 down TWWs then, but 12 up weeks followed them.

- TWWs in the second and third quarter (Worst Six Months May through October) are much weaker and the weeks following, horrendous. But in the first and fourth quarter (Best Six Months period November through April) a solid bullish bias is evident.

See more in our March 2004 *Almanac Investor Newsletter* at *stocktradersalmanac.com*.

TRIPLE-WITCHING WEEK & WEEK AFTER DOW POINT CHANGES
January 1991 — June 2004 Dow 2633.66 to 10435.48 up 296.2%

	Expiration Week Q1	Week After	Expiration Week Q2	Week After	Expiration Week Q3	Week After	Expiration Week Q4	Week After
1991	-6.93	-89.36	-34.98	-58.81	33.54	-13.19	20.12	167.04
1992	40.48	-44.95	-69.01	-2.94	21.35	-76.73	9.19	12.97
1993	43.76	-31.60	-10.24	-3.88	-8.38	-70.14	10.90	6.15
1994	32.95	-120.92	3.33	-139.84	58.54	-101.60	116.08	26.24
1995	38.04	65.02	86.80	75.05	96.85	-33.42	19.87	-78.76
1996	114.52	51.67	55.78	-50.60	49.94	-15.54	179.53	76.51
1997	-130.67	-64.20	14.47	-108.79	174.30	4.91	-82.01	-76.98
1998	303.91	-110.35	-122.07	231.67	100.16	133.11	81.87	314.36
1999	27.20	-81.31	365.05	-303.00	-224.80	-524.30	32.73	148.33
2000	666.41	517.49	-164.76	-44.55	-293.65	-79.63	-277.95	200.60
2001	-821.21	-318.63	-353.36	-19.05	-1369.70	611.75	224.19	101.65
2002	34.74	-179.56	-220.42	-10.53	-326.67	-284.57	77.61	-207.54
2003	662.26	-376.20	83.63	-211.70	173.27	-331.74	236.06	46.45
2004	-53.48	26.37	6.31	-44.57				
Up	10	4	7	2	8	3	11	10
Down	4	10	7	12	5	10	2	3

June 1982 — December 1990 Dow 819.54 to 2633.66 up 221.4%

	Expiration Week Q1	Week After	Expiration Week Q2	Week After	Expiration Week Q3	Week After	Expiration Week Q4	Week After
1982	—	—	-21.12	14.46	10.12	2.58	-7.26	33.57
1983	N/C	22.35	46.08	-0.50	-14.03	29.88	-17.89	8.34
1984	44.60	-29.52	-44.35	44.17	-35.78	4.97	23.07	5.19
1985	-22.31	20.10	23.52	10.98	-9.74	22.85	7.79	0.00
1986	-24.18	53.16	5.35	5.72	3.93	7.04	16.59	1.55
1987	74.86	2.28	43.12	16.01	-84.10	45.53	108.26	24.37
1988	52.39	-108.42	2.31	38.94	29.34	-7.47	7.22	18.22
1989	10.00	-49.10	-27.04	45.49	-34.96	7.03	8.11	-28.16
1990	57.89	-36.94	73.51	-78.71	-51.73	-59.90	39.85	-4.45
Up	5	4	6	7	3	7	7	6
Down	2	4	3	2	6	2	2	3

AUGUST

MONDAY
8

*Regulatory agencies within five years
become controlled by industries they were set up to regulate.*
— Gabriel Kolko

FOMC Meeting

TUESDAY
9

*The best minds are not in government.
If any were, business would hire them away.*
— Ronald Reagan

WEDNESDAY
10

Success is going from failure to failure without loss of enthusiasm.
— Winston Churchill (British statesman, 1874-1965)

THURSDAY
11

*For want of a nail, the shoe was lost. For want of a shoe,
the horse was lost. For want of a horse, the rider was lost.
For want of a rider, the battle was lost. For want of a battle,
the kingdom was lost. And all for the want of a nail!*
— English proverb

Mid-August stronger than beginning

FRIDAY

12

*You know a country is falling apart
when even the government will not accept its own currency.*
— Jim Rogers (Financier, *Adventure Capitalist*, b. 1942)

SATURDAY
13

SUNDAY
14

ALMANAC INVESTING 101

"How do I make money with the *Stock Trader's Almanac?*" Every year we field countless questions from Almanac Readers who want to add the calendar edge to their quiver but aren't sure how.

The Almanac is a tool to help investors gain perspective of the markets. Trading with the Almanac as your only reference is akin to planning an outdoor wedding with the *Old Farmer's Almanac*. Just because there is only a 5% chance of rain on your wedding day doesn't mean you shouldn't have a tent. Trading with any one trading tool, book, or advisor for that matter, is, in general, a bad idea.

There is no magic formula to make investing easy. Nothing can replace research, experience and a healthy dose of luck. There is, however, a methodology investors can employ to mitigate losses and enhance returns. Nineteenth-century philosopher George Santayana once quipped, "Those who cannot remember the past are condemned to repeat it." This is the cornerstone of the philosophy behind what we call Almanac Investing. Simply put, Almanac Investing relies on analyzing and studying the markets from an historical perspective. Whether a person is a short-term trader or a longer-term investor, being aware of historical and seasonal patterns and tendencies is helpful and valuable.

Almanac Investing is constantly evolving as the investment world changes. This is due to the exogenous factors that shape not only Wall Street, but Main Street. That being said, there are a few tried-and-true methods that will benefit all investors, from the novice to the professional money manager. Below is a sampling of how to unlock the power of Almanac Investing. Those who are interested in learning more are encouraged to visit *www.stocktradersalmanac.com* and peruse the archives of our newsletter the *Almanac Investor*.

SECTOR SEASONALITY: SELECTED PERCENTAGE PLAYS

One of the most popular investment strategies in the Almanac is sector seasonality. Listed on the weekly planning pages on the Sunday before each month begins are the bullish and bearish sectors for the upcoming month. This is generated from the history summarized on page 118. Until recently, this was a difficult strategy for the individual investor to employ — ETFs changed that forever!

The advent of exchange traded funds (ETFs) has facilitated Almanac Investing. Before the creation of this vehicle, investors would have to hand-pick a basket of stocks from a sector, thus incurring additional commission costs and risks or wrestle with cumbersome mutual funds and other brokerage house products. ETFs are funds that track an index, but can be traded like a stock. Basically, they bundle together the securities that are in an index. Investors can do just about anything with an ETF that they can do with a normal stock, such as short selling. Because ETFs are traded on stock exchanges, they can be bought and sold at any time during the day (unlike most mutual funds). Their prices will fluctuate from moment to moment, just like any other stock's price, and an investor will need a broker in order to purchase them.

Listed on page 189 are the top 140 ETFs by market cap. (If you look back to last year's Almanac on page 189, you will see only 96 ETFs — an indication of how quickly the universe of ETFs is growing.) Every month, we wade through the world of ETF in the *Almanac Investor* and hand-select the funds that we feel best mirror the bullish sector(s) of the month.

ALMANAC INVESTOR SWITCHING STRATEGY: THE MOTHER OF ALL SEASONAL TRADES

"Sell in May and go away." This old Wall Street proverb has merit. The flip side is "Buy
(continued on page 80)

AUGUST

MONDAY

15

I always keep these seasonal patterns in the back of my mind.
My antennae start to purr at certain times of the year.
— Kenneth Ward

TUESDAY

 16

The difference between genius and stupidity
is that genius has its limits.
— Anonymous

WEDNESDAY

17

Only buy stocks when the market declines 10%
from that date a year ago, which happens once or twice a decade.
— Eugene D. Brody (Oppenheimer Capital)

THURSDAY

 18

No profession requires more hard work, intelligence, patience,
and mental discipline than successful speculation.
— Robert Rhea

Expiration day Dow down 10 of last 14

FRIDAY

 **19**

Ignorance is not knowing something;
stupidity is not admitting your ignorance.
— Daniel Turov (*Turov on Timing*)

SATURDAY

20

SUNDAY

21

(continued from page 78)

in October and get yourself sober." Not too catchy, but nothing really rhymes with October. The simple fact is that the market makes the vast majority of its gains from the beginning of November through the end of April, while the market tends to be flat to down from May through October.

The simple switching strategy has been refined by adding a MACD timing trigger (see pages 50 & 52). Starting at the beginning of April, we employ a 12-25-9 MACD trigger to indicate and confirm a sell. And starting at the beginning of October we employ an 8-17-9 MACD trigger to indicate and confirm a buy. (For a detailed explanation go to *www.stocktradersalmanac.com* and click on the MACD tab.)

When the October MACD triggers, an Almanac Investor would go long the broad market ETFs Diamonds Trust (DIA) for the Dow, the S&P Depository Receipts (SPY) for the S&P and the Nasdaq 100 Trust (QQQ) for the NASDAQ. The April trigger would confirm that it is time to sell Diamonds and Spiders. The Qs get sold on June's "Best Eight Months" trigger.

The purpose of that signal is not to call market tops and bottoms, nor is it a trigger to dump everything in your portfolio. The sell signal represents that it is time to rotate out of our seasonal investments in broad market index positions (the QQQs, DIAs and SPYs) purchased when the *Almanac Investor* MACD buy signal triggered in October.

This sell signal is also a signal for people who are risk adverse to move a larger portion of their investment portfolios into cash or cash equivalents. It is also time to become more defensive with a portfolio, tighten stop losses and take gains when they are present.

Subscribers to our services receive all MACD buy and sell signals via email. The signals are made public on our website at a later date.

THE ONLY "FREE LUNCH" ON WALL STREET

We have been capitalizing for many years on the NYSE stocks making new 52-week lows near year-end. Many are dumped for tax-loss purposes. These stocks often bounce sharply for one to two months, creating some fast profit potential for nimble traders. We sift though the chaff and put out a list of these year-end appetizers every year (see the full strategy on page 112).

Recently the tax selling has continued to the very end of the year. The moves have come fast and furious at times, often with the stocks dropping preciptously and bouncing as fast. We have added selections from the Amex and NASDAQ to broaden opportunities. *Almanac Investor* subscribers receive the Free Lunch lists before the markets open three days before the last trading day of the year.

This is just a sampling of a typical year for an investor utilizing history and the calendar for investment decisions. For investors who are serious about historical research, we offer research tools at *www.stocktradersalmanac.com*. This allows for much deeper research by allowing custom setting of time frames, index, the manipulating of parameters and much more. There are literally dozens of new strategies generated each year. Many are discussed in the Proving Grounds section of the *Almanac Investor* (pages 8 & 9); many come from suggestions from Almanac Investors doing their own research.

On page 104 of this year's *Almanac* there is more information about the *Almanac Investor* as well as a special discount code for *Almanac* Readers.

AUGUST

MONDAY

eware the "Summer Rally" hype historically the weakest rally of all seasons Averages 9.4% on the Dow (page 70) 2003 14.3% gain bucked trend, but still weaker than Spring and Fall

22

Edison has done more toward abolishing poverty than all the reformers and statesmen.
— Henry Ford

TUESDAY

23

In this age of instant information, investors can experience both fear and greed at the exact same moment.
— Sam Stovall (Chief Investment Strategist, Standard & Poor's, October 2003)

WEDNESDAY

 ## 24

Don't be scared to take big steps — you can't cross a chasm in two small jumps.
— David Lloyd George (British Prime Minister, 1916-1922)

End of August murderous 6 of the last 8 years Average loss last 5 days of August Dow –3.4% S&P –3.1% NAS –2.7%

THURSDAY

25

Sell stocks whenever the market is 30% higher over a year ago.
— Eugene D. Brody (Oppenheimer Capital)

FRIDAY

26

The heights by great men reached and kept, were not attained by sudden flight, but they, while their companions slept, were toiling upward in the night.
— Henry Wadsworth Longfellow

SATURDAY

27

September Sector Seasonalities: Bullish: Pharmaceutical; Bearish: Semiconductor (page 118)

SUNDAY

28

SEPTEMBER ALMANAC

SEPTEMBER							OCTOBER						
S	M	T	W	T	F	S	S	M	T	W	T	F	S
				1	2	3							1
4	5	6	7	8	9	10	2	3	4	5	6	7	8
11	12	13	14	15	16	17	9	10	11	12	13	14	15
18	19	20	21	22	23	24	16	17	18	19	20	21	22
25	26	27	28	29	30		23	24	25	26	27	28	29
							30	31					

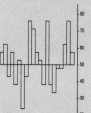

Market Probability Chart above is a graphic representation of the Market Probability Calendar on page 123.

♦ Start of business year, end of vacations, and back to school made September a leading barometer month in first 60 years of the century, now portfolio managers back after Labor Day tend to clean house ♦ Biggest % loser on the S&P, Dow and NASDAQ (pages 48 & 54) ♦ Streak of four great Septembers averaging 4.2% gains ended with five losers in a row averaging –6.9% losses (see below) ♦ Day after Labor Day Dow up 8 of last 10 ♦ Opened strong eight of last nine years but tends to close weak due to end-of-quarter mutual fund portfolio restructuring ♦ September Triple-Witching Week is dangerous, week after pitiful (see page 76).

SEPTEMBER DAILY POINT CHANGES DOW JONES INDUSTRIALS

Previous Month	1994	1995	1996	1997	1998	1999	2000	2001	2002	2003
Close	3913.42	4610.56	5616.21	7622.42	7539.07	10829.28	11215.10	9949.75	8663.50	9415.82
1	– 11.98	36.98	—	H	288.36	108.60	23.68	—	—	H
2	– 15.86	—	H	257.36	– 45.06	– 94.67	—	—	H	107.45
3	—	—	32.18	14.86	– 100.15	235.24	—	H	– 355.45	45.19
4	—	H	8.51	– 27.40	– 41.97	—	H	47.74	117.07	19.44
5	H	22.54	– 49.94	– 44.83	—	—	21.83	35.78	– 141.42	– 84.56
6	13.12	13.73	52.90	—	—	H	50.03	– 192.43	143.50	—
7	– 12.45	– 14.09	—	—	H	– 44.32	– 50.77	– 234.99	—	—
8	22.21	31.00	—	12.77	380.53	2.21	– 39.22	—	—	82.95
9	– 33.65	—	73.98	16.73	– 155.76	43.06	—	—	92.18	– 79.09
10	—	—	– 6.66	– 132.63	– 249.48	– 50.97	—	0.34	83.23	– 86.74
11	—	4.22	27.74	– 58.30	179.96	—	– 25.16	Closed*	– 21.44	39.30
12	– 14.47	42.27	17.02	81.99	—	—	37.74	Closed*	– 201.76	11.79
13	19.52	18.31	66.58	—	—	1.90	– 51.05	Closed*	– 66.72	—
14	15.47	36.28	—	—	149.85	– 120.00	– 94.71	Closed*	—	—
15	58.55	– 4.23	—	– 21.83	79.04	– 108.91	– 160.47	—	—	– 22.74
16	– 20.53	—	50.68	174.78	65.39	– 63.96	—	—	67.49	118.53
17	—	—	– 0.37	– 9.48	– 216.01	66.17	—	– 684.81	– 172.63	– 21.69
18	—	– 17.16	– 11.47	36.28	21.89	—	– 118.48	– 17.30	– 35.10	113.48
19	3.37	– 13.37	– 9.62	– 5.45	—	—	– 19.23	– 144.27	– 230.06	– 14.31
20	– 67.63	25.65	20.72	—	—	20.27	– 101.37	– 382.92	43.63	—
21	– 17.49	– 25.29	—	—	37.59	– 225.43	77.60	– 140.40	—	—
22	– 14.47	– 3.25	—	79.56	– 36.05	– 74.40	81.85	—	—	– 109.41
23	– 5.38	—	6.28	– 26.77	257.21	– 205.48	—	—	– 113.87	40.63
24	—	—	– 20.71	– 63.35	– 152.42	– 39.26	—	368.05	– 189.02	– 150.53
25	—	5.78	3.33	– 58.70	26.78	—	– 39.22	56.11	158.69	– 81.55
26	17.49	– 4.33	– 8.51	74.17	—	—	– 176.83	92.58	155.30	– 30.88
27	13.80	– 3.25	4.07	—	—	24.06	– 2.96	114.03	– 295.67	—
28	15.14	25.29	—	—	80.07	– 27.86	195.70	166.14	—	—
29	– 23.55	1.44	—	69.25	– 28.32	– 62.05	– 173.14	—	—	67.16
30	– 11.44	—	9.25	– 46.17	– 237.90	123.47	—	—	– 109.52	– 105.18
Close	3843.19	4789.08	5882.17	7945.26	7842.62	10336.95	10650.92	8847.56	7591.93	9275.06
Change	– 70.23	178.52	265.96	322.84	303.55	– 492.33	– 564.18	– 1102.19	– 1071.57	– 140.76

Market closed for four days after 9/11 terrorist attack

September is when leaves and stocks tend to fall
On Wall Street it's the worst month of all

AUGUST/SEPTEMBER

MONDAY
29

If you don't keep your employees happy,
they won't keep the customers happy.
— Red Lobster V.P. (*New York Times* April 23, 1989)

TUESDAY
30

The worst mistake investors make
is taking their profits too soon, and their losses too long.
— Michael Price (Mutual Shares Fund)

WEDNESDAY
31

Individualism, private property, the law of accumulation of
wealth and the law of competition…are the highest result of human experience,
the soil in which, so far, has produced the best fruit.
— Andrew Carnegie (Scottish-born U.S. industrialist, philanthropist,
The Gospel Of Wealth, 1835-1919)

September opened strong 8 of last 9 years but tends to close weak

THURSDAY
1

Drawing on my fine command of language, I said nothing.
— Robert Benchley

Average September losses last 33 years

NAS −1.1%	Dow −1.6%	S&P −1.3%
Up 17 Down 16	Up 9 Down 24	Up 11 Down 21
Rank #12	Rank #12	Rank #12

FRIDAY
2

There's nothing wrong with cash. It gives you time to think.
— Robert Prechter, Jr. (*Elliott Wave Theorist*)

SATURDAY
3

SUNDAY
4

A CORRECTION FOR ALL SEASONS

While there's a rally for every season (page 70), almost always there's a decline or correction, too. Fortunately, corrections tend to be smaller than rallies, and that's what gives the stock market its long-term upward bias. In each season the average bounce outdoes the average setback. On average the net gain between the rally and the correction is smallest in summer and fall.

The summer setback tends to be slightly outdone by the average correction in the fall. Tax selling and portfolio cleaning are the usual explanations – individuals sell to register a tax loss and institutions like to get rid of their losers before preparing year-end statements. The October jinx also plays a major part. Since 1964, there have been 16 fall declines of over 10%, and in nine of them (1966, 1974, 1978, 1979, 1987, 1990, 1997, 2000 and 2002) much damage was done in October, where so many bear markets end. Important October lows were also seen in 1998 and 1999. Most often, it has paid to buy after fourth quarter or late third quarter "waterfall declines" for a rally that may continue into January or even beyond. War in Iraq affected the pattern in 2003. Anticipation of our invasion put the market down in the first quarter. Quick success inspired the bulls which resumed their upward move through the summer.

SEASONAL CORRECTIONS IN DOW JONES INDUSTRIALS

	WINTER Nov/Dec High to Q1 Low	SPRING Feb/Mar High to Q2 Low	SUMMER May/Jun High to Q3 Low	FALL Aug/Sep High to Q4 Low
1964	− 0.1%	− 2.4%	− 1.0%	− 2.1%
1965	− 2.5	− 7.3	− 8.3	− 0.9
1966	− 6.0	− 13.2	− 17.7	− 12.7
1967	− 4.2	− 3.9	− 5.5	− 9.9
1968	− 8.8	− 0.3	− 5.5	+ 0.4
1969	− 8.7	− 8.7	− 17.2	− 8.1
1970	− 13.8	− 20.2	− 8.8	− 2.5
1971	− 1.4	− 4.8	− 10.7	− 13.4
1972	− 0.5	− 2.6	− 6.3	− 5.3
1973	− 11.0	− 12.8	− 10.9	− 17.3
1974	− 15.3	− 10.8	− 29.8	− 27.6
1975	− 6.3	− 5.5	− 9.9	− 6.7
1976	− 0.2	− 5.1	− 4.7	− 8.9
1977	− 8.5	− 7.2	− 11.5	− 10.2
1978	− 12.3	− 4.0	− 7.0	− 13.5
1979	− 2.5	− 5.8	− 3.7	− 10.9
1980	− 10.0	− 16.0	− 1.7	− 6.8
1981	− 6.9	− 5.1	− 18.6	− 12.9
1982	− 10.9	− 7.5	− 10.6	− 3.3
1983	− 4.1	− 2.8	− 6.8	− 3.6
1984	− 11.9	− 10.5	− 8.4	− 6.2
1985	− 4.8	− 4.4	− 2.8	− 2.3
1986	− 3.3	− 4.7	− 7.3	− 7.6
1987	− 1.4	− 6.6	− 1.7	− 36.1
1988	− 6.7	− 7.0	− 7.6	− 4.5
1989	− 1.7	− 2.4	− 3.1	− 6.6
1990	− 7.9	− 4.0	− 17.3	− 18.4
1991	− 6.3	− 3.6	− 4.5	− 6.3
1992	+ 0.1	− 3.3	− 5.4	− 7.6
1993	− 2.7	− 3.1	− 3.0	− 2.0
1994	− 4.4	− 9.6	− 4.4	− 7.1
1995	− 0.8	− 0.1	− 0.2	− 2.0
1996	− 3.5	− 4.6	− 7.5	+ 0.2
1997	− 1.8	− 9.8	− 2.2	− 13.3
1998	− 7.0	− 3.1	− 18.2	− 13.1
1999	− 2.7	− 1.7	− 8.0	− 11.5
2000	− 14.8	− 7.4	− 4.1	− 11.8
2001	− 14.5	− 13.6	− 27.4	− 16.2
2002	− 5.1	− 14.2	− 26.7	− 19.5
2003	− 15.8	− 5.3	− 3.1	− 2.1
2004	− 3.9	− 7.7		
Totals	**− 254.9%**	**− 272.7%**	**− 359.1%**	**− 370.1%**
Average	**− 6.2%**	**− 6.7%**	**− 9.0%**	**− 9.3%**

SEPTEMBER

MONDAY
5

Labor Day
(Market Closed)

*The two most abundant elements in the universe are
Hydrogen and Stupidity.*
— Harlan Ellison (Science fiction writer, b. 1934)

TUESDAY
6

Day after Labor Day Dow up 8 of last 10

*Those companies that the market expects will have the best futures,
as measured by the price/earnings ratios they are accorded,
have consistently done worst subsequently.*
— David Dreman

WEDNESDAY
7

*The usual bull market successfully weathers a number of tests
until it is considered invulnerable, whereupon it is ripe for a bust.*
— George Soros

THURSDAY
8

*If you can buy all you want of a new issue, you do not want any;
if you cannot obtain any, you want all you can buy.*
— Rod Fadem (Oppenheimer & Co.)

FRIDAY
9

*I was in search of a one-armed economist
so that the guy could never make a statement and then say:
"on the other hand."*
— Harry S. Truman

SATURDAY
10

SUNDAY
11

"In Memory"

MARKET BEHAVIOR THREE DAYS BEFORE AND THREE DAYS AFTER HOLIDAYS

We have kept track of holiday seasonality annually in the *Stock Trader's Almanac* since the first edition in 1968. Over the years the market tended to go up on the day before holidays and sell off the day after, but a transformation has taken place. Some holidays seem to be favored by the bulls, while others are not.

Eight holidays are separated into four groups: those positive the day after, those positive both the day before and after, those negative the day after, and the sole holiday that's negative both the day before and after. Notice we show average percent changes for the Dow, S&P 500, and the Zweig Unweighted Price Index.

Bear in mind that the Dow and S&P are both blue chip indices, whereas the Zweig would be more representative of smaller cap stocks. This is evident on the last day of the year with ZUPI smaller stocks having a field day, while their larger brethren in the Dow and S&P are showing losses on average. The best six-day span can be seen for ZUPI stocks on the three days before and three days after New Year's Day, a gain of about 2.2% on average. Thanks to the Santa Claus Rally the six days around Christmas are up solidly as well.

The worst day after a holiday is the day after Easter. Surprisingly, the following day is one of the best second days after a holiday, right up there with the second day after New Year's.

Presidents' Day is the least bullish of all the holidays, bearish the day before and three days after. The S&P and NASDAQ have dropped 12 of the last 13 days before Presidents' Day, Dow 11 of 13.

HOLIDAYS: 3 DAYS BEFORE, 3 DAYS AFTER (Average % Change 1980 — July 2004)

	− 3	− 2	− 1		+1	+2	+3
				Positive Day After			
S&P 500	0.09	0.35	− 0.16	New Year's	0.01	0.52	0.13
DJIA	0.06	0.27	− 0.28	Day	0.22	0.52	0.30
ZUPI	0.11	0.34	0.51	*1.1.05*	0.36	0.54	0.36
S&P 500	0.15	− 0.05	0.04	Memorial	0.38	0.17	0.18
DJIA	0.14	− 0.09	− 0.03	Day	0.47	0.20	0.12
ZUPI	− 0.07	0.07	0.18	*5.30.05*	0.14	0.11	0.19
				Positive Before & After			
S&P 500	− 0.17	− 0.31	0.25	Labor	0.09	0.06	− 0.12
DJIA	− 0.17	− 0.35	0.23	Day	0.17	0.07	− 0.17
ZUPI	0.02	− 0.04	0.25	*9.5.05*	0.01	0.02	0.14
S&P 500	− 0.02	0.00	0.24	Thanksgiving	0.22	− 0.22	0.18
DJIA	0.08	0.02	0.31	*11.24.05*	0.17	− 0.22	0.23
ZUPI	− 0.14	− 0.13	0.19		0.32	− 0.19	0.13
S&P 500	0.18	0.18	0.23	Christmas	0.21	0.06	0.35
DJIA	0.23	0.25	0.32	*12.25.05 (Closed 12.26)*	0.26	0.04	0.30
ZUPI	0.03	0.15	0.35		0.13	0.11	0.37
				Negative Day After			
S&P 500	0.24	− 0.05	0.24	Good Friday	− 0.44	0.53	0.10
DJIA	0.19	− 0.10	0.21	*3.25.05*	− 0.30	0.53	0.08
ZUPI	0.07	0.10	0.16		− 0.38	0.25	0.07
S&P 500	0.00	0.12	0.06	Independence	− 0.20	− 0.02	0.11
DJIA	0.00	0.11	0.04	Day	− 0.13	0.03	0.08
ZUPI	0.12	0.08	0.11	*7.4.05*	− 0.07	− 0.04	0.05
				Negative Before & After			
S&P 500	0.25	− 0.01	− 0.37	Presidents'	− 0.14	− 0.12	− 0.06
DJIA	0.25	0.02	− 0.31	Day	− 0.06	− 0.17	− 0.07
ZUPI	0.17	− 0.02	− 0.07	*2.21.05*	− 0.22	− 0.15	− 0.07

Data courtesy of Martin Zweig/Catherine Nolan

SEPTEMBER

Monday before Triple Witching Dow up 10 of 14

MONDAY
12

A gold mine is a hole in the ground with a liar on top.
— Mark Twain (1835-1910, pen name of Samuel Longhorne Clemens,
American novelist and satirist)

TUESDAY
13

*In this game, the market has to keep pitching,
but you don't have to swing. You can stand there with
the bat on your shoulder for six months until you get a fat pitch.*
— Warren Buffett

WEDNESDAY
14

*There are three principal means of acquiring knowledge…
observation of nature, reflection, and experimentation.
Observation collects facts; reflection combines them;
experimentation verifies the result of that combination.*
— Denis Diderot (French editor, philosopher.
He edited the first modern encyclopedia in 1745, 1713-1784)

THURSDAY
15

*You're perhaps the most accomplished confidence man since Charles Ponzi.
I'd say you were a carnival barker, except that wouldn't be fair to carnival barkers.
A carnie will at least tell you up front that he's running a shell game.*
— Senator Peter G. Fitzgerald (In comments to Kenneth L. Lay,
former chairman of Enron, February 13, 2002)

Triple-Witching Day Dow down 8 of last 14

FRIDAY

16

*A committee is a cul de sac down
which ideas are lured and then quietly strangled.*
— Sir Barnett Cocks (Member of Parliament)

SATURDAY
17

SUNDAY
18

MARKET GAINS MORE EIGHT DAYS A MONTH
THAN ON ALL 13 REMAINING DAYS COMBINED

Trading patterns have changed dramatically. For many years the last day plus the first four days were the best days of the month. Thousands took advantage of this anomaly and thrived. The market currently exhibits greater bullish bias from the last three trading days of the previous month through the first two days of the current month and now shows significant bullishness during the middle three trading days nine to eleven, due to 401(k) cash inflows (see pages 136 and 137). This pattern was not as pronounced during the boom years of the 1990s with market strength all month long. But the last four and a half years have experienced monthly bullishness at the ends, beginnings and middles of months versus losses during the rest of the month. Was 1999's "rest of month" bullishness a bearish omen?

SUPER EIGHT DAYS* DOW % CHANGES VS. REST OF MONTH

	Super 8 Days	Rest of Month	Super 8 Days	Rest of Month	Super 8 Days	Rest of Month
	1996		**1997**		**1998**	
Jan	2.10%	1.12%	0.80%	0.91%	4.18%	− 2.30%
Feb	1.07	4.46	4.19	1.46	5.43	1.55
Mar	0.65	1.24	− 3.83	1.58	3.06	2.53
Apr	2.44	− 4.20	− 4.50	2.66	2.29	− 1.47
May	0.71	1.86	5.49	3.81	2.37	− 1.79
Jun	− 1.04	1.22	1.63	2.55	− 4.64	4.47
Jul	− 2.91	− 1.36	2.85	2.65	3.55	− 3.43
Aug	3.09	1.25	− 2.39	− 1.76	− 4.75	0.17
Sep	1.07	1.84	4.51	− 3.57	− 4.92	− 0.59
Oct	2.37	− 0.74	2.45	− 6.73	0.68	3.59
Nov	2.46	6.86	6.56	− 2.84	6.19	4.57
Dec	− 3.70	3.82	2.53	− 3.57	− 2.75	2.11
Totals	**8.31%**	**17.37%**	**20.29%**	**− 2.85%**	**10.69%**	**9.41%**
Average	**0.69%**	**1.45%**	**1.69%**	**− 0.24%**	**0.89%**	**0.78%**
	1999		**2000**		**2001**	
Jan	0.98%	0.08%	− 4.09%	0.47%	2.13%	− 2.36%
Feb	0.76	1.62	0.43	− 9.10	1.41	− 3.36
Mar	− 0.68	3.74	2.76	5.62	− 1.50	− 3.30
Apr	2.84	7.09	− 2.79	4.77	− 2.61	9.56
May	− 0.83	− 1.92	0.71	− 7.86	2.02	1.53
Jun	0.20	0.01	5.99	− 4.10	− 2.46	− 2.45
Jul	5.87	− 1.74	− 0.65	0.83	2.16	2.29
Aug	− 0.35	2.41	3.08	3.75	0.24	− 2.48
Sep	− 5.83	− 2.32	− 3.27	− 2.34	− 3.62	− 12.05
Oct	− 2.86	2.97	− 0.85	− 1.47	4.51	5.36
Nov	4.25	2.45	5.81	− 4.06	1.01	2.48
Dec	0.29	3.92	− 2.96	4.44	0.19	1.99
Totals	**4.64%**	**18.31%**	**4.17%**	**− 9.05%**	**3.48%**	**− 7.37%**
Average	**0.39%**	**1.53%**	**0.35%**	**− 0.75%**	**0.29%**	**− 0.61%**
	2002		**2003**		**2004**	
Jan	− 1.92%	− 0.24%	1.00%	− 4.86%	3.79%	− 1.02%
Feb	− 1.41	4.27	2.71	− 4.82	− 1.20	0.83
Mar	4.11	− 2.64	5.22	− 0.90	− 1.65	− 1.69
Apr	− 2.46	0.08	2.87	− 1.91	3.20	− 0.60
May	3.62	− 4.07	3.17	2.46	− 2.91	− 0.51
Jun	− 2.22	− 6.51	3.09	− 0.38	1.14	1.36
Jul	− 5.04	− 4.75	1.18	1.64		
Aug	2.08	4.59	− 0.74	1.55		
Sep	− 6.58	− 5.00	3.58	− 3.47		
Oct	8.48	− 1.50	2.87	1.41		
Nov	4.74	0.99	− 0.47	0.48		
Dec	− 0.76	− 4.02	2.10	3.70		
Totals	**2.64%**	**− 18.80%**	**26.58%**	**− 5.10%**	**2.37%**	**− 1.63%**
Average	**0.22%**	**− 1.57%**	**2.22%**	**− 0.43%**	**0.40%**	**− 0.27%**

	Super 8 Days*			Rest of Month (13 Days)	
102	Net % Changes	83.17%		Net % Changes	0.29%
Month	Average Period	0.82%		Average Period	0.003%
Totals	Average Day	0.06%		Average Day	0.0002%

* Super 8 Days = Last 3 + First 2 + Middle 3

SEPTEMBER

Week after Triple Witching Dow down 11 of 14

MONDAY
19

Those who cannot remember the past are condemned to repeat it.
— George Santayana (American philosopher, poet)

FOMC Meeting

 ## TUESDAY
20

*Wall Street has a uniquely hysterical way of thinking the world
will end tomorrow but be fully recovered in the long run,
then a few years later believing the immediate future is rosy
but that the long term stinks.*
— Kenneth L. Fisher (*Wall Street Waltz*)

WEDNESDAY
21

*The only way to even begin to manage this new world is by focusing on...
nation building — helping others restructure their economies
and put in place decent non-corrupt government.*
— Thomas L. Friedman (Op-ed columnist, *New York Times*)

THURSDAY
22

*The higher a people's intelligence and moral strength,
the lower will be the prevailing rate of interest.*
— Eugen von Bohm-Bawerk
(Austrian economist, *Capital and Interest*, 1851-1914)

FRIDAY
23

*Selling a soybean contract short
is worth two years at the Harvard Business School.*
— Robert Stovall (Managing director, Wood Asset Management)

SATURDAY
24

SUNDAY
25

OCTOBER ALMANAC

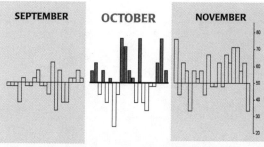

OCTOBER							NOVEMBER					
S	M	T	W	T	F	S	S	M	T	W	T	F	S
						1							1	2	3	4	5
2	3	4	5	6	7	8	6	7	8	9	10	11	12
9	10	11	12	13	14	15	13	14	15	16	17	18	19
16	17	18	19	20	21	22	20	21	22	23	24	25	26
23	24	25	26	27	28	29	27	28	29	30			
30	31												

Market Probability Chart above is a graphic representation of the Market Probability Calendar on page 123.

◆ Known as the jinx month because of crashes in 1929, 1987, the 554-point drop on October 27, 1997, back-to-back massacres in 1978 and 1979 and Friday the 13th in 1989 ◆ Yet October is a "bear killer" and turned the tide in ten post-WWII bear markets: 1946, 1957, 1960, 1962, 1966, 1974, 1987, 1990, 1998 and 2002 ◆ Worst six months of the year ends with October (page 50) ◆ No longer worst month (pages 48 & 54) ◆ Best month 1998-2003 average Dow 5.9%, S&P 5.0%, NAS 6.4% ◆ October is a great time to buy depressed high-tech stocks (page 118) ◆ Big October gains last five years after atrocious Septembers ◆ Can get into Best Six Months earlier using MACD (page 52).

OCTOBER DAILY POINT CHANGES DOW JONES INDUSTRIALS

Previous Month	1994	1995	1996	1997	1998	1999	2000	2001	2002	2003
Close	3843.19	4789.08	5882.17	7945.26	7842.62	10336.95	10650.92	8847.56	7591.93	9275.06
1	—	—	22.73	70.24	− 210.09	− 63.95	—	− 10.73	346.86	194.14
2	—	− 27.82	29.07	12.03	152.16	—	49.21	113.76	− 183.18	18.60
3	3.70	− 11.56	− 1.12	11.05	—	—	19.61	173.19	− 38.42	84.51
4	− 45.76	− 9.03	60.01	—	—	128.23	64.74	− 62.90	− 188.79	—
5	− 13.79	22.04	—	—	− 58.45	− 0.64	− 59.56	58.89	—	—
6	− 11.78	6.50	—	61.64	16.74	187.75	− 128.38	—	—	22.67
7	21.87	—	− 13.05	78.09	− 1.29	− 51.29	—	—	− 105.56	59.63
8	—	—	− 13.04	− 83.25	− 9.78	112.71	—	− 51.83	78.65	− 23.71
9	—	− 42.99	− 36.15	− 33.64	167.61	—	− 28.11	− 15.50	− 215.22	49.11
10	23.89	− 5.42	− 8.95	− 16.21	—	—	− 44.03	188.42	247.68	− 5.33
11	55.51	14.45	47.71	—	—	− 1.58	− 110.61	169.59	316.34	—
12	− 1.68	29.63	—	—	101.95	− 231.12	− 379.21	− 66.29	—	—
13	14.80	28.90	—	27.01	− 63.33	− 184.90	157.60	—	—	89.70
14	20.52	—	40.62	24.07	30.64	54.45	—	—	27.11	48.60
15	—	− 5.22	− 38.31	330.58	− 266.90	—	3.46	378.28	− 9.93
16	—	− 9.40	16.03	− 119.10	117.40	—	46.62	36.61	− 219.65	− 11.33
17	13.46	11.56	38.39	− 91.85	—	—	− 149.09	− 151.26	239.01	69.93
18	− 6.39	− 18.42	35.03	—	—	96.57	− 114.69	− 69.75	47.36	—
19	18.50	24.93	—	—	49.69	88.65	167.96	40.89	—	—
20	− 24.89	− 7.59	—	74.41	39.40	187.43	83.61	—	—	56.15
21	− 19.85	—	− 3.36	139.00	13.38	− 94.67	—	—	215.84	− 30.30
22	—	—	− 29.07	− 25.79	13.91	172.56	—	172.92	− 88.08	− 149.40
23	—	− 39.38	− 25.34	− 186.88	− 80.85	—	45.13	− 36.95	44.11	14.89
24	− 36.00	28.18	− 43.98	− 132.36	—	—	121.35	5.54	− 176.93	− 30.67
25	− 4.71	− 29.98	14.54	—	—	− 120.32	− 66.59	117.28	126.65	—
26	− 2.36	− 49.86	—	—	− 20.08	− 47.80	53.64	82.27	—	—
27	26.92	37.93	—	− 554.26	− 66.17	92.76	210.50	—	—	25.70
28	55.51	—	− 34.29	337.17	5.93	227.64	—	—	− 75.95	140.15
29	—	—	34.29	8.35	123.06	107.33	—	− 275.67	0.90	26.22
30	—	14.82	− 13.79	− 125.00	97.07	—	245.15	− 147.52	58.47	12.08
31	− 22.54	− 1.09	36.15	60.41	—	—	135.37	− 46.84	− 30.38	14.51
Close	3908.12	4755.48	6029.38	7442.08	8592.10	10729.86	10971.14	9075.14	8397.03	9801.12
Change	64.93	− 33.60	147.21	− 503.18	749.48	392.91	320.22	227.58	805.10	526.06

October has killed many a bear
Buy tech stocks and soon wear a grin ear to ear

SEPTEMBER/OCTOBER

Septembers close weak (pages 82 and 123)

MONDAY
26

To know values is to know the meaning of the market.
— Charles Dow

TUESDAY
27

*The worst crime against working people
is a company that fails to make a profit.*
— Samuel Gompers

WEDNESDAY
28

*Of a stock's move, 31% can be attributed to the general stock market,
12% to the industry influence, 37% to the influence of other groupings,
and the remaining 20% is peculiar to the one stock.*
— Benjamin F. King (*Market and Industry Factors
in Stock Price Behavior, Journal of Business*, January 1966)

THURSDAY
29

Every man with a new idea is a crank until the idea succeeds.
— Mark Twain (American novelist and satirist,
pen name of Samuel Longhorne Clemens, 1835-1910)

FRIDAY
30

The bigger a man's head gets, the easier it is to fill his shoes.
— Anonymous

SATURDAY
1

October Sector Seasonalities:
Bullish: Airline, Internet, Consumer, Cyclical, High-Tech, Telecomm, NASDAQ,
Banking, Semiconductor, Broker/Dealers; Bearish: Gold/Silver (page 118)

SUNDAY
2

EIGHT STEPS FOR DRIVING A STAKE THROUGH THE HEART OF BUREAUCRACY

From *Less is More: How Great Companies Improve Productivity Without Layoffs*
(2003, Portfolio Trade/Penguin Putman)

by Jason Jennings

"Change everything as fast as you can (which is always faster than you think you can)." One of the traits of highly productive enterprises is that when they decide to do something, they do it swiftly and decisively. People who lead extremely efficient organizations agree that slow, ponderous change leaves everyone paralyzed with fear for weeks or months. Waiting for the other shoe to drop is far more painful than moving quickly to achieve the desired result. Any manager who believes an organization will fix itself over time is delusional.

"Get the right people on the bus." A leader or manager must rapidly ascertain who believes in, supports and will enthusiastically champion the chosen destination. Those people who work against the goal must be dismissed. Managers must come to realize a brutal truth: anyone not proactively supporting a chosen destination will consciously or unconsciously work to subvert it.

"Blow up functional silos and construct cross-functional teams." As long as individual departments stand alone like impenetrable silos on the Kansas prairie, the primary efforts of the people inside them will be about defending their fortresses from attack. The company must change the minds of people who protect their individual silo/empires and where that attempt fails, replace them with people who will focus on building more productive business units.

"Decentralize to create entrepreneurship." CEO Bill Zollars of Yellow Freight describes this as getting decisions closer to the customer and out of the "Palace of Miracles" — the head office. As an example, in 1998 Yellow introduced a new service called Exact Express that promised to deliver a shipment within a one-hour window. The magic of the offer was that if the customer was unhappy for any reason about the service — even something as frivolous as not liking the driver's appearance — they could decide not to pay for it.

The product turned out to be a remarkable success in spite of the in-house grousing. Some of the remaining bureaucrats predicted that the company would go bankrupt because everyone would complain in order to get the service free. No way. According to Zollars, the amount the company writes

(continued on page 94)

OCTOBER

October best month 1998-2003
End of "Worst Six Months" and "Worst Four Months" (pages 50 and 58)

MONDAY

3

*Early in March (1960), Dr. Arthur F. Burns called on me...
Burns' conclusion was that unless some decisive action was taken,
and taken soon, we were heading for another economic dip
which would hit its low point in October, just before the elections.*
— Richard M. Nixon (37th U.S. President, Six Crises, 1913-1994)

Rosh Hashanah

TUESDAY

4

*If there's anything duller than being on a board in Corporate America,
I haven't found it.*
— Ross Perot (*New York Times*, October 28, 1992)

Average October gains last 33 years

NAS 0.5%	Dow 0.6%	S&P 1.0%
Up 17 Down 16	Up 20 Down 13	Up 19 Down 14
Rank #8	Rank #6	Rank #5

WEDNESDAY

5

*Bull markets are born on pessimism, grow on skepticism,
mature on optimism, and die on euphoria.*
— Sir John Templeton
(Founder Templeton Funds, philanthropist, 1994)

Start looking for MACD seasonal BUY Signal (pages 52 and 58)
Almanac Investor subscribers will be emailed the alert when it triggers
visit stocktradersalmanac.com for details

THURSDAY

6

*Every age has a blind eye and sees nothing wrong in
practices and institutions, which its successors view with just horror.*
— Sir Richard Livingston (*On Education*)

FRIDAY

7

*The highest reward for a person's toil is not what they get for it,
but what they become by it.*
— John Ruskin (English writer)

SATURDAY

8

SUNDAY

9

(continued from page 92)

off is infinitesimal by comparison to the additional millions in revenues linked straight back to the Exact Express initiative.

By moving the decision to the level of the customer instead of having a department of paper pushers haggling with clients, another part of bureaucracy was eliminated.

"Flatten the organization to increase responsiveness to customers and others within the company." One powerful way to check on whether an organization is too fat is by running this simple test: When calling someone in the business — whether a department head, manager, owner or CEO — note whether your efforts are hindered by countless levels of gatekeepers. If so, chances are good you've stumbled onto a company that wants to prevent contact with the bosses. And if the boss is in hiding, so are countless others. Yellow tackled this problem by flattening the organization from eight layers to five.

When the boss responds immediately to customers and fellow workers, the stage has been set for productivity. The accessibility of the heads of highly productive businesses — like Dan DiMicco, who answers his own phone; Michael O'Leary, who sends his own faxes; and Bill Zollars, who answers his own email — sends a resounding message throughout the organization that the days of bureaucracy are over.

"Create passion in the ranks: lead by visible example, show the troops you care — a lot!" The passion of a leader is demonstrated by Michael O'Leary's collecting boarding coupons and unloading luggage, Bill Zollars's nonstop years of travel to spread the message and Chairman Pat Lancaster's personally flying out to fix a customer's problem. It tempts credulity to ask any employee to be devoted to the objective of making the enterprise productive if their executives are not actively leading the way. Employees must be able to witness the passion of their leaders.

"Create and reinforce a high-performance culture." Among American workers, a frequently used response to the question "How are you?" is the downtrodden "Same s—, different day." That simply isn't the answer you'll receive in the highly charged environments of Nucor, SRC, Lantech, The Warehouse and Ryanair. The leaders of those companies know it's their singular responsibility to use every tool at their disposal, and to invent new ones if need be, to maintain an electric atmosphere. Zollars's formula: Use recognition, promotions and greed.

"View all decisions from the perspective of 'Does it help the customer?' and 'Does it make us money?' If it doesn't, it's bureaucracy. Shoot it!" We discovered the same mind-set at all productive companies committed to flattening the hierarchical structure. They've institutionalized the use of these two questions and ask them before making any decision.

OCTOBER

Columbus Day
(Bond Market Closed)

MONDAY
10

*I write an email about every week to ten days...
and within about 24 hours everyone will have read it.
The amazing thing is how I can change the direction of
the entire company within 24 hours. Ten years ago I couldn't do that.*
— Michael Marks (CEO Flextronics, *Forbes*, July 7, 2003)

Historically the worst trading day of the year (page 123)

TUESDAY
11

The years teach much which the days never know.
— Ralph Waldo Emerson

WEDNESDAY
12

*The facts are unimportant! It's what they are perceived to be
that determines the course of events.*
— R. Earl Hadady

Yom Kippur

THURSDAY
 # 13

*Never doubt that a small group of thoughtful,
committed citizens can change the world:
indeed it's the only thing that ever has.*
— Margaret Mead (American anthropologist)

FRIDAY
 # 14

*The test of success is not what you do when you are on top.
Success is how high you bounce when you hit bottom.*
— General George S. Patton, Jr. (1885-1945)

SATURDAY
15

SUNDAY
16

TRADE LIKE A HEDGE FUND

By James Altucher

THE BEST INVESTMENT BOOK OF THE YEAR

Reviewed by Yale Hirsch

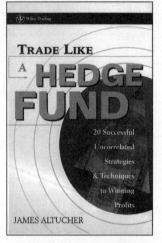

Altucher, a successful money manager, reveals his most profitable stock trading strategies and how to use them, despite strong protests from his partners and clients. I say, "Never look a gift horse in the mouth. Grab it ASAP!"

Hedging was featured in the *1968 Stock Trader's Almanac,* our first edition: "How You Can Buy a Stock 10% Cheaper…or Make up to 30% Per Year if You Don't." It involved selling a one-year put option on a blue chip like Telephone and receiving a $300 premium. Deducting this from a 25% margin deposit resulted in an outlay of $1,000. Also, a friend of mine enjoyed continually selling call options on RCA (then at about $20) until, after many premiums, he got the price he paid down to Zero! It was common knowledge then that sellers of call options earned around 15% a year.

Mathematician Edward O. Thorp wrote *Beat the Dealer* in 1962, in which he calculated ways to win at blackjack at casinos. He, together with Sheen T. Kassouf, then wrote *Beat the Market* in 1967, which demonstrated ways to earn 25% a year hedging/arbitraging various securities. One way was to sell overpriced expiring warrants short, while buying the company's common stock. The system besides warrants subsequently added similar strategies with convertible bonds, put and call options, and convertible preferreds.

Another friend, Earl Zazove, gave up his medical practice to privately manage money based on these techniques and eventually grew the fund to $1 billion. The same fund currently manages $3 billion. After meeting in 1973, Earl and Ed attempted to take over some closed-end funds, which were usually selling at discount, and then convert them to open-end funds. If the fund was selling at a 20% discount, you got an immediate 25% return. After they succeeded at opening a few funds, closed-end funds changed their constitutions to thwart the duo.

The beauty of this book is that it opens up for serious investors how very talented investing minds think and shows how they can profitably mine reams of market and stock data in this computer/broadband/wireless age. Some of the strategies:

The Bread and Butter Trade—Playing Gaps

Many traders and hedge funds short stocks that gap up and hold until they fall back to the prior day's close. When the stocks gap down they buy and hold until they move up to the previous day's close. Six different strategies are offered. In one of them you buy a stock after it is down the day before, and it gaps down more than 5% at the open the next day, and QQQ is gapping down more than a half percent. You hold the stock at least until the next morning and only sell if the stock goes lower than the prior day's close.

RESERVE YOUR *2006 ALMANAC* AT THE 2005 PRICE!

As a special service to our *Stock Trader's Almanac* readers, we offer you the opportunity to purchase the 2006 edition of the *Almanac* at a special limited time only price. Order your supply of the *2006 Almanac* before February 15th and pay the 2005 price PLUS save 20%! To order: call us toll free at 800-356-5016 (in Canada call 800-597-3299), fax us at 800-597-3299, or order online at www.wiley.com/go/sta2006. Be sure to refer to promo code PSTA6 for this special offer.

RESERVE YOUR *2006 STOCK TRADER'S ALMANAC* NOW!

☐ **Please reserve _____ copies of your *2006 Stock Trader's Almanac*.**

BEFORE 2/15/05: Pay $27.96 (20% off of the 2005 list price of $34.95) plus shipping (Promo Code: PSTA6)

AFTER 2/15/05: Pay $31.96 (20% off of the 2006 list price of $39.95) plus shipping (Promo Code: ALMA6)

Shipping: US: first item $5.00, each additional $3.00; International: first item $10.50, each additional $7.00. Bulk discounts for 5 or more copies available. Call 800-356-5016.

$_____ payment enclosed

☐ Check made payable to **John Wiley & Sons, Inc.** *(US Funds only, drawn on a US bank)*

☐ Charge Credit Card (check one):   ☐ Visa   ☐ Mastercard   ☐ AmEx

Name _____

Address _____   Account # _____

City _____   Expiration Date _____

State _____ Zip _____   Signature _____

☐ **BECOME A SUBSCRIBER! I want to stay up-to-date! Please send me future editions of the *Stock Trader's Almanac.*** You will automatically be shipped (along with the bill) future editions of the *Stock Trader's Almanac* at the yearly pre-publication discount. It's so easy and convenient!

ISBN: 0-471-70956-5

SEND ME MORE OF THE *2005 STOCK TRADER'S ALMANAC* !

☐ Send _____ additional copies of the 2005 *Stock Trader's Almanac.*

$34.95 for single copies plus shipping *(US: first item $5.00, each additional $3.00; International: first item $10.50, each additional $7.00).* Bulk discounts for 5 or more copies available. Call 201-748-6037.

☐ $_____ payment enclosed   ☐ Charge Credit Card (check one):
(US Funds only, drawn on a US bank)   ☐ Visa   ☐ Mastercard   ☐ AmEx
Check made payable to **John Wiley & Sons, Inc.**

Name _____

Address _____   Account # _____

City _____   Expiration Date _____

State _____ Zip _____   Signature _____

ISBN: 0-471-64936-8

RESERVE YOUR *2006 STOCK TRADER'S ALMANAC* NOW AND RECEIVE 20% OFF.

Mail the postage paid card below to reserve your copy.

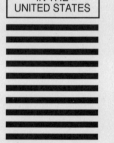

Buying Bankruptcies

Seems that when companies go bankrupt, trading in their stocks is usually halted. After they open sharply down under a dollar, they tend to more than double in days.

Playing the Bollinger Bands

These are upper and lower bands on a chart surrounding the stock's moving average. The idea here is that the price tends to be overbought when reaching the upper band and oversold when hitting the lower band. Several strategies have been devised to take advantage of these tendencies.

Buying Stocks Under $5

Buying stocks when they cross under $5, with variations, and selling one month later is a successful strategy. An example given was buying goto.com at $5 on December 21, 2001 and selling one month later for a 143% profit. This falls into the Almanac's "Free Lunch" strategy on page 112.

Buy When Month's Last Day Is Down One Percent, Sell Next Day's Open

This resulted in 11 winning trades and 2 losing. As the market tends to be up on the first day of the month (see 2005 Almanac, page 62), I did some research. I took a quick look at the Dow on the month's last day and the following day from January 1998 through June 2004 and eliminated bear year 2002. I found that there were 31 occasions the month's last day was down. The following day closed up 26 times and down 5 times, though the market went much higher intraday on most of the losing days.

Taking Advantage of Option Expiration Day

If the day before option expiration day is up 1.5% on the S&P 500, then buy the close the day before expiration and sell at the close on expiration day. Results: 12 winning trades, no losers.

However, Altucher reminds readers that using seasonal strategies does require common sense and identifying the nuance before others. If the whole wide world learns that the market soars on a particular day of the week, month, or year, you can bet it won't happen next time. Also, the threat of war can derail any pattern, as Iraq did in 2003 with our Best Six Months strategy (see Almanac pages 50, 52).

Additions and Deletions From the S&P

Several strategies are available based on studies showing that a stock tends to rise about 5% between the day of the announcement it will be included in the index, and the actual effective date.

Wednesdays as Reversal Days is fascinating and could be the base for many different strategies. Going contrary to what the public thinks about the **200-day moving average** can produce decent profits. Systems using the **TICK** or the **QQQs** are included, along with **Extreme Convertible Arbitrage** and **Spyder Spreads**, and much more.

All in all, this is one of the most truely useful investment books in 38 editions of the *Stock Trader's Almanac*. If interested in buying the book, use the "Almanac Investor Reading List" link on our website *www.stocktradersalmanac.com* and receive a 15% discount.

YEAR'S TOP INVESTMENT BOOKS

Trade Like a Hedge Fund: 20 Successful Uncorrelated Strategies & Techniques to Winning Profits, James Altucher, John Wiley & Sons, Inc., $59.95. <u>Best Investment Book of the Year</u>. Shares a number of unique trading strategies that work. (See page 96.)

The Triumph of Contrary Investing: Crowds, Manias, and Beating the Market by Going Against the Crowds, Ned Davis, McGraw-Hill, $21.95. Can't forget his forecast of "Dow 777 in '77", which was right on target. One of the true master market analysts.

All About Market Timing: The Easy Way to Get Started, Leslie N. Masonson, McGraw-Hill, Soft, $16.95. Includes some impressive chapters on our "Best Six Months" strategy combined with the four-year election/stock market cycle. Well worth it for this information alone.

Bull's Eye Investing: Targeting Real Returns in a Smoke and Mirrors Market, John Maudlin, John Wiley & Sons, Inc., $24.95. Thoroughly analyzes past bull/bear cycles to show the market and economy may not be as vibrant as some expect. Quite illuminating! Offers many sophisticated strategies for uncertain times.

The Event-Trading Phenomenon, Peter McKenna, TradeWins Publishing, $55.00. A combination of good or bad news, with overbought and/or oversold markets, produces large market reactions. This can occur several times a month and can be highly profitable. Another useful strategy for sharp traders.

A Complete Guide to Technical Trading Tactics: How to Profit Using Pivot Points, Candlesticks, & Other Indicators, John L. Person, John Wiley & Sons, Inc., $59.95. A must for any trader in futures, options, commodities and currencies by a real professional. Also covers Bollinger bands and many other indicators and strategies.

The Encyclopedia of Technical Market Indicators, Second Edition, Robert W. Colby, CMT, McGraw-Hill, $70.00. A very ambitious effort. Nothing compares to it. A treasury and analysis of over one hundred known and widely used indicators. Colby currently manages money successfully using, among other things, indicators in the book.

Technical Analysis for Dummies, Barbara Rockefeller, John Wiley & Sons, Inc., $24.99. Technical analysis made simple. An effortless read packed with instant info. Valuable for beginners and extremely valuable if you are a full-time trader in bonds, stocks, currencies, or commodities.

The Oil Factor: Protect Yourself - and Profit - from the Coming Energy Crisis, Stephen Leeb and Donna Leeb, Warner Business Books, $24.95. There is no doubt we have a serious problem with the supply of oil. How bad could it get and what are some of the solutions?

Adventure Capitalist, Jim Rogers, Random House, $26.95. His inscription reads, "Life is short; drive hard and far. Make it happen!" Rogers and his fiancée, now wife, did just that. They drove through 116 countries. His observations make for one of the most delightful reads and learning experiences about business conditions in other lands. Inadvertently omitted last year, it was on our bed stands. Providing a wealth of *Almanac* quotations.

(continued on page 100)

Monday before expiration Dow down only 3 times since 1982! **MONDAY**

17

I know nothing grander, better exercise...
more positive proof of the past, the triumphant result of faith
in human kind, than a well-contested national election.
— Walt Whitman (American poet, 1819-1892)

TUESDAY

18

Let me tell you the secret that has led me to my goal.
My strength lies solely in my tenacity.
— Louis Pasteur (French chemist,
founder of microbiology, 1822-1895)

Crash October 19, 1987, Dow down 22.6% in one day **WEDNESDAY**

19

There are very few instances in history
when any government has ever paid off debt.
— Walter Wriston (Retired CEO of Citicorp and Citibank)

THURSDAY

 ## 20

People's spending habits depend more on how wealthy they feel
than with the actual amount of their current income.
— A.C. Pigou (English economist,
The Theory of Unemployment, 1877-1959)

Expiration day 50-50 since 1980, up 12 down 12, but up 3 of last 4 **FRIDAY**

 ## 21

Cheapening the cost of necessities and conveniences of life
is the most powerful agent of civilization and progress.
— Thomas Elliott Perkins (1888)

SATURDAY

22

SUNDAY

23

YEAR'S TOP INVESTMENT BOOKS

(continued from page 98)

Intermarket Analysis: Profiting from Global Market Relationships, John J. Murphy, John Wiley & Sons, Inc., $69.95. Former CNBC technical analyst analyzes how the four different global financial markets – currencies, commodities, stocks, and bonds – interacted over 25 years.

The Great Game of Politics: Why We Elect Whom We Elect, Dick Stoken, Forge, $25.95. The constant battle between left and right. How the electorate chooses between them. Which presidents changed history? Excellent and original unbiased power concepts.

The Bond King: Investment Secrets from Pimco's Bill Gross, Timothy Middleton, John Wiley & Sons, Inc., $27.95. Gross manages the largest amount of fixed-income money on the planet and has outperformed every other fund in its class.

The Company of Strangers: A Natural History of Economic Life, Paul Seabright, Princeton University Press, $29.95. (Jacket copy) "The division of labor among strangers is humankind's most momentous invention, on which all modern society depends."

Paul Volcker: The Making of a Financial Legend, Joseph B. Treaster, John Wiley & Sons, Inc., $27.95. How one of our great central bankers broke the back of double-digit inflation in America. Provides an excellent picture of the American economy at work.

The Birth of Plenty: How the Prosperity of the Modern World Was Created, William Bernstein, McGraw-Hill, $29.95. Four conditions after 1820 led to it: property rights, scientific rationalism, capital markets, and transportation and communication. One of the best reads of the year.

Capital: The Story of Long-Term Investment Excellence, Charles D. Ellis, John Wiley & Sons, Inc., $34.95. A great investment pro writes about one of the most successful money management companies, which has outperformed the market for over 30 years.

Forge (Tom Doherty Assoc)	McGraw-Hill	Princeton University Press
175 Fifth Avenue	Two Penn Plaza	41 William Street
New York NY 10010	New York NY 10121	Princeton NJ 08540
Random House	TradeWins Publishing	Warner Business Books
1745 Broadway	375 Stewart Road	1271 Avenue of the Americas
New York NY 10019	Wilkes-Barre PA 18706	New York NY 10020

John Wiley & Sons, Inc.
111 River Street
Hoboken NJ 07030

If interested in buying any of these books, visit our "Almanac Investor Reading List" on our website *www.stocktradersalmanac.com*. Various discounts are available.

OCTOBER

Late October is time to buy depressed high tech stocks (page 90)

MONDAY
24

*Anyone who has achieved excellence knows
that it comes as a result of ceaseless concentration.*
— Louise Brooks (Writer)

TUESDAY
25

*A day will come when all nations on our continent will form a European brotherhood...
A day will come when we shall see...the United States of Europe...
reaching out for each other across the seas.*
— Victor Hugo (French novelist, playwright,
Hunchback of Notre Dame and *Les Misérables*, 1802-1885)

WEDNESDAY
26

*The word "crisis" in Chinese is composed of two characters:
the first, the symbol of danger; the second, opportunity.*
— Anonymous

THURSDAY
 ## 27

*Analysts are supposed to be critics of corporations.
They often end up being public relations spokesmen for them.*
— Ralph Wanger (Chief Investment Officer, Acorn Fund)

1929 Crash October 28 and 29, Dow down 23.0% in two days

FRIDAY
 ## 28

*Buy a stock the way you would buy a house.
Understand and like it such that you'd be content to own it
in the absence of any market.*
— Warren Buffett

SATURDAY
29

*Daylight Saving Time ends
Bullish November Sector Seasonalities:
High-Tech, Russell 2000 (page 118)*

SUNDAY
30

NOVEMBER ALMANAC

NOVEMBER						
S	M	T	W	T	F	S
		1	2	3	4	5
6	7	8	9	10	11	12
13	14	15	16	17	18	19
20	21	22	23	24	25	26
27	28	29	30			

DECEMBER						
S	M	T	W	T	F	S
					1	2	3
4	5	6	7	8	9	10
11	12	13	14	15	16	17
18	19	20	21	22	23	24
25	26	27	28	29	30	31

OCTOBER   NOVEMBER   DECEMBER

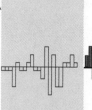
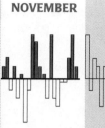
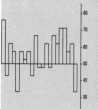

Market Probability Chart above is a graphic representation of the Market Probability Calendar on page 123.

◆ #2 S&P month and #3 on Dow since 1950, #3 on NASDAQ since 1971 (pages 48 & 54) ◆ Also start of the "Best Six Months" of the year (page 50) and NASDAQ's Best Three and Eight Months ◆ Simple timing indicator almost triples "Best Six Months" strategy (page 52) doubles NASDAQ's Best Eight (page 58) ◆ RECORD S&P up 36, down 18, Dow 36/18 ◆ Day before and after Thanksgiving Day combined, only 9 losses in 52 years (page 108) ◆ 2003 broke 11-year winning streak week before Thanksgiving ◆ Dow down only three Novembers last 14 post-election years, S&P down 4.

NOVEMBER DAILY POINT CHANGES DOW JONES INDUSTRIALS

Previous Month	1994	1995	1996	1997	1998	1999	2000	2001	2002	2003
Close	3908.12	4755.48	6029.38	7442.08	8592.10	10729.86	10971.14	9075.14	8397.03	9801.12
1	− 44.75	11.20	− 7.45	—	—	− 81.35	− 71.67	188.76	120.61	—
2	− 26.24	41.91	—	—	114.05	− 66.67	− 18.96	59.64	—	—
3	8.75	16.98	—	232.31	0.00	27.22	− 62.56	—	—	57.34
4	− 38.36	—	19.75	14.74	76.99	30.58	—	—	53.96	− 19.63
5	—	—	39.50	3.44	132.33	64.84	—	117.49	106.67	− 18.00
6	—	− 11.56	96.53	− 9.33	59.99	—	159.26	150.09	92.74	36.14
7	1.35	− 16.98	28.33	− 101.92	—	—	− 25.03	− 36.75	− 184.77	− 47.18
8	21.87	55.64	13.78	—	—	14.37	− 45.12	33.15	− 49.11	—
9	1.01	11.56	—	—	− 77.50	− 101.53	− 72.81	20.48	—	—
10	− 9.76	6.14	—	− 28.73	− 33.98	− 19.58	− 231.30	—	—	− 53.26
11	− 20.52	—	35.78	6.14	− 40.16	− 2.44	—	—	− 178.18	− 18.74
12	—	—	10.44	− 157.41	5.92	174.02	—	− 53.63	27.05	111.04
13	—	2.53	8.20	86.44	89.85	—	− 85.70	196.58	12.49	− 10.89
14	28.26	− 1.09	38.76	84.72	—	—	163.81	72.66	143.64	− 69.26
15	− 3.37	50.94	35.03	—	—	8.57	26.54	48.78	36.96	—
16	18.84	46.61	—	—	91.66	171.58	− 51.57	− 5.40	—	—
17	− 17.15	20.59	—	125.74	− 24.97	− 49.24	− 26.16	—	—	− 57.85
18	− 12.79	—	− 1.12	− 47.40	54.83	152.61	—	—	92.52	− 86.67
19	—	—	50.69	73.92	14.94	− 31.81	—	109.47	− 11.79	66.30
20	—	− 6.86	32.42	101.87	103.50	—	− 167.22	− 75.08	148.23	− 71.04
21	− 45.75	40.46	− 11.55	54.46	—	—	31.85	− 66.70	222.14	9.11
22	− 91.52	18.06	53.29	—	—	85.63	− 95.18	H	− 40.31	—
23	− 3.36	H	—	—	214.72	− 93.89	H	125.03*	—	—
24	H	7.23*	—	− 113.15	− 73.12	12.54	70.91*	—	—	119.26
25	33.64*	—	76.03	41.03	13.13	H	—	—	44.56	16.15
26	—	—	− 19.38	− 14.17	H	− 19.26*	—	23.04	− 172.98	15.63
27	—	22.04	− 29.07	H	18.80*	—	75.84	− 110.15	255.26	H
28	31.29	7.22	H	28.35*	—	—	− 38.49	− 160.74	H	2.89*
29	− 1.01	27.46	22.36*	—	—	40.99	121.53	117.56	− 35.59*	—
30	0.68	− 31.07	—	—	− 216.53	− 70.11	− 214.62	22.14	—	—
Close	3739.23	5074.49	6521.70	7823.13	9116.55	10877.81	10414.49	9851.56	8896.09	9782.46
Change	− 168.89	319.01	492.32	381.05	524.45	147.95	− 556.65	776.42	499.06	− 18.66

Shortened trading day

Astute investors always smile and remember
When stocks seasonally start soaring, and salute November

OCTOBER/NOVEMBER

Halloween

MONDAY

 31

Don't worry about people stealing your ideas.
If the ideas are any good, you'll have to ram them down people's throats.
— Howard Aiken (U.S. computer scientist, 1900-1973)

FOMC Meeting
"Best Six Months" begin Dow and S&P
"Best Eight" on NASDAQ (pages 50 and 58)

TUESDAY

 1

There is only one side of the market
and it is not the bull side or the bear side, but the right side.
— Jesse Livermore

Average November gains last 33 years
NAS 1.9% Dow 1.3% S&P 1.4%
Up 22 Down 11 Up 22 Down 11 Up 22 Down 11
Rank #3   Rank #4   Rank #3

WEDNESDAY

2

The political problem of mankind is to combine three things:
economic efficiency, social justice, and individual liberty.
— John Maynard Keynes

THURSDAY

 3

The men who can manage men manage the men who manage only things,
and the men who can manage money manage all.
— Will Durant

FRIDAY

4

Q. What kind of grad students do you take?
A. I never take a straight-A student.
A real scientist tends to be critical, and somewhere along the line,
they had to rebel against their teachers.
— Lynn Margulis (U. Mass science professor,
The Scientist, 6/30/03)

SATURDAY

5

SUNDAY

6

A POWERFUL TOOL FOR ALMANAC INVESTORS — TRY IT FREE ALONG WITH A FREE ISSUE OF *ALMANAC INVESTOR NEWSLETTER*

Investment success is a never-ending challenge. After 38 years of publishing *The Stock Trader's Almanac,* we are still working hard at monitoring market changes and incorporating them into our strategies, developing new indicators, updating the major and minor cycles — and of course, finding new opportunities in the ever-churning universe of 10,000 active stocks.

In addition to the annual *Almanac,* we have long published newsletters that keep subscribers abreast of our current research and thinking on the market. These efforts culminated three years ago in the launch of *Almanac Investor Newsletter,* a 16-page monthly guide to market patterns, cycles, fundamental developments, strategies and stock selection.

This newsletter combines our previous monthly publications in one comprehensive but easily understandable package. It is specifically designed to update and expand the proven strategies outlined in *The Stock Trader's Almanac* — and do much more besides.

HOW TO GET *INSIDE* THE MARKET

In addition to our perennial bestseller and monthly newsletter, we now offer web-based tools to traders and investors who want to do their own research and explore the market in depth. We began the development of these tools — basically an interactive database — six years ago. The original idea was to make our own research quicker, more accurate and more comprehensive. These easy-to-use research tools are now available to subscribers.

We continuously add new features and much more data to this resource. *Almanac Investor* subscribers can have unlimited use of the **Online Almanac Research Tool** for a small additional fee. But as a *Stock Trader's Almanac* reader, you are invited to try out the Research Tool, as well as our monthly newsletter, FREE of charge as explained below.

The Research Tool will integrate data and studies assembled over the 38-year history of the *Almanac* plus ongoing research and more. It's designed to be of value to the beginning investor seeking to expand his skills as well as experienced traders wanting to do their own in-depth research.

Comparable databases — if they are available at all — present users with a mass of difficult-to-use data and may cost thousands of dollars. Our Online Research Tool guides users through the process, opening the needed data step by step, graphing or calculating the results in an easily understood way.

Just go to *stocktradersalmanac.com* and try the site — FREE for one month. We do not want or need your personal information. All that is required is a valid email address and the **promotion code TRIAL5**. Refer to the insert card after page 64 in this book for more details. You will also receive one new issue emailed to you (generally emailed the third Thursday of each month). We want to make this website the best research tool available on the Internet, and in order to do that we need your comments and feedback.

NOVEMBER

MONDAY
7

From very early on, I understood that you can touch a piece of paper once...
if you touch it twice, you're dead. Therefore, paper only touches my hand once.
After that, it's either thrown away, acted on or given to somebody else.
— Manuel Fernandez (Businessman, *Investor's Business Daily*)

Election Day

TUESDAY
8

Genius is the ability to put into effect what is in your mind.
— F. Scott Fitzgerald (Author, 1896-1940)

WEDNESDAY
9

I just wait until the fourth year, when the business cycle bottoms,
and buy whatever I think will have the biggest bounce.
— Larry Tisch's investment style

THURSDAY
10

I never buy at the bottom and I always sell too soon.
— Baron Nathan Rothchild's success formula
(London financier, 1777-1836)

Veteran's Day
(Bond Market Closed)

FRIDAY
11

Those heroes of finance are like beads on a string,
when one slips off, the rest follow.
— Henrik Ibsen

SATURDAY
12

SUNDAY
13

MOST OF THE SO–CALLED "JANUARY EFFECT" TAKES PLACE IN THE LAST HALF OF DECEMBER

Over the years we reported annually on the fascinating January Effect, showing that Standard and Poor's Low-Priced Stock Index during January handily outperformed the S&P 500 Index 40 out of 43 years between 1953 and 1995. Readers saw that "Cats and Dogs" on average quadrupled the returns of blue chips in this period. Then, the January Effect disappeared over the next four years.

In addition, S&P decided to discontinue their Low-Priced Index. S&P's SmallCap 600 index was launched October 17, 1994, not giving us an historically significant set of data. Looking at the graph on page 114, which shows small-cap stocks beginning to outperform the blue chips in mid-December, made the decision simple; just compare the Russell 1000 index of large capitalization stocks to the Russell 2000 smaller capitalization stocks. Doing it in half-month segments was an inspiration and proved to be quite revealing, as you can see in the table.

17-YEAR AVERAGE RATES OF RETURN (DEC 1987- FEB 2004)

From 12/15	Russell 1000		Russell 2000	
	Change	Annualized	Change	Annualized
12/15-12/31	2.1%	73.1%	3.7%	156.4%
12/15-01/15	2.4	33.6	4.7	74.1
12/15-01/31	3.5	31.2	5.6	54.2
12/15-02/15	4.3	28.9	7.2	52.1
12/15-02/28	3.8	20.6	7.5	43.6
From 12/31				
12/31-01/15	0.3	3.6	1.0	12.3
12/31-01/31	1.3	10.8	1.8	15.1
12/31-02/15	2.2	13.6	3.4	22.2
12/31-02/28	1.6	8.5	3.6	19.4

25-YEAR AVERAGE RATES OF RETURN (DEC 1979 - FEB 2004)

From 12/15	Russell 1000		Russell 2000	
	Change	Annualized	Change	Annualized
12/15-12/31	1.8%	58.2%	3.0%	118.2%
12/15-01/15	2.5	34.8	4.9	78.2
12/15-01/31	3.5	31.9	5.8	56.6
12/15-02/15	4.2	28.3	7.3	52.9
12/15-02/28	4.0	21.5	7.6	44.2
From 12/31				
12/31-01/15	0.7	9.2	1.8	24.3
12/31-01/31	1.7	14.7	2.6	23.1
12/31-02/15	2.5	15.6	4.2	27.6
12/31-02/28	2.2	11.4	4.4	23.9

Small-cap strength in the last half of December became even more magnified after the 1987 market crash. Note the dramatic shift in gains in the last half of December during the 17-year period starting in 1987, versus the 25 years from 1979 to 2004. With all the beaten down small stocks being dumped for tax loss purposes, it surely pays to get a head start on the January Effect in mid-December.

NOVEMBER

Monday before expiration
Dow down 5 straight after being up 5 straight

MONDAY

 14

Every successful enterprise requires three people —
a dreamer, a businessman, and a son-of-a-bitch.
— Peter McArthur (1904)

Week before Thanksgiving week,
S&P up 11 of 12, 2003 broke 11-year run

TUESDAY

15

I cannot give you a formula for success
but I can give you a formula for failure: Try to please everybody.
— Herbert Swope (American journalist, 1882-1958)

WEDNESDAY

16

Moses Shapiro (of General Instrument) told me,
"Son, this is Talmudic wisdom. Always ask the question 'If not?'
Few people have good strategies for when their assumptions
are wrong." That's the best business advice I ever got.
— John Malone (CEO of cable giant TCI, Fortune, Feb. 16, 1998)

THURSDAY

 17

Big money is made in the stock market
by being on the right side of major moves.
I don't believe in swimming against the tide.
— Martin Zweig

Expiration day Dow up 9 of last 14

FRIDAY

 18

Central bankers are brought up pulling the legs off ants.
— Paul Volker (Quoted by William Grieder, Secrets of the Temple)

SATURDAY

19

SUNDAY

20

TRADING THE THANKSGIVING MARKET

For 35 years the combination of the Wednesday before Thanksgiving and the Friday after had a great track record, except for two occasions. Attributing this phenomenon to the warm "holiday spirit" was a no-brainer. But publishing it in the 1987 Almanac was the "kiss of death." Wednesday through Monday were all crushed, down 6.6% over the three days in 1987. Since 1988 Wednesday-Friday lost six of sixteen times with a total Dow point-gain of 412.59 versus a Wednesday-Monday total Dow point-gain of 669.96 with only three losses. The best strategy seems to be going long into weakness Tuesday or Wednesday and staying in through the following Monday or exiting into strength.

DOW JONES INDUSTRIALS BEFORE AND AFTER THANKSGIVING

	Tuesday Before	Wednesday Before		Friday After	Total Gain Dow Points	Dow Close	Next Monday
1952	− 0.18	1.54		1.22	2.76	283.66	0.04
1953	1.71	0.65		2.45	3.10	280.23	1.14
1954	3.27	1.89		3.16	5.05	387.79	0.72
1955	4.61	0.71		0.26	0.97	482.88	− 1.92
1956	− 4.49	− 2.16		4.65	2.49	472.56	− 2.27
1957	− 9.04	10.69		3.84	14.53	449.87	− 2.96
1958	− 4.37	8.63		8.31	16.94	557.46	2.61
1959	2.94	1.41		1.42	2.83	652.52	6.66
1960	− 3.44	1.37		4.00	5.37	606.47	− 1.04
1961	− 0.77	1.10		2.18	3.28	732.60	− 0.61
1962	6.73	4.31	T	7.62	11.93	644.87	− 2.81
1963	32.03	− 2.52		9.52	7.00	750.52	1.39
1964	− 1.68	− 5.21	H	− 0.28	− 5.49	882.12	− 6.69
1965	2.56	N/C		− 0.78	− 0.78	948.16	− 1.23
1966	− 3.18	1.84	A	6.52	8.36	803.34	− 2.18
1967	13.17	3.07		3.58	6.65	877.60	4.51
1968	8.14	− 3.17	N	8.76	5.59	985.08	− 1.74
1969	− 5.61	3.23		1.78	5.01	812.30	− 7.26
1970	5.21	1.98	K	6.64	8.62	781.35	12.74
1971	− 5.18	0.66		17.96	18.62	816.59	13.14
1972	8.21	7.29	S	4.67	11.96	1025.21	− 7.45
1973	− 17.76	10.08		− 0.98	9.10	854.00	− 29.05
1974	5.32	2.03	G	− 0.63	1.40	618.66	− 15.64
1975	9.76	3.15		2.12	5.27	860.67	− 4.33
1976	− 6.57	1.66	I	5.66	7.32	956.62	− 6.57
1977	6.41	0.78		1.12	1.90	844.42	− 4.85
1978	− 1.56	2.95	V	3.12	6.07	810.12	3.72
1979	− 6.05	− 1.80		4.35	2.55	811.77	16.98
1980	3.93	7.00	I	3.66	10.66	993.34	− 23.89
1981	18.45	7.90		7.80	15.70	885.94	3.04
1982	− 9.01	9.01	N	7.36	16.37	1007.36	− 4.51
1983	7.01	− 0.20		1.83	1.63	1277.44	− 7.62
1984	9.83	6.40	G	18.78	25.18	1220.30	− 7.95
1985	0.12	18.92		− 3.56	15.36	1472.13	− 14.22
1986	6.05	4.64		− 2.53	2.11	1914.23	− 1.55
1987	40.45	− 16.58		− 36.47	− 53.05	1910.48	− 76.93
1988	11.73	14.58		− 17.60	− 3.02	2074.68	6.76
1989	7.25	17.49	D	18.77	36.26	2675.55	19.42
1990	− 35.15	9.16		− 12.13	− 2.97	2527.23	5.94
1991	14.08	− 16.10	A	− 5.36	− 21.46	2894.68	40.70
1992	25.66	17.56		15.94	33.50	3282.20	22.96
1993	3.92	13.41	Y	− 3.63	9.78	3683.95	− 6.15
1994	− 91.52	− 3.36		33.64	30.28	3708.27	31.29
1995	40.46	18.06		7.23*	25.29	5048.84	22.04
1996	− 19.38	− 29.07		22.36*	− 6.71	6521.70	N/C
1997	41.03	− 14.17		28.35*	14.18	7823.13	189.98
1998	− 73.12	13.13		18.80*	31.93	9333.08	− 216.53
1999	− 93.89	12.54		− 19.26*	− 6.72	10988.91	− 40.99
2000	31.85	− 95.18		70.91*	− 24.27	10470.23	75.84
2001	− 75.08	− 66.70		125.03*	58.33	9959.71	23.04
2002	− 172.98	255.26		− 35.59*	219.67	8896.09	− 33.52
2003	16.15	15.63		2.89*	18.52	9899.05	116.59

*Shortened trading day

NOVEMBER

MONDAY
 21

English stocks...are springing up like mushrooms this year...
forced up to a quite unreasonable level and then, for most part, collapse.
In this way, I have made over 400 pounds...[Speculating] makes small demands on one's time,
and it's worthwhile running some risk in order to relieve the enemy of his money.
— Karl Marx (German social philosopher and revolutionary,
in an 1864 letter to his uncle, 1818-1883)

TUESDAY
 22

The possession of gold has ruined fewer men than the lack of it.
— Thomas Bailey Aldridge (1903)

(Bond Market Closes Early)   WEDNESDAY
 23

Never overpay for a stock.
More money is lost than in any other way
by projecting above-average growth and paying an extra multiple for it.
— Charles Neuhauser (Bear Stearns)

Thanksgiving   THURSDAY
(Market Closed)
24

Look for an impending crash in the economy
when the bestseller lists are filled with books
on business strategies and quick-fix management ideas.
— Peter Drucker

(Shortened Trading Day)   FRIDAY
 25

Big Business breeds bureaucracy and bureaucrats
exactly as big government does.
— T.K. Quinn

SATURDAY
26

Bullish December Sector Seasonalities: Oil, Gold/Silver   SUNDAY
27

DECEMBER ALMANAC

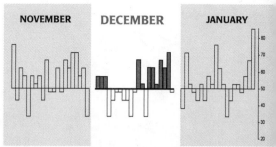

DECEMBER							JANUARY						
S	M	T	W	T	F	S	S	M	T	W	T	F	S
				1	2	3	1	2	3	4	5	6	7
4	5	6	7	8	9	10	8	9	10	11	12	13	14
11	12	13	14	15	16	17	15	16	17	18	19	20	21
18	19	20	21	22	23	24	22	23	24	25	26	27	28
25	26	27	28	29	30	31	29	30	31				

Market Probability Chart above is a graphic representation of the Market Probability Calendar on page 123.

◆ #1 S&P month average gain 1.7%, #2 Dow 1.8% since 1950 (page 48), #2 NAS-DAQ 2.1% since 1971 ◆ 2002 worst December since 1931, down over 6% Dow and S&P, –9.7% on NASDAQ (pages 141, 145 & 151) ◆ "Free lunch" served on Wall Street at month end (page 112) ◆ Small caps start to outperform larger caps near middle of month (page 114) ◆ "Santa Claus Rally" visible in graph above and on page 116 ◆ In 1998 was part of best fourth quarter since 1928 ◆ S&P down only three Decembers last 15 post-election years; Dow down 4.

◆ DECEMBER DAILY POINT CHANGES DOW JONES INDUSTRIALS

Previous Month	1994	1995	1996	1997	1998	1999	2000	2001`	2002	2003
Close	3739.23	5074.49	6521.70	7823.13	9116.55	10877.81	10414.49	9851.56	8896.09	9782.46
1	– 38.36	12.64	—	189.98	16.99	120.58	– 40.95	—	—	116.59
2	44.75	—	N/C	5.72	– 69.00	40.67	—	—	– 33.52	– 45.41
3	—	—	– 79.01	13.18	– 184.86	247.12	—	– 87.60	– 119.64	19.78
4	—	52.39	– 19.75	18.15	136.46	—	186.56	129.88	– 5.08	57.40
5	– 3.70	37.93	14.16	98.97	—	—	338.62	220.45	– 114.57	– 68.14
6	4.03	21.68	– 55.16	—	—	– 61.17	– 234.34	– 15.15	22.49	—
7	– 10.43	– 39.74	—	—	54.33	– 118.36	– 47.02	– 49.68	—	—
8	– 49.79	2.53	—	– 38.29	– 42.49	– 38.53	95.55	—	—	102.59
9	5.38	—	82.00	– 61.18	– 18.79	66.67	—	—	– 172.36	– 41.85
10	—	—	9.31	– 70.87	– 167.61	89.91	—	– 128.01	100.85	– 1.56
11	—	27.46	– 70.73	– 129.80	– 19.82	—	12.89	– 33.08	14.88	86.30
12	27.26	– 9.40	– 98.81	– 10.69	—	—	42.47	6.44	– 50.74	34.00
13	– 3.03	41.55	1.16	—	—	– 32.11	26.17	– 128.36	– 104.69	—
14	30.95	– 34.32	—	—	– 126.16	– 32.42	– 119.45	44.70	—	—
15	19.18	– 5.42	—	84.29	127.70	65.15	– 240.03	—	—	– 19.34
16	41.72	—	– 36.52	53.72	– 32.70	19.57	—	80.82	193.69	106.74
17	—	—	39.98	– 18.90	85.22	12.54	—	80.82	– 92.01	15.70
18	—	– 101.52	38.44	– 110.91	27.81	—	210.46	106.42	– 88.04	102.82
19	– 16.49	34.68	126.87	– 90.21	—	—	– 61.05	72.10	– 82.55	30.14
20	– 23.55	– 50.57	10.76	—	—	– 113.16	– 265.44	– 85.31	146.52	—
21	34.65	37.21	—	—	85.22	56.27	168.36	50.16	—	—
22	13.12	1.44	—	63.02	55.61	3.06	148.27	—	—	59.78
23	18.51	—	4.62	– 127.54	157.57	202.16	—	—	– 18.03	3.26
24	—	—	33.83*	– 31.64*	15.96*	Closed	—	N/C*	– 45.18*	– 36.07*
25	H	H	H	H	H	H	H	H	H	H
26	Closed	12.29	23.83	19.18*	—	—	56.88	52.80	– 15.50	19.48*
27	28.26	– 4.34	14.23	—	—	– 14.68	110.72	43.17	– 128.83	—
28	– 22.20	– 10.12	—	—	8.76	85.63	65.60	5.68	—	—
29	– 6.06	21.32	—	113.10	94.23	7.95	– 81.91	—	—	125.33
30	1.01	—	– 11.54	123.56	– 46.34	– 31.80	—	—	29.07	– 24.96
31	—	—	– 101.10	– 7.72	– 93.21	44.26	—	– 115.49	8.78	28.88
Close	3834.44	5117.12	6448.27	7908.25	9181.43	11497.12	10786.85	10021.50	8341.63	10453.92
Change	95.21	42.63	– 73.43	85.12	64.88	619.31	372.36	169.94	– 554.46	671.46

* Shortened trading day

If Santa Claus should fail to call
Bears may come to Broad and Wall

MONDAY
28

*If all the economists in the world were laid end to end,
they still wouldn't reach a conclusion.*
— George Bernard Shaw (Irish dramatist, 1856-1950)

TUESDAY
 # 29

Don't put all your eggs in one basket.
— Market maxim

WEDNESDAY
30

Put your eggs in one basket and watch the basket.
— An alternate strategy

2003 broke 3-year Dow losing streak first trading day of December ## THURSDAY
1

*Learn from the mistakes of others;
you can't live long enough to make them all yourself.*
— Eleanor Roosevelt (First Lady, 1884-1962)

FRIDAY
2

Average December gains last 33 years		
NAS 2.1%	*Dow 1.8%*	*S&P 1.7%*
Up 20 Down 13	*Up 24 Down 9*	*Up 25 Down 8*
Rank #2	*Rank #3*	*Rank #2*

*The way a young man spends his evenings
is a part of that thin area between success and failure.*
— Robert R. Young

SATURDAY
3

SUNDAY
4

WALL STREET'S ONLY "FREE LUNCH" SERVED AT YEAR-END

Investors tend to get rid of their losers near year-end for tax purposes, often hammering these stocks down to bargain levels. Over the years the Almanac has shown that NYSE stocks selling at their lows on December 15 will usually outperform the market by February 15 in the following year. Preferred stocks, closed-end funds, splits and new issues are eliminated. When there are a huge number of new lows, stocks down the most are selected, even though there are usually good reasons why some stocks have been battered.

BARGAIN STOCKS VS. THE MARKET**

Short Span Late Dec - Jan/Feb	New Lows Late Dec	% Change Jan/Feb	% Change NYSE Composite	Bargain Stocks Advantage
1974-75	112	48.9%	22.1%	26.8%
1975-76	21	34.9	14.9	20.0
1976-77	2	1.3	− 3.3	4.6
1977-78	15	2.8	− 4.5	7.3
1978-79	43	11.8	3.9	7.9
1979-80	5	9.3	6.1	3.2
1980-81	14	7.1	− 2.0	9.1
1981-82	21	− 2.6	− 7.4	4.8
1982-83	4	33.0	9.7	23.3
1983-84	13	− 3.2	− 3.8	0.6
1984-85	32	19.0	12.1	6.9
1985-86	4	− 22.5	3.9	− 26.4
1986-87	22	9.3	12.5	− 3.2
1987-88	23	13.2	6.8	6.4
1988-89	14	30.0	6.4	23.6
1989-90	25	− 3.1	− 4.8	1.7
1990-91	18	18.8	12.6	6.2
1991-92	23	51.1	7.7	43.4
1992-93	9	8.7	0.6	8.1
1993-94	10	− 1.4	2.0	− 3.4
1994-95	25	14.6	5.7	8.9
1995-96	5	− 11.3	4.5	−15.8
1996-97	16	13.9	11.2	2.7
1997-98	29	9.9	5.7	4.2
1998-99	40	− 2.8	4.3	− 7.1
1999-00	26*	8.9	− 5.4	14.3
2000-01	51[1]	44.4	0.1	44.3
2001-02	12[2]	31.4	− 2.3	33.7
2002-03	33[3]	28.7	3.9	24.8
2003-04	15[4]	16.7	2.3	14.4
30-Year Totals		**420.8%**	**125.5%**	**295.3%**
Average		**14.0%**	**4.2%**	**9.8%**

** Dec 15 - Feb 15 (1974-1999) * Chosen 12/29/99 [1] Chosen 12/27/00 [2] 12/26/01-1/16/02, incl NAS stocks
[3] 12/26/02-1/14/03, incl NAS & AMEX stocks [4] 12/26/03-1/13/04, incl NAS, AMEX & OTCBB stocks

However, as tax selling in recent years seems to be continuing down to the last few days of the year, we've altered the strategy the last five years to make our selections from stocks making new lows on the fourth-to-last trading day of the year. We tweaked the strategy further the last three years as few NYSE stocks were left after our screens, adding selections from NASDAQ, AMEX and the OTC Bulletin Board, and emailed them to our *Almanac Investor* newsletter subscribers. Over the past few years these stocks tend to start giving back their gains in January. We have advised subscribers to sell in mid-January. Subscribers will receive the list of stocks selected December 28, 2004, via email.

This "Free Lunch" strategy is only an extremely short-term strategy reserved for the nimblest traders. It has performed better after market corrections and when there are more New Lows at year-end. The object is to buy bargain stocks near their 52-week lows and sell any quick, generous gains, as they can often be real dogs.

Examination of December trades by NYSE members through the years shows they tend to buy on balance during this month, contrary to other months. See more in our February 2004 *Almanac Investor Newsletter* at *stocktradersalmanac.com*.

DECEMBER

MONDAY
5

The greatest lie ever told:
Build a better mousetrap
and the world will beat a path to your door.
— Yale Hirsch

TUESDAY
6

What counts more than luck is determination and perseverance.
If the talent is there, it will come through. Don't be too impatient.
— Fred Astaire (The report from his first screen test stated,
"Can't act. Can't sing. Balding. Can dance a little.")

WEDNESDAY
7

Patriotism is when love of your own people comes first. Nationalism is
when hate for people other than your own comes first.
— Charles De Gaulle (French president and WWII general,
1890-1970, May 1969)

THURSDAY
8

If there were only one religion in England
there would be danger of despotism; if there were two,
they would be at each other's throats;
but there are thirty and they live in peace and happiness.
— Voltaire

FRIDAY
9

The most valuable executive
is one who is training somebody to be a better man than he is.
— Robert G. Ingersoll (American lawyer and orator,
"the Great Agnostic," 1833-1899)

SATURDAY
10

SUNDAY
11

JANUARY EFFECT NOW STARTS IN MID-DECEMBER

Small-cap stocks tend to outperform big caps in January. Known as the "January Effect," the graph below reveals that it does indeed exist. Ned Davis Research has taken the 26 years of daily data for the Russell 2000 index of smaller companies and divided it by the Russell 1000 index of largest companies. Then they compressed the 26 years into a single year to show an idealized yearly pattern. When the graph is descending, big blue chips are outperforming smaller companies; when the graph is rising, smaller companies are moving up faster than their larger brethren.

In a typical year the smaller fry stay on the sidelines while the big boys are on the field; suddenly, in mid-December, the smaller fry take over and take off. So many year-end dividends, payouts and bonuses could be a factor. Other major moves are quite evident just before Labor Day – possibly because individual investors are back from vacations – and off the low points in late October and November. After a pause in mid-January, small caps take the lead through the end of February.

RUSSELL 2000/RUSSELL 1000 ONE-YEAR SEASONAL PATTERN

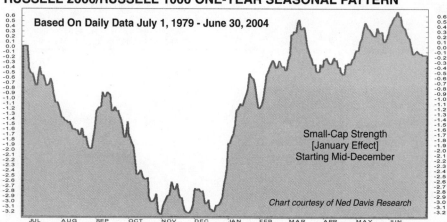

Data for the bottom graph was provided by Global Financial Data and shows the actual ratio of the Russell 2000 divided by the Russell 1000 from 1979. Smaller companies had the upper hand for five years into 1983 as the last major bear trend wound to a close and the nascent bull market logged its first year. After falling behind for about eight years, they came back after the Persian Gulf War bottom in 1990, moving up until 1994 when big caps ruled the latter stages of the millennial bull. For six years the picture was bleak for small fry as the blue chips and tech stocks moved to stratospheric PE ratios. Small caps spiked in late 1999 and early 2000 and have been rising since 2001 with bursts after the bear market ended in October 2002 and the successful test in March 2003. As this first stage of the recovery matures, stocks with lower market capitalizations may pause – but watch for them to outperform first when the next bull phase is imminent.

RUSSELL 2000/RUSSELL 1000 (1979 - JUNE 2004)

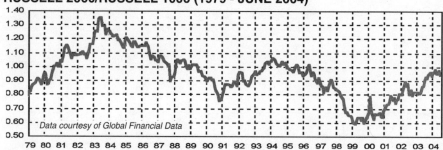

DECEMBER

MONDAY

12

Beware of inside information…all inside information.
— Jesse Livermore (*How to Trade in Stocks*)

FOMC Meeting   **TUESDAY**

13

*A fanatic is one who can't change his mind
and won't change the subject.*
— Winston Churchill (British statesman, 1874-1965)

WEDNESDAY

14

*I'm always turned off by an overly optimistic letter
from the president in the annual report.
If his letter is mildly pessimistic, to me that's a good sign.*
— Philip Carret (Centenarian, Founded Pioneer Fund in 1928, 1896-1998)

Small cap strength starts in mid-December   **THURSDAY**

15

An autobiography must be such that one can sue oneself for libel.
— Thomas Hoving (Museum director)

Triple-Witching Day Dow up 10 of last 13   **FRIDAY**

    # 16

*The average man desires to be told specifically
which particular stock to buy or sell. He wants to get something for nothing.
He does not wish to work.*
— William Lefevre (*Reminiscences of a Stock Operator*)

SATURDAY

17

SUNDAY

18

IF SANTA CLAUS SHOULD FAIL TO CALL
BEARS MAY COME TO BROAD & WALL

Santa Claus tends to come to Wall Street nearly every year, bringing a short, sweet respectable rally within the last five days of the year and the first two in January. This has been good for an average 1.7% gain since 1969 (1.5% since 1950). Santa's failure to show tends to precede bear markets, or times stocks could be purchased later in the year at much lower prices. Such occasions provide opportunities for long-term players to at least write options on their stocks. We discovered this phenomenon in 1972.

DAILY % CHANGE IN S&P 500 AT YEAR END

	Trading Days Before Year-End						First Days in January			Rally %
	6	5	4	3	2	1	1	2	3	Change
1969	− 0.4	1.1	0.8	− 0.7	0.4	0.5	1.0	0.5	− 0.7	3.6
1970	0.1	0.6	0.5	1.1	0.2	− 0.1	− 1.1	0.7	0.6	1.9
1971	− 0.4	0.2	1.0	0.3	− 0.4	0.3	− 0.4	0.4	1.0	1.3
1972	− 0.3	− 0.7	0.6	0.4	0.5	1.0	0.9	0.4	− 0.1	3.1
1973	− 1.1	− 0.7	3.1	2.1	− 0.2	0.01	0.1	2.2	− 0.9	6.7
1974	− 1.4	1.4	0.8	− 0.4	0.03	2.1	2.4	0.7	0.5	7.2
1975	0.7	0.8	0.9	− 0.1	− 0.4	0.5	0.8	1.8	1.0	4.3
1976	0.1	1.2	0.7	− 0.4	0.5	0.5	− 0.4	− 1.2	− 0.9	0.8
1977	0.8	0.9	N/C	0.1	0.2	0.2	− 1.3	− 0.3	− 0.8	− 0.3
1978	0.03	1.7	1.3	− 0.9	− 0.4	− 0.2	0.6	1.1	0.8	3.3
1979	− 0.6	0.1	0.1	0.2	− 0.1	0.1	− 2.0	− 0.5	1.2	− 2.2
1980	− 0.4	0.4	0.5	− 1.1	0.2	0.3	0.4	1.2	0.1	2.0
1981	− 0.5	0.2	− 0.2	− 0.5	0.5	0.2	0.2	− 2.2	− 0.7	− 1.8
1982	0.6	1.8	− 1.0	0.3	− 0.7	0.2	− 1.6	2.2	0.4	1.2
1983	− 0.2	− 0.03	0.9	0.3	− 0.2	0.05	− 0.5	1.7	1.2	2.1
1984	− 0.5	0.8	− 0.2	− 0.4	0.3	0.6	− 1.1	− 0.5	− 0.5	− 0.6
1985	− 1.1	− 0.7	0.2	0.9	0.5	0.3	− 0.8	0.6	− 0.1	1.1
1986	− 1.0	0.2	0.1	− 0.9	− 0.5	− 0.5	1.8	2.3	0.2	2.4
1987	1.3	− 0.5	− 2.6	− 0.4	1.3	− 0.3	3.6	1.1	0.1	2.2
1988	− 0.2	0.3	− 0.4	0.1	0.8	− 0.6	− 0.9	1.5	0.2	0.9
1989	0.6	0.8	− 0.2	0.6	0.5	0.8	1.8	− 0.3	− 0.9	4.1
1990	0.5	− 0.6	0.3	− 0.8	0.1	0.5	− 1.1	− 1.4	− 0.3	− 3.0
1991	2.5	0.6	1.4	0.4	2.1	0.5	0.04	0.5	− 0.3	5.7
1992	− 0.3	0.2	− 0.1	− 0.3	0.2	− 0.7	− 0.1	− 0.2	0.04	− 1.1
1993	0.01	0.7	0.1	− 0.1	− 0.4	− 0.5	− 0.2	0.3	0.1	− 0.1
1994	0.01	0.2	0.4	− 0.3	0.1	− 0.4	− 0.03	0.3	− 0.1	0.2
1995	0.8	0.2	0.4	0.04	− 0.1	0.3	0.8	0.1	− 0.6	1.8
1996	− 0.3	0.5	0.6	0.1	− 0.4	− 1.7	− 0.5	1.5	− 0.1	0.1
1997	− 1.5	− 0.7	0.4	1.8	1.8	− 0.04	0.5	0.2	− 1.1	4.0
1998	2.1	− 0.2	− 0.1	1.3	− 0.8	− 0.2	− 0.1	1.4	2.2	1.3
1999	1.6	− 0.1	0.04	0.4	0.1	0.3	− 1.0	− 3.8	0.2	− 4.0
2000	0.8	2.4	0.7	1.0	0.4	− 1.0	− 2.8	5.0	− 1.1	5.7
2001	0.4	− 0.02	0.4	0.7	0.3	− 1.1	0.6	0.9	0.6	1.8
2002	0.2	− 0.5	− 0.3	− 1.6	0.5	0.05	3.3	− 0.05	2.2	1.2
2003	0.3	− 0.2	0.2	1.2	0.01	0.2	− 0.3	1.2	0.1	2.4
Avg	0.09	0.35	0.33	0.13	0.20	0.06	0.07	0.55	0.10	1.7

The couplet above was certainly on the mark in 2000, as the period suffered a horrendous 4.0% loss. On January 14, 2000, the Dow started its 33-month 37.8% slide to the October 2002 midterm election year bottom. NASDAQ cracked eight weeks later, falling 37.3% in 10 weeks, eventually dropping 77.9% by October 2002. This is reminiscent of the Dow during the Depression, when the Dow initially fell 47.9% in just over two months from 381.17 September 3, 1929, only to end down 89.2% at its 20th century low of 41.22 on July 8, 1932. Perhaps October 9, 2002, will prove to be the low for the 21st century. Saddam Hussein cancelled Christmas by invading Kuwait in 1990. Less bullishness on last day is due to last-minute portfolio restructuring. Pushing gains and losses into the next tax year often affects year's first trading day.

DECEMBER

MONDAY
19

One determined person can make a significant difference;
a small group of determined people can change the course of history.
— Sonia Johnson (Author, lecturer)

TUESDAY
20

In business, the competition will bite you if you keep running;
if you stand still, they will swallow you.
— William Knudsen (Former President of GM)

WEDNESDAY
 # 21

History shows that once the United States fully recognizes
an economic problem and thereby places all its efforts on
solving it, the problem is about to be solved by natural forces.
— James L. Fraser (Contrary Investor)

Watch for Santa Claus Rally (page 116)

THURSDAY
 # 22

The mind is not a vessel to be filled but a fire to be kindled.
— Plutarch (Greek biographer and philosopher,
Parallel Lives, 46-120 AD)

Last trading day before Christmas Dow up 8 of last 13, but last 3 weak

FRIDAY
23

It is a funny thing about life; if you refuse to accept anything
but the best, you very often get it.
— W. Somerset Maugham

SATURDAY
24

Christmas Day

SUNDAY
25

SECTOR SEASONALITY: SELECTED PERCENTAGE PLAYS

Sector seasonality was featured in the first 1968 Almanac. A Merrill Lynch study showed that buying seven sectors around September or October and selling in the first few months of 1954-1964 tripled the gains of holding them for ten years.

Seasonality studies on sectors by Jon D. Markman, senior investment strategist and portfolio manager at Pinnacle Investment Advisors, in his book *Online Investing* and his online *SuperModels* on CNBC on MSN Money inspired the sector index seasonality table below (Reminiscent of our "Best Six Months," page 50, see Exchange Traded Funds on page 189.)

Major changes this year: six-month-longer Airline streak, October-June, 26.8% and we've cut all Forest/Paper trades. New August-September Gold/Silver run, 6.1%; fresh March-May Oil spurt, 8.2%; bonus April-June Internet spike, 6.9%; October-May Consumer spree, 13.5%; and May-September Semiconductor crash, –4.3% have been added. Results employing these sector seasonalities with ETFs appear in the August 2004 *Almanac Investor Newsletter* at stocktradersalmanac.com.

SECTOR INDEX SEASONALITY TABLE

Symbol	Sector Index		Months of Streak Start	End	Avg.% Return
XNG	Natural Gas	(Bearish)	January	January	– 3.3
BKX	PHLX Banking		January	May	8.1
SOX	PHLX Semiconductor		January	January	8.2
UTY	PHLX Utility	(Bearish)	January	March	– 2.4
IIX	Internet	(Bearish)	February	February	– 5.3
XNG	Natural Gas		February	May	15.9
XAL	Airline		March	June	14.8
BTK	Biotechnology	(Bearish)	March	March	– 5.4
XOI	Oil		March	May	8.2
XBD	Securities Broker/Dealer		March	July	11.0
BTK	Biotechnology		April	June	7.5
IIX	Internet		April	June	6.9
SOX	PHLX Semiconductor		April	April	5.3
UTY	PHLX Utility		April	December	6.5
SOX	PHLX Semiconductor	(Bearish)	May	September	– 4.3
XNG	Natural Gas	(Bearish)	June	July	– 6.4
XAL	Airline	(Bearish)	July	September	–18.1
IIX	Internet	(Bearish)	July	August	– 5.1
RUT	Russell 2000	(Bearish)	July	October	– 4.1
BTK	Biotechnology		August	February	28.2
CYC	Morgan Stanley Cyclical	(Bearish)	August	September	– 5.3
XAU	PHLX Gold/Silver		August	September	6.1
DRG	Pharmaceutical		September	January	13.3
SOX	PHLX Semiconductor	(Bearish)	September	September	– 7.5
XAL	Airline		October	June	26.8
IIX	Internet		October	January	22.2
CMR	Morgan Stanley Consumer		October	May	13.5
CYC	Morgan Stanley Cyclical		October	April	13.7
MSH	Morgan/Stanley High-Tech		October	January	19.1
XTC	N. Amer Telecomm		October	January	14.3
NDX	Nasdaq 100		October	January	12.5
NDX	Nasdaq 100		October	June	18.4
COMP	Nasdaq Composite		October	January	11.0
COMP	Nasdaq Composite		October	June	15.1
BKX	PHLX Banking		October	May	14.0
XAU	PHLX Gold/Silver	(Bearish)	October	October	– 6.0
SOX	PHLX Semiconductor		October	April	29.3
XBD	Securities Broker/Dealer		October	January	18.2
PSE	Pacfic SE High-Tech		November	January	12.9
RUT	Russell 2000		November	May	12.5
XOI	Oil		December	May	11.5
XAU	PHLX Gold/Silver		December	May	6.6

Chanukah
(Market Closed)

MONDAY

26

The power to tax involves the power to destroy.
— John Marshall (U. S. Supreme Court, 1819)

First trading day after Christmas Dow up 11 of last 13
New Lows perform better when selected last
settlement day of year (page 112)

TUESDAY

 # 27

There is nothing like a ticker tape except a woman —
nothing that promises, hour after hour, day after day,
such sudden developments; nothing that disappoints so often
or occasionally fulfils with such unbelievable, passionate magnificence.
— Walter K. Gutman (Financial analyst, described as the "Proust of Wall Street"
by New Yorker, You Only Have to Get Rich Once, 1961, The Gutman Letter, 1903-1986)

Imanac Investor FREE LUNCH Menu of New Lows served to subscribers,
visit stocktradersalmanac.com for details

WEDNESDAY

 # 28

The stock market is that creation of man
which humbles him the most.
— Anonymous

THURSDAY

 # 29

The big guys are the status quo, not the innovators.
— Kenneth L. Fisher (Forbes columnist)

Last day of year NASDAQ up 29 of 33, but down last 4
Dow down 5 of last 8, with some big losers

FRIDAY

30

If you don't know who you are,
the stock market is an expensive place to find out.
— George Goodman (1959)

SATURDAY

31

New Year's Day
January Sector Seasonalities: Bullish: Banking, Semiconductor;
Bearish: Natural Gas, Utilities (page 118)

SUNDAY

1

NASDAQ COMPOSITE MARKET PROBABILITY CALENDAR 2005

% CHANCE OF THE MARKET RISING ON ANY TRADING DAY OF THE YEAR

(Based on the number of times the NASDAQ rose on a particular trading day during January 1971-December 2003)

Date	Jan	Feb	Mar	Apr	May	Jun	Jul	Aug	Sep	Oct	Nov	Dec
1	H	66.7	63.6	39.4	S	57.6	54.6	51.5	54.6	S	69.7	63.6
2	S	69.7	60.6	S	57.6	78.8	S	39.4	66.7	S	48.5	60.6
3	51.5	63.6	75.8	S	72.7	63.6	S	48.5	S	48.5	75.8	S
4	75.8	66.7	54.6	60.6	63.6	S	H	63.6	S	63.6	54.6	S
5	60.6	S	S	60.6	54.6	S	51.5	63.6	H	54.6	S	63.6
6	66.7	S	S	54.6	54.6	60.6	42.4	S	60.6	63.6	S	57.6
7	51.5	51.5	57.6	54.6	S	57.6	51.5	S	57.6	63.6	42.4	45.5
8	S	51.5	60.6	63.6	S	45.5	63.6	39.4	57.6	S	51.5	51.5
9	S	48.5	60.6	S	57.6	45.5	S	51.5	42.4	S	63.6	42.4
10	60.6	63.6	51.5	S	57.6	60.6	S	54.6	S	60.6	63.6	S
11	54.6	54.6	72.7	66.7	42.4	S	63.6	57.6	S	45.5	48.5	S
12	60.6	S	S	57.6	57.6	S	60.6	63.6	42.4	51.5	S	42.4
13	66.7	S	S	54.6	60.6	63.6	72.7	S	57.6	75.8	S	45.5
14	72.7	60.6	48.5	66.7	S	60.6	75.8	S	54.6	63.6	57.6	36.4
15	S	60.6	57.6	54.6	S	51.5	66.7	57.6	36.4	S	39.4	45.5
16	S	48.5	66.7	S	60.6	48.5	S	51.5	39.4	S	42.4	57.6
17	H	57.6	51.5	S	54.6	48.5	S	54.6	S	48.5	54.6	S
18	69.7	39.4	63.6	60.6	51.5	S	45.5	51.5	S	48.5	51.5	S
19	63.6	S	S	60.6	45.5	S	45.5	36.4	54.6	36.4	S	54.6
20	48.5	S	S	51.5	54.6	48.5	54.6	S	66.7	72.7	S	54.6
21	51.5	H	39.4	54.6	S	60.6	45.5	S	51.5	39.4	54.6	57.6
22	S	48.5	60.6	54.6	S	48.5	54.6	63.6	57.6	S	66.7	66.7
23	S	57.6	54.6	S	48.5	51.5	S	57.6	45.5	S	60.6	66.7
24	54.6	57.6	36.4	S	57.6	51.5	S	51.5	S	42.4	H	S
25	42.4	54.6	H	48.5	48.5	S	57.6	51.5	S	33.3	57.6	S
26	66.7	S	S	51.5	57.6	S	48.5	57.6	51.5	39.4	S	H
27	57.6	S	S	69.7	51.5	42.4	48.5	S	45.5	54.6	S	72.7
28	60.6	60.6	51.5	60.6	S	57.6	48.5	S	45.5	57.6	69.7	54.6
29	S		54.6	75.8	S	69.7	57.6	54.6	48.5	S	66.7	72.7
30	S		48.5	S	H	75.8	S	60.6	51.5	S	69.7	87.9
31	69.7		69.7		72.7		S	72.7		69.7		S

DOW JONES INDUSTRIALS MARKET PROBABILITY CALENDAR 2005

% CHANCE OF THE MARKET RISING ON ANY TRADING DAY OF THE YEAR

(Based on the number of times the DJIA rose on a particular trading day during January 1953-December 2003)

Date	Jan	Feb	Mar	Apr	May	Jun	Jul	Aug	Sep	Oct	Nov	Dec
1	H	54.9	66.7	56.9	S	54.9	62.8	45.1	62.8	S	64.7	45.1
2	S	54.9	70.6	S	54.9	52.9	S	45.1	58.8	S	51.0	56.9
3	56.9	39.2	58.8	S	62.8	56.9	S	45.1	S	49.0	68.6	S
4	74.5	51.0	51.0	54.9	52.9	S	H	54.9	S	62.8	54.9	S
5	49.0	S	S	51.0	49.0	S	64.7	56.9	H	51.0	S	62.8
6	54.9	S	S	60.8	43.1	56.9	60.8	S	58.8	58.8	S	58.8
7	47.1	43.1	45.1	54.9	S	52.9	56.9	S	43.1	49.0	41.2	45.1
8	S	41.2	56.9	58.8	S	39.2	62.8	45.1	47.1	S	60.8	41.2
9	S	43.1	60.8	S	49.0	35.3	S	47.1	41.2	S	54.9	52.9
10	47.1	60.8	52.9	S	51.0	58.8	S	52.9	S	52.9	60.8	S
11	45.1	43.1	54.9	62.8	47.1	S	54.9	47.1	S	39.2	43.1	S
12	49.0	S	S	62.8	49.0	S	51.0	64.7	51.0	39.2	S	58.8
13	58.8	S	S	56.9	54.9	58.8	35.3	S	56.9	56.9	S	41.2
14	56.9	51.0	49.0	72.6	S	54.9	64.7	S	45.1	58.8	49.0	49.0
15	S	52.9	60.8	62.8	S	49.0	47.1	56.9	52.9	S	56.9	47.1
16	S	35.3	62.8	S	52.9	49.0	S	51.0	49.0	S	49.0	58.8
17	H	49.0	54.9	S	43.1	49.0	S	41.2	S	52.9	51.0	S
18	58.8	52.9	51.0	54.9	54.9	S	45.1	54.9	S	51.0	49.0	S
19	41.2	S	S	54.9	47.1	S	47.1	45.1	39.2	43.1	S	52.9
20	37.3	S	S	49.0	49.0	43.1	47.1	S	47.1	62.8	S	54.9
21	41.2	H	39.2	45.1	S	52.9	45.1	S	45.1	39.2	62.8	54.9
22	S	37.3	49.0	49.0	S	51.0	47.1	58.8	45.1	S	66.7	47.1
23	S	47.1	37.3	S	31.4	43.1	S	51.0	43.1	S	58.8	62.8
24	47.1	60.8	47.1	S	54.9	41.2	S	49.0	S	49.0	H	S
25	56.9	47.1	H	51.0	39.2	S	58.8	49.0	S	27.5	64.7	S
26	58.8	S	S	58.8	43.1	S	54.9	45.1	51.0	49.0	S	H
27	49.0	S	S	52.9	51.0	49.0	47.1	S	54.9	56.9	S	70.6
28	64.7	52.9	47.1	47.1	S	45.1	60.8	S	47.1	60.8	56.9	51.0
29	S		56.9	54.9	S	54.9	56.9	51.0	47.1	S	52.9	58.8
30	S		39.2	S	H	54.9	S	43.1	41.2	S	52.9	58.8
31	62.8		41.2		64.7		S	60.8		52.9		S

S&P 500 MARKET PROBABILITY CALENDAR 2005

% CHANCE OF THE MARKET RISING ON ANY TRADING DAY OF THE YEAR*

(Based on the number of times the S&P 500 rose on a particular trading day during January 1953-December 2003)

Date	Jan	Feb	Mar	Apr	May	Jun	Jul	Aug	Sep	Oct	Nov	Dec
1	H	56.9	60.8	60.8	S	52.9	68.6	47.1	62.8	S	64.7	49.0
2	S	56.9	64.7	S	54.9	60.8	S	43.1	56.9	S	52.9	52.9
3	47.1	51.0	60.8	S	70.6	56.9	S	47.1	S	49.0	70.6	S
4	74.5	45.1	47.1	54.9	58.8	S	H	54.9	S	70.6	51.0	S
5	51.0	S	S	51.0	43.1	S	60.8	58.8	H	52.9	S	60.8
6	47.1	S	S	56.9	41.2	54.9	52.9	S	58.8	60.8	S	58.8
7	43.1	47.1	47.1	56.9	S	51.0	60.8	S	43.1	51.0	43.1	41.2
8	S	41.2	58.8	60.8	S	39.2	62.8	43.1	51.0	S	60.8	47.1
9	S	39.2	60.8	S	51.0	41.2	S	52.9	49.0	S	64.7	52.9
10	49.0	62.8	49.0	S	49.0	60.8	S	49.0	S	51.0	58.8	S
11	49.0	49.0	62.8	62.8	51.0	S	52.9	47.1	S	37.3	43.1	S
12	54.9	S	S	51.0	47.1	S	49.0	66.7	51.0	45.1	S	47.1
13	60.8	S	S	51.0	54.9	62.8	45.1	S	60.8	54.9	S	45.1
14	64.7	43.1	45.1	62.8	S	54.9	72.6	S	49.0	52.9	51.0	41.2
15	S	51.0	64.7	60.8	S	52.9	54.9	60.8	52.9	S	51.0	47.1
16	S	33.3	62.8	S	54.9	47.1	S	52.9	51.0	S	49.0	58.8
17	H	52.9	52.9	S	47.1	54.9	S	49.0	S	51.0	54.9	S
18	52.9	45.1	51.0	54.9	56.9	S	43.1	52.9	S	54.9	52.9	S
19	52.9	S	S	52.9	41.2	S	43.1	45.1	47.1	39.2	S	47.1
20	47.1	S	S	52.9	54.9	39.2	47.1	S	52.9	68.6	S	45.1
21	45.1	H	45.1	49.0	S	51.0	43.1	S	51.0	35.3	60.8	51.0
22	S	43.1	43.1	43.1	S	54.9	43.1	56.9	52.9	S	64.7	45.1
23	S	39.2	52.9	S	41.2	43.1	S	49.0	39.2	S	60.8	60.8
24	60.8	56.9	39.2	S	52.9	39.2	S	49.0	S	41.2	H	S
25	51.0	51.0	H	47.1	43.1	S	56.9	47.1	S	33.3	68.6	S
26	52.9	S	S	58.8	43.1	S	54.9	43.1	49.0	56.9	S	H
27	45.1	S	S	49.0	51.0	39.2	51.0	S	52.9	60.8	S	70.6
28	66.7	60.8	49.0	45.1	S	51.0	62.8	S	54.9	58.8	58.8	54.9
29	S		56.9	60.8	S	58.8	68.6	51.0	49.0	S	56.9	66.7
30	S		33.3	S	H	51.0	S	47.1	45.1	S	51.0	70.6
31	68.6		41.2		62.8		S	64.7		52.9		S

See new trends developing on pages 60, 88 and 136

RECENT S&P 500 MARKET PROBABILITY CALENDAR 2005

% CHANCE OF THE MARKET RISING ON ANY TRADING DAY OF THE YEAR*

(Based on the number of times the S&P 500 rose on a particular trading day during January 1983-December 2003**)

Date	Jan	Feb	Mar	Apr	May	Jun	Jul	Aug	Sep	Oct	Nov	Dec
1	H	47.6	47.6	57.1	S	61.9	81.0	42.9	47.6	S	76.2	57.1
2	S	57.1	61.9	S	57.1	71.4	S	42.9	47.6	S	42.9	57.1
3	38.1	66.7	61.9	S	71.4	57.1	S	47.6	S	57.1	61.9	S
4	71.4	38.1	47.6	52.4	52.4	S	H	52.4	S	61.9	57.1	S
5	52.4	S	S	42.9	28.6	S	52.4	61.9	H	42.9	S	57.1
6	47.6	S	S	61.9	28.6	52.4	38.1	S	47.6	57.1	S	33.3
7	42.9	47.6	47.6	47.6	S	42.9	57.1	S	38.1	38.1	33.3	42.9
8	S	47.6	61.9	61.9	S	28.6	61.9	47.6	52.4	S	57.1	47.6
9	S	38.1	47.6	S	52.4	47.6	S	42.9	47.6	S	52.4	47.6
10	52.4	71.4	42.9	S	61.9	52.4	S	52.4	S	52.4	57.1	S
11	42.9	61.9	61.9	57.1	52.4	S	38.1	42.9	S	23.8	42.9	S
12	57.1	S	S	47.6	66.7	S	57.1	71.4	47.6	42.9	S	42.9
13	52.4	S	S	52.4	66.7	57.1	66.7	S	52.4	76.2	S	42.9
14	76.2	47.6	42.9	61.9	S	66.7	85.7	S	57.1	71.4	66.7	33.3
15	S	66.7	71.4	66.7	S	57.1	47.6	57.1	47.6	S	47.6	47.6
16	S	28.6	66.7	S	57.1	61.9	S	66.7	47.6	S	47.6	66.7
17	H	38.1	52.4	S	42.9	57.1	S	57.1	S	57.1	61.9	S
18	61.9	42.9	57.1	57.1	66.7	S	47.6	61.9	S	52.4	47.6	S
19	52.4	S	S	47.6	52.4	S	42.9	47.6	42.9	38.1	S	52.4
20	33.3	S	S	57.1	52.4	42.9	52.4	S	61.9	76.2	S	33.3
21	42.9	H	47.6	38.1	S	52.4	28.6	S	33.3	38.1	66.7	61.9
22	S	52.4	42.9	52.4	S	71.4	38.1	57.1	57.1	S	61.9	61.9
23	S	42.9	57.1	S	33.3	28.6	S	52.4	38.1	S	71.4	52.4
24	52.4	52.4	47.6	S	76.2	38.1	S	61.9	S	33.3	H	S
25	52.4	57.1	H	33.3	52.4	S	81.0	47.6	S	47.6	71.4	S
26	47.6	S	S	61.9	47.6	S	57.1	57.1	38.1	47.6	S	H
27	57.1	S	S	57.1	52.4	28.6	47.6	S	52.4	61.9	S	66.7
28	66.7	61.9	47.6	57.1	S	52.4	66.7	S	52.4	76.2	57.1	61.9
29	S		57.1	66.7	S	71.4	71.4	52.4	57.1	S	61.9	71.4
30	S		28.6	S	H	47.6	S	42.9	52.4	S	33.3	47.6
31	85.7		47.6		57.1		S	52.4		57.1		S

* See new trends developing on pages 60, 88 and 136   ** Based on most recent 21-year period

2006 STRATEGY CALENDAR
(Option expiration dates encircled)

	MONDAY	TUESDAY	WEDNESDAY	THURSDAY	FRIDAY	SATURDAY	SUNDAY
JANUARY	26	27	28	29	30	31	1 JANUARY New Year's Day
	2	3	4	5	6	7	8
	9	10	11	12	13	14	15
	16 Martin Luther King Day	17	18	19	(20)	21	22
	23	24	25	26	27	28	29
FEBRUARY	30	31	1 FEBRUARY	2	3	4	5
	6	7	8	9	10	11	12
	13	14 ♥	15	16	(17)	18	19
	20 Presidents' Day	21	22	23	24	25	26
MARCH	27	28	1 MARCH Ash Wednesday	2	3	4	5
	6	7	8	9	10	11	12
	13	14	15	16	(17) ☘ St. Patrick's Day	18	19
	20	21	22	23	24	25	26
APRIL	27	28	29	30	31	1 APRIL	2 Daylight Saving Time Begins
	3	4	5	6	7	8	9
	10	11	12	13 Passover	14 Good Friday	15	16 Easter
	17	18	19	20	(21)	22	23
	24	25	26	27	28	29	30
MAY	1 MAY	2	3	4	5	6	7
	8	9	10	11	12	13	14 Mother's Day
	15	16	17	18	(19)	20	21
	22	23	24	25	26	27	28
JUNE	29 Memorial Day	30	31	1 JUNE	2	3	4
	5	6	7	8	9	10	11
	12	13	14	15	(16)	17	18 Father's Day
	19	20	21	22	23	24	25
	26	27	28	29	30	1 JULY	2

Market closed on shaded weekdays; closes early when half-shaded.

2006 STRATEGY CALENDAR

(Option expiration dates encircled)

MONDAY	TUESDAY	WEDNESDAY	THURSDAY	FRIDAY	SATURDAY	SUNDAY	
3	4 Independence Day	5	6	7	8	9	JULY
10	11	12	13	14	15	16	JULY
17	18	19	20	(21)	22	23	JULY
24	25	26	27	28	29	30	JULY
31	1 AUGUST	2	3	4	5	6	AUGUST
7	8	9	10	11	12	13	AUGUST
14	15	16	17	(18)	19	20	AUGUST
21	22	23	24	25	26	27	AUGUST
28	29	30	31	1 SEPTEMBER	2	3	SEPTEMBER
4 Labor Day	5	6	7	8	9	10	SEPTEMBER
11	12	13	14	(15)	16	17	SEPTEMBER
18	19	20	21	22	23 Rosh Hashanah	24	SEPTEMBER
25	26	27	28	29	30	1 OCTOBER	OCTOBER
2 Yom Kippur	3	4	5	6	7	8	OCTOBER
9 Columbus Day	10	11	12	13	14	15	OCTOBER
16	17	18	19	(20)	21	22	OCTOBER
23	24	25	26	27	28	29 Daylight Saving Time Ends	OCTOBER
30	31 🎃	1 NOVEMBER	2	3	4	5	NOVEMBER
6	7 Election Day	8	9	10	11 Veterans' Day	12	NOVEMBER
13	14	15	16	(17)	18	19	NOVEMBER
20	21	22	23 Thanksgiving	24	25	26	NOVEMBER
27	28	29	30	1 DECEMBER	2	3	DECEMBER
4	5	6	7	8	9	10	DECEMBER
11	12	13	14	(15)	16 Chanukah	17	DECEMBER
18	19	20	21	22	23	24	DECEMBER
25 Christmas	26	27	28	29	30	31	DECEMBER

DECENNIAL CYCLE: A MARKET PHENOMENON

By arranging each year's market gain or loss so the first and succeeding years of each decade fall into the same column, certain interesting patterns emerge — strong fifth and eighth years, weak seventh and zero years.

This fascinating phenomenon was first presented by Edgar Lawrence Smith in *Common Stocks and Business Cycles* (William-Frederick Press, 1959). Anthony Gaubis co-pioneered the decennial pattern with Smith.

When Smith first cut graphs of market prices into ten-year segments and placed them above one another, he observed that each decade tended to have three bull market cycles and that the longest and strongest bull markets seem to favor the middle years of a decade.

Don't place too much emphasis on the decennial cycle nowadays, other than the extraordinary fifth and zero years, as the stock market is more influenced by the quadrennial presidential election cycle, shown on page 127. Also, the last half-century, which has been the most prosperous in U.S. history, has distributed the returns among most years of the decade. Interestingly, NASDAQ suffered its worst bear market ever in a zero year, giving us the rare experience of witnessing a bubble burst.

Though fifth years are the strongest and have a twelve-and-zero winning streak, we don't expect 2005 to be huge gainer year-over-year. We look for perhaps one more surge to new recovery highs in early 2005 as the first bull cycle of the millennium runs its course. Post-election years are historically the worst of the 4-year cycle. (See post-election year column on page 127.)

THE TEN-YEAR STOCK MARKET CYCLE
Annual % Change In Dow Jones Industrial Average
Year Of Decade

DECADES	1st	2nd	3rd	4th	5th	6th	7th	8th	9th	10th
1881-1890	3.0%	− 2.9%	− 8.5%	−18.8%	20.1%	12.4%	− 8.4%	4.8%	5.5%	−14.1%
1891-1900	17.6	− 6.6	−24.6	− 0.6	2.3	− 1.7	21.3	22.5	9.2	7.0
1901-1910	− 8.7	− 0.4	−23.6	41.7	38.2	− 1.9	−37.7	46.6	15.0	−17.9
1911-1920	0.4	7.6	−10.3	− 5.4	81.7	− 4.2	−21.7	10.5	30.5	−32.9
1921-1930	12.7	21.7	− 3.3	26.2	30.0	0.3	28.8	48.2	−17.2	−33.8
1931-1940	−52.7	−23.1	66.7	4.1	38.5	24.8	−32.8	28.1	− 2.9	−12.7
1941-1950	−15.4	7.6	13.8	12.1	26.6	− 8.1	2.2	− 2.1	12.9	17.6
1951-1960	14.4	8.4	− 3.8	44.0	20.8	2.3	−12.8	34.0	16.4	− 9.3
1961-1970	18.7	−10.8	17.0	14.6	10.9	−18.9	15.2	4.3	−15.2	4.8
1971-1980	6.1	14.6	−16.6	−27.6	38.3	17.9	−17.3	− 3.1	4.2	14.9
1981-1990	− 9.2	19.6	20.3	− 3.7	27.7	22.6	2.3	11.8	27.0	− 4.3
1991-2000	20.3	4.2	13.7	2.1	33.5	26.0	22.6	16.1	25.2	− 6.2
2001-2010	− 7.1	−16.8	25.3							
Total % Change	0.1%	23.1%	66.1%	88.7%	368.6%	71.5%	−38.3%	221.7%	110.6%	−86.9%
Avg % Change	0.01%	1.8%	5.1%	7.4%	30.7%	6.0%	− 3.2%	18.5%	9.2%	−7.2%
Up Years	8	7	6	7	12	7	6	10	9	4
Down Years	5	6	7	5	0	5	6	2	3	8

Based on annual close; Cowles indices 1881-1885; 12 Mixed Stocks, 10 Rails, 2 Inds 1886-1889;

20 Mixed Stocks, 18 Rails, 2 Inds 1890-1896; Railroad average 1897 (First industrial average published May 26, 1896)

PRESIDENTIAL ELECTION/STOCK MARKET CYCLE
THE 171-YEAR SAGA CONTINUES

It is no mere coincidence that the last two years (pre-election year and election year) of the 43 administrations since 1833 produced a total net market gain of 742.8%, dwarfing the 227.6% gain of the first two years of these administrations.

Presidential elections every four years have a profound impact on the economy and the stock market. Wars, recessions and bear markets tend to start or occur in the first half of the term; prosperous times and bull markets, in the latter half.

STOCK MARKET ACTION SINCE 1833
Annual % Change In Dow Jones Industrial Average[1]

4-Year Cycle Beginning	Elected President	Post-Election Year	Mid-Term Year	Pre-Election Year	Election Year
1833	Jackson (D)	− 0.9	13.0	3.1	− 11.7
1837	Van Buren (D)	− 11.5	1.6	− 12.3	5.5
1841*	W.H. Harrison (W)**	− 13.3	− 18.1	45.0	15.5
1845*	Polk (D)	8.1	− 14.5	1.2	− 3.6
1849*	Taylor (W)	N/C	18.7	− 3.2	19.6
1853*	Pierce (D)	− 12.7	− 30.2	1.5	4.4
1857	Buchanan (D)	− 31.0	14.3	− 10.7	14.0
1861*	Lincoln (R)	− 1.8	55.4	38.0	6.4
1865	Lincoln (R)**	− 8.5	3.6	1.6	10.8
1869	Grant (R)	1.7	5.6	7.3	6.8
1873	Grant (R)	− 12.7	2.8	− 4.1	− 17.9
1877	Hayes (R)	− 9.4	6.1	43.0	18.7
1881	Garfield (R)**	3.0	− 2.9	− 8.5	− 18.8
1885*	Cleveland (D)	20.1	12.4	− 8.4	4.8
1889*	B. Harrison (R)	5.5	− 14.1	17.6	− 6.6
1893*	Cleveland (D)	− 24.6	− 0.6	2.3	− 1.7
1897*	McKinley (R)	21.3	22.5	9.2	7.0
1901	McKinley (R)**	− 8.7	− 0.4	− 23.6	41.7
1905	T. Roosevelt (R)	38.2	− 1.9	− 37.7	46.6
1909	Taft (R)	15.0	− 17.9	0.4	7.6
1913*	Wilson (D)	− 10.3	− 5.4	81.7	− 4.2
1917	Wilson (D)	− 21.7	10.5	30.5	− 32.9
1921*	Harding (R)**	12.7	21.7	− 3.3	26.2
1925	Coolidge (R)	30.0	0.3	28.8	48.2
1929	Hoover (R)	− 17.2	− 33.8	− 52.7	− 23.1
1933*	F. Roosevelt (D)	66.7	4.1	38.5	24.8
1937	F. Roosevelt (D)	− 32.8	28.1	− 2.9	− 12.7
1941	F. Roosevelt (D)	− 15.4	7.6	13.8	12.1
1945	F. Roosevelt (D)**	26.6	− 8.1	2.2	− 2.1
1949	Truman (D)	12.9	17.6	14.4	8.4
1953*	Eisenhower (R)	− 3.8	44.0	20.8	2.3
1957	Eisenhower (R)	− 12.8	34.0	16.4	− 9.3
1961*	Kennedy (D)**	18.7	− 10.8	17.0	14.6
1965	Johnson (D)	10.9	− 18.9	15.2	4.3
1969*	Nixon (R)	− 15.2	4.8	6.1	14.6
1973	Nixon (R)***	− 16.6	− 27.6	38.3	17.9
1977*	Carter (D)	− 17.3	− 3.1	4.2	14.9
1981*	Reagan (R)	− 9.2	19.6	20.3	− 3.7
1985	Reagan (R)	27.7	22.6	2.3	11.8
1989	G. H. W. Bush (R)	27.0	− 4.3	20.3	4.2
1993*	Clinton (D)	13.7	2.1	33.5	26.0
1997	Clinton (D)	22.6	16.1	25.2	− 6.2
2001*	G. W. Bush (R)	− 7.1	− 16.8	25.3	
Total % Gain		**67.9 %**	**159.7%**	**457.6%**	**285.2%**
Average % Gain		**1.6 %**	**3.7%**	**10.6%**	**6.8%**
# Up		19	25	32	28
# Down		23	18	11	14

*Party in power ousted   **Death in office   ***Resigned   **D**—Democrat, **W**—Whig, **R**—Republican
[1] Based on annual close; Prior to 1886 based on Cowles and other indices; 12 Mixed Stocks, 10 Rails, 2 Inds 1886-1889; 20 Mixed Stocks, 18 Rails, 2 Inds 1890-1896; Railroad average 1897 (First industrial average published May 26, 1896)

BULL AND BEAR MARKETS SINCE 1900

— Beginning —		— Ending —		Bull		Bear	
Date	DJIA	Date	DJIA	% Gain	Days	% Change	Days
9/24/00	38.80	6/17/01	57.33	47.8%	266	− 46.1%	875
11/9/03	30.88	1/19/06	75.45	144.3	802	− 48.5	665
11/15/07	38.83	11/19/09	73.64	89.6	735	− 27.4	675
9/25/11	53.43	9/30/12	68.97	29.1	371	− 24.1	668
7/30/14	52.32	11/21/16	110.15	110.5	845	− 40.1	393
12/19/17	65.95	11/3/19	119.62	81.4	684	− 46.6	660
8/24/21	63.90	3/20/23	105.38	64.9	573	− 18.6	221
10/27/23	85.76	9/3/29	381.17	344.5	2138	− 47.9	71
11/13/29	198.69	4/17/30	294.07	48.0	155	− 86.0	813
7/8/32	41.22	9/7/32	79.93	93.9	61	− 37.2	173
2/27/33	50.16	2/5/34	110.74	120.8	343	− 22.8	171
7/26/34	85.51	3/10/37	194.40	127.3	958	− 49.1	386
3/31/38	98.95	11/12/38	158.41	60.1	226	− 23.3	147
4/8/39	121.44	9/12/39	155.92	28.4	157	− 40.4	959
4/28/42	92.92	5/29/46	212.50	128.7	1492	− 23.2	353
5/17/47	163.21	6/15/48	193.16	18.4	395	− 16.3	363
6/13/49	161.60	1/5/53	293.79	81.8	1302	− 13.0	252
9/14/53	255.49	4/6/56	521.05	103.9	935	− 19.4	564
10/22/57	419.79	1/5/60	685.47	63.3	805	− 17.4	294
10/25/60	566.05	12/13/61	734.91	29.8	414	− 27.1	195
6/26/62	535.76	2/9/66	995.15	85.7	1324	− 25.2	240
10/7/66	744.32	12/3/68	985.21	32.4	788	− 35.9	539
5/26/70	631.16	4/28/71	950.82	50.6	337	− 16.1	209
11/23/71	797.97	1/11/73	1051.70	31.8	415	− 45.1	694
12/6/74	577.60	9/21/76	1014.79	75.7	655	− 26.9	525
2/28/78	742.12	9/8/78	907.74	22.3	192	− 16.4	591
4/21/80	759.13	4/27/81	1024.05	34.9	371	− 24.1	472
8/12/82	776.92	11/29/83	1287.20	65.7	474	− 15.6	238
7/24/84	1086.57	8/25/87	2722.42	150.6	1127	− 36.1	55
10/19/87	1738.74	7/17/90	2999.75	72.5	1002	− 21.2	86
10/11/90	2365.10	7/17/98	9337.97	294.8	2836	− 19.3	45
8/31/98	7539.07	1/14/00	11722.98	55.5	501	− 29.7	616
9/21/01	8235.81	3/19/02	10635.25	29.1	179	− 31.5	204
10/9/02	7286.27	2/17/04	10714.88	47.1*	496*	*At Press Time	
			Average	**84.3%**	**716**	**−30.8%**	**406**

Based on Dow Jones industrial average
1900-2000 Data: Ned Davis Research
The NYSE was closed from 7/31/1914 to 12/11/1914 due to World War I.
DJIA figures were then adjusted back to reflect the composition change from 12 to 20 stocks in September 1916.

Bear markets begin at the end of one bull market and end at the start of the next bull market (7/17/90 to 10/11/90 as an example). The high at Dow 3978.36 on January 31, 1994, was followed by a 9.7 percent correction. A 10.3 percent correction occurred between the May 22, 1996, closing high of 5778 and the intraday low on July 16, 1996. The longest bull market on record ended on July 17, 1998, and the shortest bear market on record ended on August 31, 1998, when the new bull market began. The greatest bull super cycle in history that began 8/12/82 ended in 2000 after the Dow gained 1409% and NASDAQ climbed 3072%. The Dow gained only 497% in the eight-year super bull from 1921 to the top in 1929. NASDAQ suffered its worst loss ever, down 77.9%, nearly as much as the 89.2% drop in the Dow from 1929 to the bottom in 1932.

DIRECTORY OF TRADING PATTERNS & DATABANK

CONTENTS

A TYPICAL DAY IN THE MARKET

Half-hourly data became available for the Dow Jones industrial average starting in January 1987. The NYSE switched 10:00am openings to 9:30am in October 1985. Below is the comparison between half-hourly performance 1987-July 2, 2004 and hourly November 1963-June 1985. Stronger openings and closings in a more bullish climate are evident. Morning and afternoon weaknesses appear an hour earlier.

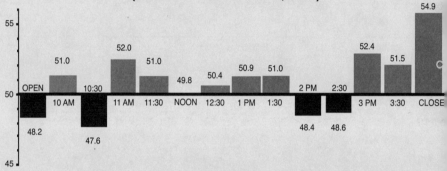

MARKET % PERFORMANCE EACH HALF-HOUR OF THE DAY (JANUARY 1987 - JULY 2, 2004)

Based on the number of times the Dow Jones Industrial Average increased over previous half-hour

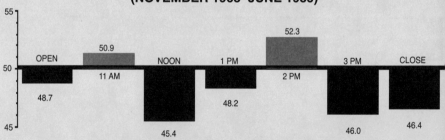

MARKET % PERFORMANCE EACH HOUR OF THE DAY (NOVEMBER 1963–JUNE 1985)

Based on the number of times the Dow Jones Industrial Average increased over previous hour

On the opposite page, half-hourly movements since January 1987 are separated by day of the week. From 1953 to 1989 Monday was the worst day of the week, especially during long bear markets, but times changed. Monday reversed positions and became the best day of the week and on the plus side twelve years in a row from 1990 to 2000. Monday was a net loser in 2001 and 2002 but not the worst day of the week, best day in 2003 and 2004 so far. (See pages 60, 66, 132-135.) Fridays were down 2000-2002 on the S&P and Dow, 2001-2003 on NASDAQ during the bear. Dow and S&P gains spread out in 2003 except for a net loss on Wednesday. Dow and S&P up Monday and Tuesday in 2004, down rest of week. Monday and Friday are best for NASDAQ in 2004 to date. On all days stocks do tend to firm up near the close with weakness early morning and from 2 to 2:30 frequently.

THROUGH THE WEEK ON A HALF-HOURLY BASIS

From the chart showing the percentage of times the Dow Jones industrial average rose over the preceding half-hour (January 1987—July 2, 2004*) the typical week unfolds.

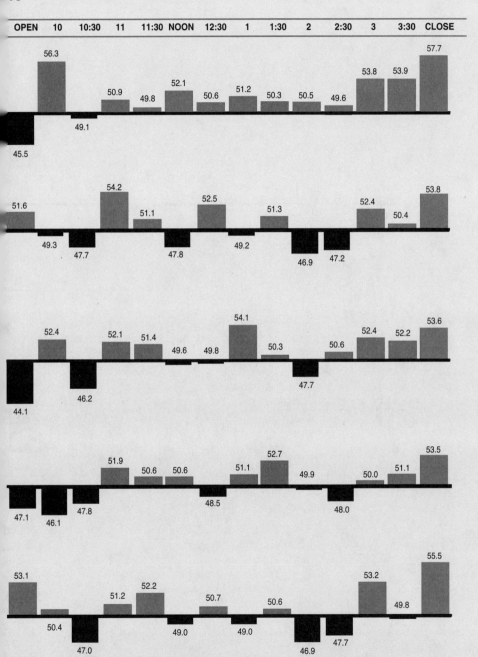

OPEN	10	10:30	11	11:30	NOON	12:30	1	1:30	2	2:30	3	3:30	CLOSE

*Research indicates that where Tuesday is the first trading day of the week, it follows the Monday pattern. Therefore, all such Tuesdays were combined with the Mondays here. Thursdays that are the final trading day of a given week behave like Fridays, and were similarly grouped with Fridays.

MONDAY NOW MOST PROFITABLE DAY OF WEEK

Between 1952 and 1989 Monday was the worst trading day of the week. The first trading day of the week (including Tuesday, when Monday is a holiday) rose only 44.3% of the time, while the other trading days closed higher 54.8% of the time. (NYSE Saturday trading discontinued June 1952.)

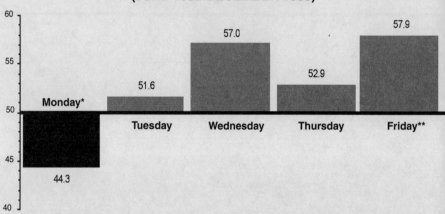

**MARKET % PERFORMANCE EACH DAY OF THE WEEK
(JUNE 1952-DECEMBER 1989)**

A dramatic reversal occurred in 1990 — Monday became the most powerful day of the week. Throughout the recent bear market (2001-2002) Monday returned to its old ways and Friday has become a day to avoid, as traders were not inclined to stay long over the weekend during uncertain market times. See pages 60 and 134.

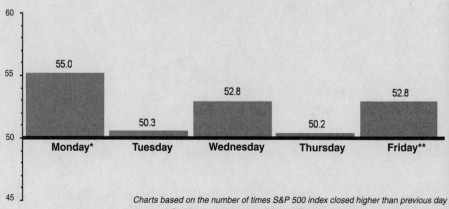

**MARKET % PERFORMANCE EACH DAY OF THE WEEK
(JANUARY 1990-JULY 2, 2004)**

Charts based on the number of times S&P 500 index closed higher than previous day
* On Monday holidays, the following Tuesday is included in the Monday figure
** On Friday holidays, the preceding Thursday is included in the Friday figure

NASDAQ DAYS OF THE WEEK

Despite 20 years less data, daily trading patterns on NASDAQ through 1989 appear to be fairly similar to the S&P across on page 132 except for more bullishness on Thursdays. During the mostly flat markets of the 1970s and early 1980s, it would appear that apprehensive investors decided to throw in the towel over weekends and sell on Mondays and Tuesdays.

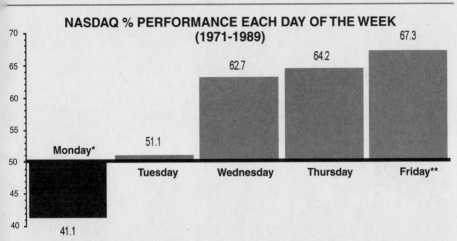

NASDAQ % PERFORMANCE EACH DAY OF THE WEEK (1971-1989)

Monday* 41.1 — Tuesday 51.1 — Wednesday 62.7 — Thursday 64.2 — Friday** 67.3

Notice the vast difference in the daily trading pattern between NASDAQ and S&P from January 1, 1990 to recent times. The reason for so much more bullishness is that NASDAQ moved up 1010%, over three times as much during the 1990-2000 period. The gain for the S&P was 332% and for the Dow Jones industrials, 326%. NASDAQ's weekly patterns are beginning to move in step with the rest of the market. Notice on page 135 Monday's weakness during the 2000 to 2002 bear market.

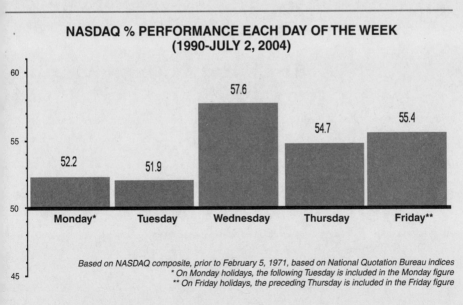

NASDAQ % PERFORMANCE EACH DAY OF THE WEEK (1990-JULY 2, 2004)

Monday* 52.2 — Tuesday 51.9 — Wednesday 57.6 — Thursday 54.7 — Friday** 55.4

Based on NASDAQ composite, prior to February 5, 1971, based on National Quotation Bureau indices
* On Monday holidays, the following Tuesday is included in the Monday figure
** On Friday holidays, the preceding Thursday is included in the Friday figure

S&P DAILY PERFORMANCE EACH YEAR SINCE 1952

To determine if market trend alters performance of different days of the week, w
separated twenty bear years of 1953, '56, '57, '60, '62, '66, '69, '70, '73, '74, '77, '78
'81, '84, '87, '90, '94, 2000, 2001 and 2002 from 33 bull market years. While Tuesday
and Thursday did not vary much between bull and bear years, Mondays and Friday;
were sharply affected. There was a swing of 10.2 percentage points in Monday's an(
11.1 in Friday's performance. Mondays have been much stronger since 1990.

PERCENTAGE OF TIMES MARKET CLOSED HIGHER THAN PREVIOUS DAY
(1953 - JULY 1, 2004)

	Monday*	Tuesday	Wednesday	Thursday	Friday*
1952	48.4%	55.6%	58.1%	51.9%	66.7%
1953	32.7	50.0	54.9	57.5	56.6
1954	50.0	57.5	63.5	59.2	73.1
1955	50.0	45.7	63.5	60.0	78.9
1956	36.5	39.6	46.9	50.0	59.6
1957	25.0	54.0	66.7	48.9	44.2
1958	59.6	52.0	59.6	68.1	72.6
1959	42.3	53.1	55.8	48.9	69.8
1960	34.6	50.0	44.2	54.0	59.6
1961	52.9	54.4	64.7	56.0	67.3
1962	28.3	52.1	54.0	51.0	50.0
1963	46.2	63.3	51.0	57.5	69.2
1964	40.4	48.0	61.5	58.7	77.4
1965	44.2	57.5	55.8	51.0	71.2
1966	36.5	47.8	53.9	42.0	57.7
1967	38.5	50.0	60.8	64.0	69.2
1968	49.1	57.5	64.3	42.6	54.9
1969	30.8	45.8	50.0	67.4	50.0
1970	38.5	46.0	63.5	48.9	52.8
1971	44.2	64.6	57.7	55.1	51.9
1972	38.5	60.9	57.7	51.0	67.3
1973	32.1	51.1	52.9	44.9	44.2
1974	32.7	57.1	51.0	36.7	30.8
1975	53.9	38.8	61.5	56.3	55.8
1976	55.8	55.3	55.8	40.8	58.5
1977	40.4	40.4	46.2	53.1	53.9
1978	51.9	43.5	59.6	54.0	48.1
1979	54.7	53.2	58.8	66.0	44.2
1980	55.8	54.2	71.7	35.4	59.6
1981	44.2	38.8	55.8	53.2	47.2
1982	46.2	39.6	44.2	44.9	50.0
1983	55.8	46.8	61.5	52.0	55.8
1984	39.6	63.8	31.4	46.0	44.2
1985	44.2	61.2	54.9	56.3	53.9
1986	51.9	44.9	67.3	58.3	55.8
1987	51.9	57.1	63.5	61.7	49.1
1988	51.9	61.7	51.9	48.0	59.6
1989	51.9	47.8	69.2	58.0	69.2
1990	67.9	53.2	52.9	40.0	51.9
1991	44.2	46.9	52.9	49.0	51.9
1992	51.9	49.0	53.9	56.3	45.3
1993	65.4	41.7	55.8	44.9	48.1
1994	55.8	46.8	52.9	48.0	59.6
1995	63.5	56.5	63.5	62.0	63.5
1996	54.7	44.9	51.0	57.1	63.5
1997	67.3	67.4	42.3	41.7	57.7
1998	57.7	62.5	57.7	38.3	60.4
1999	46.2	29.8	67.3	53.1	57.7
2000	51.9	43.5	40.4	56.0	46.2
2001	45.3	51.1	44.0	59.2	43.1
2002	40.4	37.5	56.9	38.8	48.1
2003	59.6	62.5	42.3	58.3	50.0
2004¹	53.9	60.9	57.7	50.0	44.4
Average	**47.2%**	**50.8%**	**55.9%**	**52.0%**	**56.6%**
33 Bull Years	**51.1%**	**52.6%**	**58.0%**	**53.1%**	**60.9%**
20 Bear Years	**40.9%**	**48.5%**	**52.1%**	**50.6%**	**49.8%**

Based on S&P 500

¹ Six months only. Not included in averages.
* On Monday holidays, the following Tuesday is included in the Monday figure
** On Friday holidays, the preceding Thursday is included in the Friday figure

NASDAQ DAILY PERFORMANCE EACH YEAR SINCE 1971

After dropping a hefty 77.9% from its 2000 high (versus -37.8% on the Dow and -49.1% on the S&P 500), NASDAQ tech stocks still outpace the blue chips and big caps — but not by nearly as much as they did. From January 1, 1971, through July 30, 2004, NASDAQ moved up an impressive 2006%. The Dow (up 1109%) and the S&P (up 1096%) gained just over half as much.

Monday's performance on NASDAQ was lackluster during the three-year bear market of 2000-2002. As NASDAQ rebounded sharply in 2003, up 50% for the year, strength returned to Monday as well as on Tuesday and Thursday. Wednesday and Friday were weak in 2003 with Friday losing the most ground though Wednesday was down more frequently. Wednesday and Thursday are the soft spots so far in 2004.

PERCENTAGE OF TIMES NASDAQ CLOSED HIGHER THAN PREVIOUS DAY
(1971-JULY 2, 2004)

	Monday*	Tuesday	Wednesday	Thursday	Friday**
1971	51.9%	52.1%	59.6%	65.3%	71.2%
1972	30.8	60.9	63.5	57.1	78.9
1973	34.0	48.9	52.9	53.1	48.1
1974	30.8	44.9	52.9	51.0	42.3
1975	44.2	42.9	63.5	64.6	63.5
1976	50.0	63.8	67.3	59.2	58.5
1977	51.9	40.4	53.9	63.3	73.1
1978	48.1	47.8	73.1	72.0	84.6
1979	45.3	53.2	64.7	86.0	82.7
1980	46.2	64.6	84.9	52.1	73.1
1981	42.3	32.7	67.3	76.6	69.8
1982	34.6	47.9	59.6	51.0	63.5
1983	42.3	44.7	67.3	68.0	73.1
1984	22.6	53.2	35.3	52.0	51.9
1985	36.5	59.2	62.8	68.8	66.0
1986	38.5	55.1	65.4	72.9	75.0
1987	42.3	49.0	65.4	68.1	66.0
1988	50.0	55.3	61.5	66.0	63.5
1989	38.5	54.4	71.2	72.0	75.0
1990	54.7	42.6	60.8	46.0	55.8
1991	51.9	59.2	66.7	65.3	51.9
1992	44.2	53.1	59.6	60.4	45.3
1993	55.8	56.3	69.2	57.1	67.3
1994	51.9	46.8	54.9	52.0	55.8
1995	50.0	52.2	63.5	64.0	63.5
1996	50.9	57.1	64.7	61.2	63.5
1997	65.4	59.2	53.9	52.1	55.8
1998	59.6	58.3	65.4	44.7	58.5
1999	61.5	40.4	63.5	57.1	65.4
2000	40.4	41.3	42.3	60.0	57.7
2001	41.5	57.8	52.0	55.1	47.1
2002	44.2	37.5	56.9	46.9	46.2
2003	57.7	60.4	40.4	60.4	46.2
2004¹	53.9	56.5	50.0	37.5	51.9
Average	**45.4%**	**51.0%**	**61.4%**	**60.7%**	**62.9%**
23 Bull Years	**48.1%**	**53.5%**	**64.8%**	**62.7%**	**66.9%**
10 Bear Years	**40.5%**	**45.5%**	**54.1%**	**56.1%**	**54.1%**

Based on NASDAQ composite, prior to February 5, 1971, based on National Quotation Bureau indices
¹ Six months only. Not included in averages.
* On Monday holidays, the following Tuesday is included in the Monday figure
** On Friday holidays, the preceding Thursday is included in the Friday figure

MONTHLY CASH INFLOWS INTO S&P STOCKS

For many years, the last trading day of the month plus the first four of th
following month were the best market days of the month. This pattern is quit
clear in the first chart showing these five consecutive trading days towering
above the other 16 trading days of the average month in the 1953-1981 period
The rationale was that individuals and institutions tended to operate similarly
causing a massive flow of cash into stocks near beginnings of months.

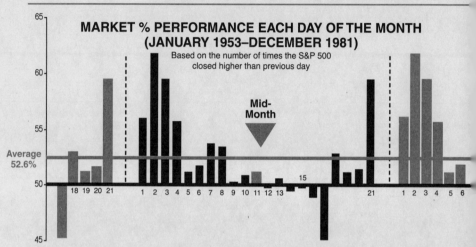

Clearly, "front-running" traders took advantage of this phenomenon, drastically
altering the previous pattern. The second chart from 1982 onward shows the trading shift caused by these "anticipators" to the last three trading days of the month
plus the first two. Another astonishing development shows the ninth, tenth, and
eleventh trading days rising strongly as well. Perhaps the enormous growth of
401(k) retirement plans (participants' salaries are usually paid twice monthly) is
responsible for this new mid-month bulge. First trading days of the month have
produced the greatest gains in recent years (see page 62).

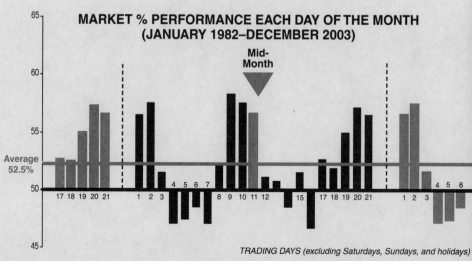

TRADING DAYS (excluding Saturdays, Sundays, and holidays)

136

MONTHLY CASH INFLOWS INTO NASDAQ STOCKS

NASDAQ stocks moved up 58.1% of the time through 1981 compared to 52.6% for the S&P across the page. Ends and beginnings of the month are fairly similar, specifically the last plus the first four trading days. But notice how investors kept piling into NASDAQ stocks for six additional days. NASDAQ rose 118.5% from January 1, 1971, to December 31, 1981, compared to 33.0% for the S&P.

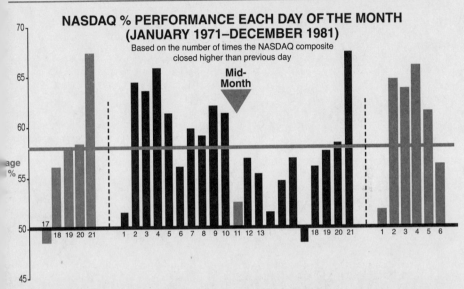

After the air was let out of the market 2000-2002, S&P's 807.3% gain over the last 22 years is more evenly matched with NASDAQ's 923.0% gain. Last three, first three, and middle ninth and tenth days rose the most. Where the S&P has six days of the month that go down more often than up, NASDAQ has none. NASDAQ exhibits the most strength on the last trading day of the month.

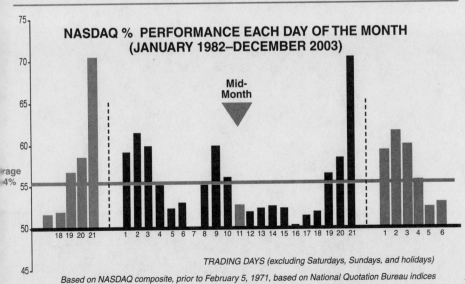

TRADING DAYS (excluding Saturdays, Sundays, and holidays)

Based on NASDAQ composite, prior to February 5, 1971, based on National Quotation Bureau indices

137

NOVEMBER, DECEMBER, AND JANUARY YEAR'S BEST THREE-MONTH SPAN

The most important observation to be made from a chart showing the average monthly percent change in market prices since 1950 is that institutions (mutual funds, pension funds, banks, etc.) determine the trading patterns in today's market.

The "investment calendar" reflects the annual, semi-annual and quarterly operations of institutions during January, April and July. October, besides being the last campaign month before elections, is also the time when most bear markets seem to end, as in 1946, 1957, 1960, 1966, 1974, 1987, 1990, 1998 and 2002. (August and September tend to combine to make the worst consecutive two-month period.)

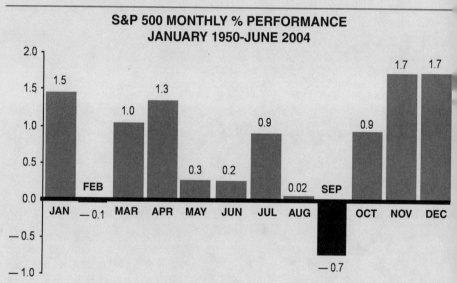

S&P 500 MONTHLY % PERFORMANCE
JANUARY 1950-JUNE 2004

Average month-to-month % change in S&P 500
(Based on monthly closing prices)

Unusual year-end strength comes from corporate and private pension funds, producing a 4.9% gain on average between November 1 and January 31. September's dismal performance makes it the worst month of the year. In the last twenty years it has only been up six times — four in a row 1995-1998. October is the top month 1998-2003.

Best months in post-election years since 1950: July +1.4% (7-6), May +1.3% (7-6), January +1.3% (7-6).

See page 48 for monthly performance tables for the S&P 500 and the Dow Jones industrials. See pages 50 and 52 for unique six-month switching strategies.

On page 74 you can see how the first month of the first three quarters far outperforms the second and the third months since 1950 and note the improvement in May's and October's performance since 1991.

NOVEMBER THROUGH JUNE
NASDAQ'S EIGHT-MONTH RUN

The two-and-a-half-year plunge of 77.9% in NASDAQ stocks between March 10, 2000, and October 9, 2002, brought several horrendous monthly losses. The two greatest were in November 2000 (-22.9%) and February 2001 (-22.4), which trimmed their average performance over the $33\frac{1}{2}$-year period. Solid gains five of the last six years plus two huge turnaround Octobers in 2001 (+12.8%) and 2002 (+13.5%) has put bear-killing October in the positive. January's 3.9% average gain is still awesome, and 2.6 times better than what the S&P did in January.

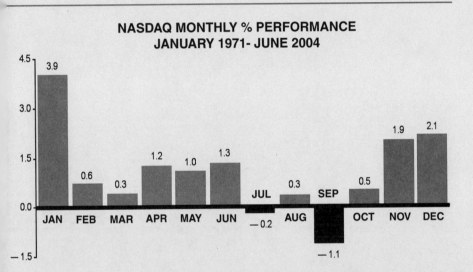

NASDAQ MONTHLY % PERFORMANCE
JANUARY 1971- JUNE 2004

Average month-to-month % change in NASDAQ composite,
prior to February 5, 1971, based on National Quotation Bureau indices
(Based on monthly closing prices)

Bear in mind when comparing NASDAQ to the S&P across the page that there are 21 fewer years of data here. During this $33\frac{1}{2}$-year (1971-June 2004) period, NASDAQ gained 2185%, while the S&P and the Dow rose only 1138% and 1144%, respectively. On page 54 you can see a statistical monthly comparison between NASDAQ and the Dow.

Year-end strength is even more pronounced in NASDAQ, producing a 7.9% gain on average between November 1 and January 31—1.6 times greater than that of the S&P 500 across the page. September is the worst month of the year for the over-the-counter index as well posting a deeper average loss of -1.1%. These extremes underscore the NAS's higher volatility — and potential for moves of greater magnitude.

Best months in post-election years since 1971: January +3.9% (5-3), May +2.9% (6-2), July +2.1% (6-2), April +2.0% (6-2). See page 58 for NASDAQ's impressive eight-month switching strategy using MACD timing.

STANDARD & POOR'S 500
MONTHLY PERCENT CHANGES

	JAN	FEB	MAR	APR	MAY	JUN
1950	1.7%	1.0%	0.4%	4.5%	3.9%	− 5.8%
1951	6.1	0.6	− 1.8	4.8	− 4.1	− 2.6
1952	1.6	− 3.6	4.8	− 4.3	2.3	4.6
1953	− 0.7	− 1.8	− 2.4	− 2.6	− 0.3	− 1.6
1954	5.1	0.3	3.0	4.9	3.3	0.1
1955	1.8	0.4	− 0.5	3.8	− 0.1	8.2
1956	− 3.6	3.5	6.9	− 0.2	− 6.6	3.9
1957	− 4.2	− 3.3	2.0	3.7	3.7	− 0.1
1958	4.3	− 2.1	3.1	3.2	1.5	2.6
1959	0.4	− 0.02	0.1	3.9	1.9	− 0.4
1960	− 7.1	0.9	− 1.4	− 1.8	2.7	2.0
1961	6.3	2.7	2.6	0.4	1.9	− 2.9
1962	− 3.8	1.6	− 0.6	− 6.2	− 8.6	− 8.2
1963	4.9	− 2.9	3.5	4.9	1.4	− 2.0
1964	2.7	1.0	1.5	0.6	1.1	1.6
1965	3.3	− 0.1	− 1.5	3.4	− 0.8	− 4.9
1966	0.5	− 1.8	− 2.2	2.1	− 5.4	− 1.6
1967	7.8	0.2	3.9	4.2	− 5.2	1.8
1968	− 4.4	− 3.1	0.9	8.2	1.1	0.9
1969	− 0.8	− 4.7	3.4	2.1	− 0.2	− 5.6
1970	− 7.6	5.3	0.1	− 9.0	− 6.1	− 5.0
1971	4.0	0.9	3.7	3.6	− 4.2	0.1
1972	1.8	2.5	0.6	0.4	1.7	− 2.2
1973	− 1.7	− 3.7	− 0.1	− 4.1	− 1.9	− 0.7
1974	− 1.0	− 0.4	− 2.3	− 3.9	− 3.4	− 1.5
1975	12.3	6.0	2.2	4.7	4.4	4.4
1976	11.8	− 1.1	3.1	− 1.1	− 1.4	4.1
1977	− 5.1	− 2.2	− 1.4	0.02	− 2.4	4.5
1978	− 6.2	− 2.5	2.5	8.5	0.4	− 1.8
1979	4.0	− 3.7	5.5	0.2	− 2.6	3.9
1980	5.8	− 0.4	−10.2	4.1	4.7	2.7
1981	− 4.6	1.3	3.6	− 2.3	− 0.2	− 1.0
1982	− 1.8	− 6.1	− 1.0	4.0	− 3.9	− 2.0
1983	3.3	1.9	3.3	7.5	− 1.2	3.5
1984	− 0.9	− 3.9	1.3	0.5	− 5.9	1.7
1985	7.4	0.9	− 0.3	− 0.5	5.4	1.2
1986	0.2	7.1	5.3	− 1.4	5.0	1.4
1987	13.2	3.7	2.6	− 1.1	0.6	4.8
1988	4.0	4.2	− 3.3	0.9	0.3	4.3
1989	7.1	− 2.9	2.1	5.0	3.5	− 0.8
1990	− 6.9	0.9	2.4	− 2.7	9.2	− 0.9
1991	4.2	6.7	2.2	0.03	3.9	− 4.8
1992	− 2.0	1.0	− 2.2	2.8	0.1	− 1.7
1993	0.7	1.0	1.9	− 2.5	2.3	0.1
1994	3.3	− 3.0	− 4.6	1.2	1.2	− 2.7
1995	2.4	3.6	2.7	2.8	3.6	2.1
1996	3.3	0.7	0.8	1.3	2.3	0.2
1997	6.1	0.6	− 4.3	5.8	5.9	4.3
1998	1.0	7.0	5.0	0.9	− 1.9	3.9
1999	4.1	− 3.2	3.9	3.8	− 2.5	5.4
2000	− 5.1	− 2.0	9.7	− 3.1	− 2.2	2.4
2001	3.5	− 9.2	− 6.4	7.7	0.5	− 2.5
2002	− 1.6	− 2.1	3.7	− 6.1	− 0.9	− 7.2
2003	− 2.7	− 1.7	1.0	8.0	5.1	1.1
2004	1.7	1.2	− 1.6	− 1.7	1.2	1.8
TOTALS	80.0%	− 2.9%	57.3%	73.8%	14.2%	13.5%
AVG.	1.5%	− 0.1%	1.0%	1.3%	0.3%	0.2%
# Up	35	29	36	37	31	30
# Down	20	26	19	18	24	25

JUL	AUG	SEP	OCT	NOV	DEC		Year's Change
0.8%	3.3%	5.6%	0.4%	− 0.1%	4.6%	1950	21.8%
6.9	3.9	− 0.1	− 1.4	− 0.3	3.9	1951	16.5
1.8	− 1.5	− 2.0	− 0.1	4.6	3.5	1952	11.8
2.5	− 5.8	0.1	5.1	0.9	0.2	1953	− 6.6
5.7	− 3.4	8.3	− 1.9	8.1	5.1	1954	45.0
6.1	− 0.8	1.1	− 3.0	7.5	− 0.1	1955	26.4
5.2	− 3.8	− 4.5	0.5	− 1.1	3.5	1956	2.6
1.1	− 5.6	− 6.2	− 3.2	1.6	− 4.1	1957	− 14.3
4.3	1.2	4.8	2.5	2.2	5.2	1958	38.1
3.5	− 1.5	− 4.6	1.1	1.3	2.8	1959	8.5
− 2.5	2.6	− 6.0	− 0.2	4.0	4.6	1960	− 3.0
3.3	2.0	− 2.0	2.8	3.9	0.3	1961	23.1
6.4	1.5	− 4.8	0.4	10.2	1.3	1962	− 11.8
− 0.3	4.9	− 1.1	3.2	− 1.1	2.4	1963	18.9
1.8	− 1.6	2.9	0.8	− 0.5	0.4	1964	13.0
1.3	2.3	3.2	2.7	− 0.9	0.9	1965	9.1
− 1.3	− 7.8	− 0.7	4.8	0.3	− 0.1	1966	− 13.1
4.5	− 1.2	3.3	− 2.9	0.1	2.6	1967	20.1
− 1.8	1.1	3.9	0.7	4.8	− 4.2	1968	7.7
− 6.0	4.0	− 2.5	4.4	− 3.5	− 1.9	1969	− 11.4
7.3	4.4	3.3	− 1.1	4.7	5.7	1970	0.1
− 4.1	3.6	− 0.7	− 4.2	− 0.3	8.6	1971	10.8
0.2	3.4	− 0.5	0.9	4.6	1.2	1972	15.6
3.8	− 3.7	4.0	− 0.1	−11.4	1.7	1973	− 17.4
− 7.8	− 9.0	−11.9	16.3	− 5.3	− 2.0	1974	− 29.7
− 6.8	− 2.1	− 3.5	6.2	2.5	− 1.2	1975	31.5
− 0.8	− 0.5	2.3	− 2.2	− 0.8	5.2	1976	19.1
− 1.6	− 2.1	− 0.2	− 4.3	2.7	0.3	1977	− 11.5
5.4	2.6	− 0.7	− 9.2	1.7	1.5	1978	1.1
0.9	5.3	NC	− 6.9	4.3	1.7	1979	12.3
6.5	0.6	2.5	1.6	10.2	− 3.4	1980	25.8
− 0.2	− 6.2	− 5.4	4.9	3.7	− 3.0	1981	− 9.7
− 2.3	11.6	0.8	11.0	3.6	1.5	1982	14.8
− 3.3	1.1	1.0	− 1.5	1.7	− 0.9	1983	17.3
− 1.6	10.6	− 0.3	− 0.01	− 1.5	2.2	1984	1.4
− 0.5	− 1.2	− 3.5	4.3	6.5	4.5	1985	26.3
− 5.9	7.1	− 8.5	5.5	2.1	− 2.8	1986	14.6
4.8	3.5	− 2.4	−21.8	− 8.5	7.3	1987	2.0
− 0.5	− 3.9	4.0	2.6	− 1.9	1.5	1988	12.4
8.8	1.6	− 0.7	− 2.5	1.7	2.1	1989	27.3
− 0.5	− 9.4	− 5.1	− 0.7	6.0	2.5	1990	− 6.6
4.5	2.0	− 1.9	1.2	− 4.4	11.2	1991	26.3
3.9	− 2.4	0.9	0.2	3.0	1.0	1992	4.5
− 0.5	3.4	− 1.0	1.9	− 1.3	1.0	1993	7.1
3.1	3.8	− 2.7	2.1	− 4.0	1.2	1994	− 1.5
3.2	− 0.03	4.0	− 0.5	4.1	1.7	1995	34.1
− 4.6	1.9	5.4	2.6	7.3	− 2.2	1996	20.3
7.8	− 5.7	5.3	− 3.4	4.5	1.6	1997	31.0
− 1.2	−14.6	6.2	8.0	5.9	5.6	1998	26.7
− 3.2	− 0.6	− 2.9	6.3	1.9	5.8	1999	19.5
− 1.6	6.1	− 5.3	− 0.5	− 8.0	0.4	2000	− 10.1
− 1.1	− 6.4	− 8.2	1.8	7.5	0.8	2001	− 13.0
− 7.9	0.5	−11.0	8.6	5.7	− 6.0	2002	− 23.4
1.6	1.8	− 1.2	5.5	0.7	5.1	2003	26.4
49.1%	0.8%	−39.2%	49.4%	91.5%	92.5%		
0.9%	0.02%	− 0.7%	0.9%	1.7%	1.7%		
29	29	21	32	36	41		
25	25	32	22	18	13		

STANDARD & POOR'S 500
MONTHLY CLOSING PRICES

	JAN	FEB	MAR	APR	MAY	JUN
1950	17.05	17.22	17.29	18.07	18.78	17.69
1951	21.66	21.80	21.40	22.43	21.52	20.96
1952	24.14	23.26	24.37	23.32	23.86	24.96
1953	26.38	25.90	25.29	24.62	24.54	24.14
1954	26.08	26.15	26.94	28.26	29.19	29.21
1955	36.63	36.76	36.58	37.96	37.91	41.03
1956	43.82	45.34	48.48	48.38	45.20	46.97
1957	44.72	43.26	44.11	45.74	47.43	47.37
1958	41.70	40.84	42.10	43.44	44.09	45.24
1959	55.42	55.41	55.44	57.59	58.68	58.47
1960	55.61	56.12	55.34	54.37	55.83	56.92
1961	61.78	63.44	65.06	65.31	66.56	64.64
1962	68.84	69.96	69.55	65.24	59.63	54.75
1963	66.20	64.29	66.57	69.80	70.80	69.37
1964	77.04	77.80	78.98	79.46	80.37	81.69
1965	87.56	87.43	86.16	89.11	88.42	84.12
1966	92.88	91.22	89.23	91.06	86.13	84.74
1967	86.61	86.78	90.20	94.01	89.08	90.64
1968	92.24	89.36	90.20	97.59	98.68	99.58
1969	103.01	98.13	101.51	103.69	103.46	97.71
1970	85.02	89.50	89.63	81.52	76.55	72.72
1971	95.88	96.75	100.31	103.95	99.63	99.70
1972	103.94	106.57	107.20	107.67	109.53	107.14
1973	116.03	111.68	111.52	106.97	104.95	104.26
1974	96.57	96.22	93.98	90.31	87.28	86.00
1975	76.98	81.59	83.36	87.30	91.15	95.19
1976	100.86	99.71	102.77	101.64	100.18	104.28
1977	102.03	99.82	98.42	98.44	96.12	100.48
1978	89.25	87.04	89.21	96.83	97.24	95.53
1979	99.93	96.28	101.59	101.76	99.08	102.91
1980	114.16	113.66	102.09	106.29	111.24	114.24
1981	129.55	131.27	136.00	132.81	132.59	131.21
1982	120.40	113.11	111.96	116.44	111.88	109.61
1983	145.30	148.06	152.96	164.42	162.39	168.11
1984	163.41	157.06	159.18	160.05	150.55	153.18
1985	179.63	181.18	180.66	179.83	189.55	191.85
1986	211.78	226.92	238.90	235.52	247.35	250.84
1987	274.08	284.20	291.70	288.36	290.10	304.00
1988	257.07	267.82	258.89	261.33	262.16	273.50
1989	297.47	288.86	294.87	309.64	320.52	317.98
1990	329.08	331.89	339.94	330.80	361.23	358.02
1991	343.93	367.07	375.22	375.35	389.83	371.16
1992	408.79	412.70	403.69	414.95	415.35	408.14
1993	438.78	443.38	451.67	440.19	450.19	450.53
1994	481.61	467.14	445.77	450.91	456.50	444.27
1995	470.42	487.39	500.71	514.71	533.40	544.75
1996	636.02	640.43	645.50	654.17	669.12	670.63
1997	786.16	790.82	757.12	801.34	848.28	885.14
1998	980.28	1049.34	1101.75	1111.75	1090.82	1133.84
1999	1279.64	1238.33	1286.37	1335.18	1301.84	1372.71
2000	1394.46	1366.42	1498.58	1452.43	1420.60	1454.60
2001	1366.01	1239.94	1160.33	1249.46	1255.82	1224.42
2002	1130.20	1106.73	1147.39	1076.92	1067.14	989.82
2003	855.70	841.15	849.18	916.92	963.59	974.50
2004	1131.13	1144.94	1126.21	1107.30	1120.68	1140.84

STANDARD & POOR'S 500
MONTHLY CLOSING PRICES

JUL	AUG	SEP	OCT	NOV	DEC	
17.84	18.42	19.45	19.53	19.51	20.41	1950
22.40	23.28	23.26	22.94	22.88	23.77	1951
25.40	25.03	24.54	24.52	25.66	26.57	1952
24.75	23.32	23.35	24.54	24.76	24.81	1953
30.88	29.83	32.31	31.68	34.24	35.98	1954
43.52	43.18	43.67	42.34	45.51	45.48	1955
49.39	47.51	45.35	45.58	45.08	46.67	1956
47.91	45.22	42.42	41.06	41.72	39.99	1957
47.19	47.75	50.06	51.33	52.48	55.21	1958
60.51	59.60	56.88	57.52	58.28	59.89	1959
55.51	56.96	53.52	53.39	55.54	58.11	1960
66.76	68.07	66.73	68.62	71.32	71.55	1961
58.23	59.12	56.27	56.52	62.26	63.10	1962
69.13	72.50	71.70	74.01	73.23	75.02	1963
83.18	81.83	84.18	84.86	84.42	84.75	1964
85.25	87.17	89.96	92.42	91.61	92.43	1965
83.60	77.10	76.56	80.20	80.45	80.33	1966
94.75	93.64	96.71	93.90	94.00	96.47	1967
97.74	98.86	102.67	103.41	108.37	103.86	1968
91.83	95.51	93.12	97.24	93.81	92.06	1969
78.05	81.52	84.21	83.25	87.20	92.15	1970
95.58	99.03	98.34	94.23	93.99	102.09	1971
107.39	111.09	110.55	111.58	116.67	118.05	1972
108.22	104.25	108.43	108.29	95.96	97.55	1973
79.31	72.15	63.54	73.90	69.97	68.56	1974
88.75	86.88	83.87	89.04	91.24	90.19	1975
103.44	102.91	105.24	102.90	102.10	107.46	1976
98.85	96.77	96.53	92.34	94.83	95.10	1977
100.68	103.29	102.54	93.15	94.70	96.11	1978
103.81	109.32	109.32	101.82	106.16	107.94	1979
121.67	122.38	125.46	127.47	140.52	135.76	1980
130.92	122.79	116.18	121.89	126.35	122.55	1981
107.09	119.51	120.42	133.71	138.54	140.64	1982
162.56	164.40	166.07	163.55	166.40	164.93	1983
150.66	166.68	166.10	166.09	163.58	167.24	1984
190.92	188.63	182.08	189.82	202.17	211.28	1985
236.12	252.93	231.32	243.98	249.22	242.17	1986
318.66	329.80	321.83	251.79	230.30	247.08	1987
272.02	261.52	271.91	278.97	273.70	277.72	1988
346.08	351.45	349.15	340.36	345.99	353.40	1989
356.15	322.56	306.05	304.00	322.22	330.22	1990
387.81	395.43	387.86	392.46	375.22	417.09	1991
424.21	414.03	417.80	418.68	431.35	435.71	1992
448.13	463.56	458.93	467.83	461.79	466.45	1993
458.26	475.49	462.69	472.35	453.69	459.27	1994
562.06	561.88	584.41	581.50	605.37	615.93	1995
639.95	651.99	687.31	705.27	757.02	740.74	1996
954.29	899.47	947.28	914.62	955.40	970.43	1997
1120.67	957.28	1017.01	1098.67	1163.63	1229.23	1998
1328.72	1320.41	1282.71	1362.93	1388.91	1469.25	1999
1430.83	1517.68	1436.51	1429.40	1314.95	1320.28	2000
1211.23	1133.58	1040.94	1059.78	1139.45	1148.08	2001
911.62	916.07	815.28	885.76	936.31	879.82	2002
990.31	1008.01	995.97	1050.71	1058.20	1111.92	2003
						2004

DOW JONES INDUSTRIALS
MONTHLY PERCENT CHANGES

	JAN	FEB	MAR	APR	MAY	JUN
1950	0.8%	0.8%	1.3%	4.0%	4.2%	− 6.4%
1951	5.7	1.3	− 1.6	4.5	− 3.7	− 2.8
1952	0.5	− 3.9	3.6	− 4.4	2.1	4.3
1953	− 0.7	− 1.9	− 1.5	− 1.8	− 0.9	− 1.5
1954	4.1	0.7	3.0	5.2	2.6	1.8
1955	1.1	0.7	− 0.5	3.9	− 0.2	6.2
1956	− 3.6	2.7	5.8	0.8	− 7.4	3.1
1957	− 4.1	− 3.0	2.2	4.1	2.1	− 0.3
1958	3.3	− 2.2	1.6	2.0	1.5	3.3
1959	1.8	1.6	− 0.3	3.7	3.2	−0.03
1960	− 8.4	1.2	− 2.1	− 2.4	4.0	2.4
1961	5.2	2.1	2.2	0.3	2.7	− 1.8
1962	− 4.3	1.1	− 0.2	− 5.9	− 7.8	− 8.5
1963	4.7	− 2.9	3.0	5.2	1.3	− 2.8
1964	2.9	1.9	1.6	− 0.3	1.2	1.3
1965	3.3	0.1	− 1.6	3.7	− 0.5	− 5.4
1966	1.5	− 3.2	− 2.8	1.0	− 5.3	− 1.6
1967	8.2	− 1.2	3.2	3.6	− 5.0	0.9
1968	− 5.5	− 1.7	0.02	8.5	− 1.4	− 0.1
1969	0.2	− 4.3	3.3	1.6	− 1.3	− 6.9
1970	− 7.0	4.5	1.0	− 6.3	− 4.8	− 2.4
1971	3.5	1.2	2.9	4.1	− 3.6	− 1.8
1972	1.3	2.9	1.4	1.4	0.7	− 3.3
1973	− 2.1	− 4.4	− 0.4	− 3.1	− 2.2	− 1.1
1974	0.6	0.6	− 1.6	− 1.2	− 4.1	0.03
1975	14.2	5.0	3.9	6.9	1.3	5.6
1976	14.4	− 0.3	2.8	− 0.3	− 2.2	2.8
1977	− 5.0	− 1.9	− 1.8	0.8	− 3.0	2.0
1978	− 7.4	− 3.6	2.1	10.6	0.4	− 2.6
1979	4.2	− 3.6	6.6	− 0.8	− 3.8	2.4
1980	4.4	− 1.5	− 9.0	4.0	4.1	2.0
1981	− 1.7	2.9	3.0	− 0.6	− 0.6	− 1.5
1982	− 0.4	− 5.4	− 0.2	3.1	− 3.4	− 0.9
1983	2.8	3.4	1.6	8.5	− 2.1	1.8
1984	− 3.0	− 5.4	0.9	0.5	− 5.6	2.5
1985	6.2	− 0.2	− 1.3	− 0.7	4.6	1.5
1986	1.6	8.8	6.4	− 1.9	5.2	0.9
1987	13.8	3.1	3.6	− 0.8	0.2	5.5
1988	1.0	5.8	− 4.0	2.2	− 0.1	5.4
1989	8.0	− 3.6	1.6	5.5	2.5	− 1.6
1990	− 5.9	1.4	3.0	− 1.9	8.3	0.1
1991	3.9	5.3	1.1	− 0.9	4.8	− 4.0
1992	1.7	1.4	− 1.0	3.8	1.1	− 2.3
1993	0.3	1.8	1.9	− 0.2	2.9	− 0.3
1994	6.0	− 3.7	− 5.1	1.3	2.1	− 3.5
1995	0.2	4.3	3.7	3.9	3.3	2.0
1996	5.4	1.7	1.9	− 0.3	1.3	0.2
1997	5.7	0.9	− 4.3	6.5	4.6	4.7
1998	− 0.02	8.1	3.0	3.0	− 1.8	0.6
1999	1.9	− 0.6	5.2	10.2	− 2.1	3.9
2000	− 4.8	− 7.4	7.8	− 1.7	− 2.0	− 0.7
2001	0.9	− 3.6	− 5.9	8.7	1.6	− 3.8
2002	− 1.0	1.9	2.9	− 4.4	− 0.2	− 6.9
2003	− 3.5	− 2.0	1.3	6.1	4.4	1.5
2004	0.3	0.9	− 2.1	− 1.3	− 0.4	2.4
TOTALS	77.5%	8.7%	52.7%	102.1%	2.9%	− 3.4%
AVG.	1.4%	0.2%	1.0%	1.9%	0.1%	− 0.1%
# Up	37	31	35	34	28	28
# Down	18	24	20	21	27	27

DOW JONES INDUSTRIALS
MONTHLY PERCENT CHANGES

JUL	AUG	SEP	OCT	NOV	DEC		Year's Change
0.1%	3.6%	4.4%	− 0.6%	1.2%	3.4%	1950	17.6%
6.3	4.8	0.3	− 3.2	− 0.4	3.0	1951	14.4
1.9	− 1.6	− 1.6	− 0.5	5.4	2.9	1952	8.4
2.7	− 5.1	1.1	4.5	2.0	− 0.2	1953	− 3.8
4.3	− 3.5	7.3	− 2.3	9.8	4.6	1954	44.0
3.2	0.5	− 0.3	− 2.5	6.2	1.1	1955	20.8
5.1	− 3.0	− 5.3	1.0	− 1.5	5.6	1956	2.3
1.0	− 4.8	− 5.8	− 3.3	2.0	− 3.2	1957	−12.8
5.2	1.1	4.6	2.1	2.6	4.7	1958	34.0
4.9	− 1.6	− 4.9	2.4	1.9	3.1	1959	16.4
− 3.7	1.5	− 7.3	0.04	2.9	3.1	1960	− 9.3
3.1	2.1	− 2.6	0.4	2.5	1.3	1961	18.7
6.5	1.9	− 5.0	1.9	10.1	0.4	1962	−10.8
− 1.6	4.9	0.5	3.1	− 0.6	1.7	1963	17.0
1.2	− 0.3	4.4	− 0.3	0.3	− 0.1	1964	14.6
1.6	1.3	4.2	3.2	− 1.5	2.4	1965	10.9
− 2.6	− 7.0	− 1.8	4.2	− 1.9	− 0.7	1966	−18.9
5.1	− 0.3	2.8	− 5.1	− 0.4	3.3	1967	15.2
− 1.6	1.5	4.4	1.8	3.4	− 4.2	1968	4.3
− 6.6	2.6	− 2.8	5.3	− 5.1	− 1.5	1969	−15.2
7.4	4.1	− 0.5	− 0.7	5.1	5.6	1970	4.8
− 3.7	4.6	− 1.2	− 5.4	− 0.9	7.1	1971	6.1
− 0.5	4.2	− 1.1	0.2	6.6	0.2	1972	14.6
3.9	− 4.2	6.7	1.0	−14.0	3.5	1973	−16.6
− 5.6	−10.4	−10.4	9.5	− 7.0	− 0.4	1974	−27.6
− 5.4	0.5	− 5.0	5.3	2.9	− 1.0	1975	38.3
− 1.8	− 1.1	1.7	− 2.6	− 1.8	6.1	1976	17.9
− 2.9	− 3.2	− 1.7	− 3.4	1.4	0.2	1977	−17.3
5.3	1.7	− 1.3	− 8.5	0.8	0.7	1978	− 3.1
0.5	4.9	− 1.0	− 7.2	0.8	2.0	1979	4.2
7.8	− 0.3	−0.02	− 0.9	7.4	− 3.0	1980	14.9
− 2.5	− 7.4	− 3.6	0.3	4.3	− 1.6	1981	− 9.2
− 0.4	11.5	− 0.6	10.7	4.8	0.7	1982	19.6
− 1.9	1.4	1.4	− 0.6	4.1	− 1.4	1983	20.3
− 1.5	9.8	− 1.4	0.1	− 1.5	1.9	1984	− 3.7
0.9	− 1.0	− 0.4	3.4	7.1	5.1	1985	27.7
− 6.2	6.9	− 6.9	6.2	1.9	− 1.0	1986	22.6
6.3	3.5	− 2.5	−23.2	− 8.0	5.7	1987	2.3
− 0.6	− 4.6	4.0	1.7	− 1.6	2.6	1988	11.8
9.0	2.9	− 1.6	− 1.8	2.3	1.7	1989	27.0
0.9	−10.0	− 6.2	− 0.4	4.8	2.9	1990	− 4.3
4.1	0.6	− 0.9	1.7	− 5.7	9.5	1991	20.3
2.3	− 4.0	0.4	− 1.4	2.4	− 0.1	1992	4.2
0.7	3.2	− 2.6	3.5	0.1	1.9	1993	13.7
3.8	4.0	− 1.8	1.7	− 4.3	2.5	1994	2.1
3.3	− 2.1	3.9	− 0.7	6.7	0.8	1995	33.5
− 2.2	1.6	4.7	2.5	8.2	− 1.1	1996	26.0
7.2	− 7.3	4.2	− 6.3	5.1	1.1	1997	22.6
− 0.8	−15.1	4.0	9.6	6.1	0.7	1998	16.1
− 2.9	1.6	− 4.5	3.8	1.4	5.7	1999	25.2
0.7	6.6	− 5.0	3.0	− 5.1	3.6	2000	− 6.2
0.2	− 5.4	−11.1	2.6	8.6	1.7	2001	− 7.1
− 5.5	− 0.8	−12.4	10.6	5.9	− 6.2	2002	−16.8
2.8	2.0	− 1.5	5.7	− 0.2	6.9	2003	25.3
						2004	
58.7%	− 3.0%	−57.5%	32.0%	87.7%	95.5%		
1.1%	− 0.1%	− 1.1%	0.6%	1.6%	1.8%		
33	30	19	32	36	39		
21	24	35	22	18	15		

DOW JONES INDUSTRIALS MONTHLY POINT CHANGES

	JAN	FEB	MAR	APR	MAY	JUN
1950	1.66	1.65	2.61	8.28	9.09	− 14.31
1951	13.42	3.22	− 4.11	11.19	− 9.48	− 7.01
1952	1.46	− 10.61	9.38	− 11.83	5.31	11.32
1953	− 2.13	− 5.50	− 4.40	− 5.12	− 2.47	− 4.02
1954	11.49	2.15	8.97	15.82	8.16	6.04
1955	4.44	3.04	− 2.17	15.95	− 0.79	26.52
1956	− 17.66	12.91	28.14	4.33	− 38.07	14.73
1957	− 20.31	− 14.54	10.19	19.55	10.57	− 1.64
1958	14.33	− 10.10	6.84	9.10	6.84	15.48
1959	10.31	9.54	− 1.79	22.04	20.04	− 0.19
1960	− 56.74	7.50	− 13.53	− 14.89	23.80	15.12
1961	32.31	13.88	14.55	2.08	18.01	− 12.76
1962	− 31.14	8.05	− 1.10	− 41.62	− 51.97	− 52.08
1963	30.75	− 19.91	19.58	35.18	9.26	− 20.08
1964	22.39	14.80	13.15	− 2.52	9.79	10.94
1965	28.73	0.62	− 14.43	33.26	− 4.27	− 50.01
1966	14.25	− 31.62	− 27.12	8.91	− 49.61	− 13.97
1967	64.20	− 10.52	26.61	31.07	− 44.49	7.70
1968	− 49.64	− 14.97	0.17	71.55	− 13.22	− 1.20
1969	2.30	− 40.84	30.27	14.70	− 12.62	− 64.37
1970	− 56.30	33.53	7.98	− 49.50	− 35.63	− 16.91
1971	29.58	10.33	25.54	37.38	− 33.94	− 16.67
1972	11.97	25.96	12.57	13.47	6.55	− 31.69
1973	− 21.00	− 43.95	− 4.06	− 29.58	− 20.02	− 9.70
1974	4.69	4.98	− 13.85	− 9.93	− 34.58	0.24
1975	87.45	35.36	29.10	53.19	10.95	46.70
1976	122.87	− 2.67	26.84	− 2.60	− 21.62	27.55
1977	− 50.28	− 17.95	− 17.29	7.77	− 28.24	17.64
1978	− 61.25	− 27.80	15.24	79.96	3.29	− 21.66
1979	34.21	− 30.40	53.36	− 7.28	− 32.57	19.65
1980	37.11	− 12.71	− 77.39	31.31	33.79	17.07
1981	− 16.72	27.31	29.29	− 6.12	− 6.00	− 14.87
1982	− 3.90	− 46.71	− 1.62	25.59	− 28.82	− 7.61
1983	29.16	36.92	17.41	96.17	− 26.22	21.98
1984	− 38.06	− 65.95	10.26	5.86	− 65.90	27.55
1985	75.20	− 2.76	− 17.23	− 8.72	57.35	20.05
1986	24.32	138.07	109.55	− 34.63	92.73	16.01
1987	262.09	65.95	80.70	− 18.33	5.21	126.96
1988	19.39	113.40	− 83.56	44.27	− 1.21	110.59
1989	173.75	− 83.93	35.23	125.18	61.35	− 40.09
1990	−162.66	36.71	79.96	− 50.45	219.90	4.03
1991	102.73	145.79	31.68	− 25.99	139.63	−120.75
1992	54.56	44.28	− 32.20	123.65	37.76	− 78.36
1993	8.92	60.78	64.30	− 7.56	99.88	− 11.35
1994	224.27	−146.34	−196.06	45.73	76.68	−133.41
1995	9.42	167.19	146.64	163.58	143.87	90.96
1996	278.18	90.32	101.52	− 18.06	74.10	11.45
1997	364.82	64.65	−294.26	425.51	322.05	341.75
1998	− 1.75	639.22	254.09	263.56	−163.42	52.07
1999	177.40	− 52.25	479.58	1002.88	−229.30	411.06
2000	−556.59	−812.22	793.61	−188.01	−211.58	− 74.44
2001	100.51	−392.08	−616.50	856.19	176.97	−409.54
2002	−101.50	186.13	297.81	−457.72	− 20.97	−681.99
2003	−287.82	−162.73	101.05	487.96	370.17	135.18
2004	34.15	95.85	−226.22	−132.13	− 37.12	247.03
TOTALS	983.34	41.03	1324.88	3069.63	828.97	− 57.31
# Up	37	31	35	34	28	28
# Down	18	24	20	21	27	27

JUL	AUG	SEP	OCT	NOV	DEC	Year's Close	
0.29	7.47	9.49	− 1.35	2.59	7.81	235.41	1950
15.22	12.39	0.91	− 8.81	− 1.08	7.96	269.23	1951
5.30	− 4.52	− 4.43	− 1.38	14.43	8.24	291.90	1952
7.12	− 14.16	2.82	11.77	5.56	− 0.47	280.90	1953
14.39	− 12.12	24.66	− 8.32	34.63	17.62	404.39	1954
14.47	2.33	− 1.56	− 11.75	28.39	5.14	488.40	1955
25.03	− 15.77	− 26.79	4.60	− 7.07	26.69	499.47	1956
5.23	− 24.17	− 28.05	− 15.26	8.83	− 14.18	435.69	1957
24.81	5.64	23.46	11.13	14.24	26.19	583.65	1958
31.28	− 10.47	− 32.73	14.92	12.58	20.18	679.36	1959
− 23.89	9.26	− 45.85	0.22	16.86	18.67	615.89	1960
21.41	14.57	− 18.73	2.71	17.68	9.54	731.14	1961
36.65	11.25	− 30.20	10.79	59.53	2.80	652.10	1962
− 11.45	33.89	3.47	22.44	− 4.71	12.43	762.95	1963
9.60	− 2.62	36.89	− 2.29	2.35	− 1.30	874.13	1964
13.71	11.36	37.48	30.24	− 14.11	22.55	969.26	1965
− 22.72	− 58.97	− 14.19	32.85	− 15.48	− 5.90	785.69	1966
43.98	− 2.95	25.37	− 46.92	− 3.93	29.30	905.11	1967
− 14.80	13.01	39.78	16.60	32.69	− 41.33	943.75	1968
− 57.72	21.25	− 23.63	42.90	− 43.69	− 11.94	800.36	1969
50.59	30.46	− 3.90	− 5.07	38.48	44.83	838.92	1970
− 32.71	39.64	− 10.88	− 48.19	− 7.66	58.86	890.20	1971
− 4.29	38.99	− 10.46	2.25	62.69	1.81	1020.02	1972
34.69	− 38.83	59.53	9.48	−134.33	28.61	850.86	1973
− 44.98	− 78.85	− 70.71	57.65	− 46.86	− 2.42	616.24	1974
− 47.48	3.83	− 41.46	42.16	24.63	− 8.26	852.41	1975
− 18.14	10.90	16.45	− 25.26	− 17.71	57.43	1004.65	1976
− 26.23	− 28.58	− 14.38	− 28.76	11.35	1.47	831.17	1977
43.32	14.55	− 11.00	− 73.37	6.58	5.98	805.01	1978
4.44	41.21	− 9.05	− 62.88	6.65	16.39	838.74	1979
67.40	− 2.73	− 0.17	− 7.93	68.85	− 29.35	963.99	1980
− 24.54	− 70.87	− 31.49	2.57	36.43	− 13.98	875.00	1981
− 3.33	92.71	− 5.06	95.47	47.56	7.26	1046.54	1982
− 22.74	16.94	16.97	− 7.93	50.82	− 17.38	1258.64	1983
− 17.12	109.10	− 17.67	0.67	− 18.44	22.63	1211.57	1984
11.99	− 13.44	− 5.38	45.68	97.82	74.54	1546.67	1985
−117.41	123.03	−130.76	110.23	36.42	− 18.28	1895.95	1986
153.54	90.88	− 66.67	−602.75	−159.98	105.28	1938.83	1987
− 12.98	− 97.08	81.26	35.74	− 34.14	54.06	2168.57	1988
220.60	76.61	− 44.45	− 47.74	61.19	46.93	2753.20	1989
24.51	− 290.84	−161.88	− 10.15	117.32	74.01	2633.66	1990
118.07	18.78	− 26.83	52.33	−174.42	274.15	3168.83	1991
75.26	− 136.43	14.31	− 45.38	78.88	− 4.05	3301.11	1992
23.39	111.78	− 96.13	125.47	3.36	70.14	3754.09	1993
139.54	148.92	− 70.23	64.93	−168.89	95.21	3834.44	1994
152.37	− 97.91	178.52	− 33.60	319.01	42.63	5117.12	1995
−125.72	87.30	265.96	147.21	492.32	− 73.43	6448.27	1996
549.82	− 600.19	322.84	−503.18	381.05	85.12	7908.25	1997
− 68.73	−1344.22	303.55	749.48	524.45	64.88	9181.43	1998
−315.65	174.13	−492.33	392.91	147.95	619.31	11497.12	1999
74.09	693.12	−564.18	320.22	−556.65	372.36	10786.85	2000
20.41	− 573.06	−1102.19	227.58	776.42	169.94	10021.50	2001
−506.67	− 73.09	−1071.57	805.10	499.06	−554.46	8341.63	2002
248.36	182.02	−140.76	526.06	− 18.66	671.46	10453.92	2003
							2004
761.58	**−1366.35**	**−2962.03**	**2416.09**	**2711.84**	**2483.68**		
33	30	19	32	36	39		
21	24	35	22	18	15		

147

DOW JONES INDUSTRIALS MONTHLY CLOSING PRICES

	JAN	FEB	MAR	APR	MAY	JUN
1950	201.79	203.44	206.05	214.33	223.42	209.11
1951	248.83	252.05	247.94	259.13	249.65	242.64
1952	270.69	260.08	269.46	257.63	262.94	274.26
1953	289.77	284.27	279.87	274.75	272.28	268.26
1954	292.39	294.54	303.51	319.33	327.49	333.53
1955	408.83	411.87	409.70	425.65	424.86	451.38
1956	470.74	483.65	511.79	516.12	478.05	492.78
1957	479.16	464.62	474.81	494.36	504.93	503.29
1958	450.02	439.92	446.76	455.86	462.70	478.18
1959	593.96	603.50	601.71	623.75	643.79	643.60
1960	622.62	630.12	616.59	601.70	625.50	640.62
1961	648.20	662.08	676.63	678.71	696.72	683.96
1962	700.00	708.05	706.95	665.33	613.36	561.28
1963	682.85	662.94	682.52	717.70	726.96	706.88
1964	785.34	800.14	813.29	810.77	820.56	831.50
1965	902.86	903.48	889.05	922.31	918.04	868.03
1966	983.51	951.89	924.77	933.68	884.07	870.10
1967	849.89	839.37	865.98	897.05	852.56	860.26
1968	855.47	840.50	840.67	912.22	899.00	897.80
1969	946.05	905.21	935.48	950.18	937.56	873.19
1970	744.06	777.59	785.57	736.07	700.44	683.53
1971	868.50	878.83	904.37	941.75	907.81	891.14
1972	902.17	928.13	940.70	954.17	960.72	929.03
1973	999.02	955.07	951.01	921.43	901.41	891.71
1974	855.55	860.53	846.68	836.75	802.17	802.41
1975	703.69	739.05	768.15	821.34	832.29	878.99
1976	975.28	972.61	999.45	996.85	975.23	1002.78
1977	954.37	936.42	919.13	926.90	898.66	916.30
1978	769.92	742.12	757.36	837.32	840.61	818.95
1979	839.22	808.82	862.18	854.90	822.33	841.98
1980	875.85	863.14	785.75	817.06	850.85	867.92
1981	947.27	974.58	1003.87	997.75	991.75	976.88
1982	871.10	824.39	822.77	848.36	819.54	811.93
1983	1075.70	1112.62	1130.03	1226.20	1199.98	1221.96
1984	1220.58	1154.63	1164.89	1170.75	1104.85	1132.40
1985	1286.77	1284.01	1266.78	1258.06	1315.41	1335.46
1986	1570.99	1709.06	1818.61	1783.98	1876.71	1892.72
1987	2158.04	2223.99	2304.69	2286.36	2291.57	2418.53
1988	1958.22	2071.62	1988.06	2032.33	2031.12	2141.71
1989	2342.32	2258.39	2293.62	2418.80	2480.15	2440.06
1990	2590.54	2627.25	2707.21	2656.76	2876.66	2880.69
1991	2736.39	2882.18	2913.86	2887.87	3027.50	2906.75
1992	3223.39	3267.67	3235.47	3359.12	3396.88	3318.52
1993	3310.03	3370.81	3435.11	3427.55	3527.43	3516.08
1994	3978.36	3832.02	3635.96	3681.69	3758.37	3624.96
1995	3843.86	4011.05	4157.69	4321.27	4465.14	4556.10
1996	5395.30	5485.62	5587.14	5569.08	5643.18	5654.63
1997	6813.09	6877.74	6583.48	7008.99	7331.04	7672.79
1998	7906.50	8545.72	8799.81	9063.37	8899.95	8952.02
1999	9358.83	9306.58	9786.16	10789.04	10559.74	10970.80
2000	10940.53	10128.31	10921.92	10733.91	10522.33	10447.89
2001	10887.36	10495.28	9878.78	10734.97	10911.94	10502.40
2002	9920.00	10106.13	10403.94	9946.22	9925.25	9243.26
2003	8053.81	7891.08	7992.13	8480.09	8850.26	8985.44
2004	10488.07	10583.92	10357.70	10225.57	10188.45	10435.48

JUL	AUG	SEP	OCT	NOV	DEC	
209.40	216.87	226.36	225.01	227.60	235.41	**1950**
257.86	270.25	271.16	262.35	261.27	269.23	**1951**
279.56	275.04	270.61	269.23	283.66	291.90	**1952**
275.38	261.22	264.04	275.81	281.37	280.90	**1953**
347.92	335.80	360.46	352.14	386.77	404.39	**1954**
465.85	468.18	466.62	454.87	483.26	488.40	**1955**
517.81	502.04	475.25	479.85	472.78	499.47	**1956**
508.52	484.35	456.30	441.04	449.87	435.69	**1957**
502.99	508.63	532.09	543.22	557.46	583.65	**1958**
674.88	664.41	631.68	646.60	659.18	679.36	**1959**
616.73	625.99	580.14	580.36	597.22	615.89	**1960**
705.37	719.94	701.21	703.92	721.60	731.14	**1961**
597.93	609.18	578.98	589.77	649.30	652.10	**1962**
695.43	729.32	732.79	755.23	750.52	762.95	**1963**
841.10	838.48	875.37	873.08	875.43	874.13	**1964**
881.74	893.10	930.58	960.82	946.71	969.26	**1965**
847.38	788.41	774.22	807.07	791.59	785.69	**1966**
904.24	901.29	926.66	879.74	875.81	905.11	**1967**
883.00	896.01	935.79	952.39	985.08	943.75	**1968**
815.47	836.72	813.09	855.99	812.30	800.36	**1969**
734.12	764.58	760.68	755.61	794.09	838.92	**1970**
858.43	898.07	887.19	839.00	831.34	890.20	**1971**
924.74	963.73	953.27	955.52	1018.21	1020.02	**1972**
926.40	887.57	947.10	956.58	822.25	850.86	**1973**
757.43	678.58	607.87	665.52	618.66	616.24	**1974**
831.51	835.34	793.88	836.04	860.67	852.41	**1975**
984.64	973.74	990.19	964.93	947.22	1004.65	**1976**
890.07	861.49	847.11	818.35	829.70	831.17	**1977**
862.27	876.82	865.82	792.45	799.03	805.01	**1978**
846.42	887.63	878.58	815.70	822.35	838.74	**1979**
935.32	932.59	932.42	924.49	993.34	963.99	**1980**
952.34	881.47	849.98	852.55	888.98	875.00	**1981**
808.60	901.31	896.25	991.72	1039.28	1046.54	**1982**
1199.22	1216.16	1233.13	1225.20	1276.02	1258.64	**1983**
1115.28	1224.38	1206.71	1207.38	1188.94	1211.57	**1984**
1347.45	1334.01	1328.63	1374.31	1472.13	1546.67	**1985**
1775.31	1898.34	1767.58	1877.81	1914.23	1895.95	**1986**
2572.07	2662.95	2596.28	1993.53	1833.55	1938.83	**1987**
2128.73	2031.65	2112.91	2148.65	2114.51	2168.57	**1988**
2660.66	2737.27	2692.82	2645.08	2706.27	2753.20	**1989**
2905.20	2614.36	2452.48	2442.33	2559.65	2633.66	**1990**
3024.82	3043.60	3016.77	3069.10	2894.68	3168.83	**1991**
3393.78	3257.35	3271.66	3226.28	3305.16	3301.11	**1992**
3539.47	3651.25	3555.12	3680.59	3683.95	3754.09	**1993**
3764.50	3913.42	3843.19	3908.12	3739.23	3834.44	**1994**
4708.47	4610.56	4789.08	4755.48	5074.49	5117.12	**1995**
5528.91	5616.21	5882.17	6029.38	6521.70	6448.27	**1996**
8222.61	7622.42	7945.26	7442.08	7823.13	7908.25	**1997**
8883.29	7539.07	7842.62	8592.62	9116.55	9181.43	**1998**
10655.15	10829.28	10336.95	10729.86	10877.81	11497.12	**1999**
10521.98	11215.10	10650.92	10971.14	10414.49	10786.85	**2000**
10522.81	9949.75	8847.56	9075.14	9851.56	10021.50	**2001**
8736.59	8663.50	7591.93	8397.03	8896.09	8341.63	**2002**
9233.80	9415.82	9275.06	9801.12	9782.46	10453.92	**2003**
						2004

NASDAQ COMPOSITE
MONTHLY PERCENT CHANGES

	JAN	FEB	MAR	APR	MAY	JUN
1971	10.2%	2.6%	4.6%	6.0%	− 3.6%	− 0.4%
1972	4.2	5.5	2.2	2.5	0.9	− 1.8
1973	− 4.0	− 6.2	− 2.4	− 8.2	− 4.8	− 1.6
1974	3.0	− 0.6	− 2.2	− 5.9	− 7.7	− 5.3
1975	16.6	4.6	3.6	3.8	5.8	4.7
1976	12.1	3.7	0.4	− 0.6	− 2.3	2.6
1977	− 2.4	− 1.0	− 0.5	1.4	0.1	4.3
1978	− 4.0	0.6	4.7	8.5	4.4	0.05
1979	6.6	− 2.6	7.5	1.6	− 1.8	5.1
1980	7.0	− 2.3	− 17.1	6.9	7.5	4.9
1981	− 2.2	0.1	6.1	3.1	3.1	− 3.5
1982	− 3.8	− 4.8	− 2.1	5.2	− 3.3	− 4.1
1983	6.9	5.0	3.9	8.2	5.3	3.2
1984	− 3.7	− 5.9	− 0.7	− 1.3	− 5.9	2.9
1985	12.7	2.0	− 1.7	0.5	3.6	1.9
1986	3.3	7.1	4.2	2.3	4.4	1.3
1987	12.2	8.4	1.2	− 2.8	− 0.3	2.0
1988	4.3	6.5	2.1	1.2	− 2.3	6.6
1989	5.2	− 0.4	1.8	5.1	4.4	− 2.4
1990	− 8.6	2.4	2.3	− 3.6	9.3	0.7
1991	10.8	9.4	6.5	0.5	4.4	− 6.0
1992	5.8	2.1	− 4.7	− 4.2	1.1	− 3.7
1993	2.9	− 3.7	2.9	− 4.2	5.9	0.5
1994	3.0	− 1.0	− 6.2	− 1.3	0.2	− 4.0
1995	0.4	5.1	3.0	3.3	2.4	8.0
1996	0.7	3.8	0.1	8.1	4.4	− 4.7
1997	6.9	− 5.1	− 6.7	3.2	11.1	3.0
1998	3.1	9.3	3.7	1.8	− 4.8	6.5
1999	14.3	− 8.7	7.6	3.3	− 2.8	8.7
2000	− 3.2	19.2	− 2.6	− 15.6	− 11.9	16.6
2001	12.2	−22.4	− 14.5	15.0	− 0.3	2.4
2002	− 0.8	−10.5	6.6	− 8.5	− 4.3	− 9.4
2003	− 1.1	1.3	0.3	9.2	9.0	1.7
2004	3.1	− 1.8	− 1.8	− 3.7	3.5	3.1
TOTALS	134.0%	21.7%	11.9%	40.7%	34.7%	43.8%
AVG.	3.9%	0.6%	0.3%	1.2%	1.0%	1.3%
# Up	24	19	21	22	20	22
# Down	10	15	13	12	14	12

Based on NASDAQ composite, prior to February 5, 1971, based on National Quotation Bureau indices

NASDAQ COMPOSITE
MONTHLY PERCENT CHANGES

JUL	AUG	SEP	OCT	NOV	DEC		Year's Change
— 2.3%	3.0%	0.6%	— 3.6%	— 1.1%	9.8%	**1971**	27.4%
— 1.8	1.7	— 0.3	0.5	2.1	0.6	**1972**	17.2
7.6	— 3.5	6.0	— 0.9	— 15.1	— 1.4	**1973**	— 31.1
— 7.9	— 10.9	— 10.7	17.2	— 3.5	— 5.0	**1974**	— 35.1
— 4.4	— 5.0	— 5.9	3.6	2.4	— 1.5	**1975**	29.8
1.1	— 1.7	1.7	— 1.0	0.9	7.4	**1976**	26.1
0.9	— 0.5	0.7	— 3.3	5.8	1.8	**1977**	7.3
5.0	6.9	— 1.6	— 16.4	3.2	2.9	**1978**	12.3
2.3	6.4	— 0.3	— 9.6	6.4	4.8	**1979**	28.1
8.9	5.7	3.4	2.7	8.0	— 2.8	**1980**	33.9
— 1.9	— 7.5	— 8.0	8.4	3.1	— 2.7	**1981**	— 3.2
— 2.3	6.2	5.6	13.3	9.3	0.04	**1982**	18.7
— 4.6	— 3.8	1.4	— 7.4	4.1	— 2.5	**1983**	19.9
— 4.2	10.9	— 1.8	— 1.2	— 1.8	2.0	**1984**	— 11.2
1.7	— 1.2	— 5.8	4.4	7.3	3.5	**1985**	31.4
— 8.4	3.1	— 8.4	2.9	— 0.3	— 2.8	**1986**	7.5
2.4	4.6	— 2.3	— 27.2	— 5.6	8.3	**1987**	— 5.4
— 1.9	— 2.8	3.0	— 1.4	— 2.9	2.7	**1988**	15.4
4.3	3.4	0.8	— 3.7	0.1	— 0.3	**1989**	19.3
— 5.2	— 13.0	— 9.6	— 4.3	8.9	4.1	**1990**	— 17.8
5.5	4.7	0.2	3.1	— 3.5	11.9	**1991**	56.8
3.1	— 3.0	3.6	3.8	7.9	3.7	**1992**	15.5
0.1	5.4	2.7	2.2	— 3.2	3.0	**1993**	14.7
2.3	6.0	— 0.2	1.7	— 3.5	0.2	**1994**	— 3.2
7.3	1.9	2.3	— 0.7	2.2	— 0.7	**1995**	39.9
— 8.8	5.6	7.5	— 0.4	5.8	— 0.1	**1996**	22.7
10.5	— 0.4	6.2	— 5.5	0.4	— 1.9	**1997**	21.6
— 1.2	— 19.9	13.0	4.6	10.1	12.5	**1998**	39.6
— 1.8	3.8	0.2	8.0	12.5	22.0	**1999**	85.6
— 5.0	11.7	— 12.7	— 8.3	— 22.9	— 4.9	**2000**	— 39.3
— 6.2	— 10.9	— 17.0	12.8	14.2	1.0	**2001**	— 21.1
— 9.2	— 1.0	— 10.9	13.5	11.2	— 9.7	**2002**	— 31.5
6.9	4.3	— 1.3	8.1	1.5	2.2	**2003**	50.0
						2004	
— 7.2%	10.1%	— 37.9%	15.7%	63.7%	68.1%		
— 0.2%	0.3%	— 1.1%	0.5%	1.9%	2.1%		
16	18	17	17	22	20		
17	15	16	16	11	13		

NASDAQ COMPOSITE
MONTHLY CLOSING PRICES

	JAN	FEB	MAR	APR	MAY	JUN
1971	98.77	101.34	105.97	112.30	108.25	107.80
1972	118.87	125.38	128.14	131.33	132.53	130.08
1973	128.40	120.41	117.46	107.85	102.64	100.98
1974	94.93	94.35	92.27	86.86	80.20	75.96
1975	69.78	73.00	75.66	78.54	83.10	87.02
1976	87.05	90.26	90.62	90.08	88.04	90.32
1977	95.54	94.57	94.13	95.48	95.59	99.73
1978	100.84	101.47	106.20	115.18	120.24	120.30
1979	125.82	122.56	131.76	133.82	131.42	138.13
1980	161.75	158.03	131.00	139.99	150.45	157.78
1981	197.81	198.01	210.18	216.74	223.47	215.75
1982	188.39	179.43	175.65	184.70	178.54	171.30
1983	248.35	260.67	270.80	293.06	308.73	318.70
1984	268.43	252.57	250.78	247.44	232.82	239.65
1985	278.70	284.17	279.20	280.56	290.80	296.20
1986	335.77	359.53	374.72	383.24	400.16	405.51
1987	392.06	424.97	430.05	417.81	416.54	424.67
1988	344.66	366.95	374.64	379.23	370.34	394.66
1989	401.30	399.71	406.73	427.55	446.17	435.29
1990	415.81	425.83	435.54	420.07	458.97	462.29
1991	414.20	453.05	482.30	484.72	506.11	475.92
1992	620.21	633.47	603.77	578.68	585.31	563.60
1993	696.34	670.77	690.13	661.42	700.53	703.95
1994	800.47	792.50	743.46	733.84	735.19	705.96
1995	755.20	793.73	817.21	843.98	864.58	933.45
1996	1059.79	1100.05	1101.40	1190.52	1243.43	1185.02
1997	1379.85	1309.00	1221.70	1260.76	1400.32	1442.07
1998	1619.36	1770.51	1835.68	1868.41	1778.87	1894.74
1999	2505.89	2288.03	2461.40	2542.85	2470.52	2686.12
2000	3940.35	4696.69	4572.83	3860.66	3400.91	3966.11
2001	2772.73	2151.83	1840.26	2116.24	2110.49	2160.54
2002	1934.03	1731.49	1845.35	1688.23	1615.73	1463.21
2003	1320.91	1337.52	1341.17	1464.31	1595.91	1622.80
2004	2066.15	2029.82	1994.22	1920.15	1986.74	2047.79

Based on NASDAQ composite, prior to February 5, 1971, based on National Quotation Bureau indices

NASDAQ COMPOSITE
MONTHLY CLOSING PRICES

JUL	AUG	SEP	OCT	NOV	DEC	
105.27	108.42	109.03	105.10	103.97	114.12	**1971**
127.75	129.95	129.61	130.24	132.96	133.73	**1972**
108.64	104.87	111.20	110.17	93.51	92.19	**1973**
69.99	62.37	55.67	65.23	62.95	59.82	**1974**
83.19	79.01	74.33	76.99	78.80	77.62	**1975**
91.29	89.70	91.26	90.35	91.12	97.88	**1976**
100.65	100.10	100.85	97.52	103.15	105.05	**1977**
126.32	135.01	132.89	111.12	114.69	117.98	**1978**
141.33	150.44	149.98	135.53	144.26	151.14	**1979**
171.81	181.52	187.76	192.78	208.15	202.34	**1980**
211.63	195.75	180.03	195.24	201.37	195.84	**1981**
167.35	177.71	187.65	212.63	232.31	232.41	**1982**
303.96	292.42	296.65	274.55	285.67	278.60	**1983**
229.70	254.64	249.94	247.03	242.53	247.35	**1984**
301.29	297.71	280.33	292.54	313.95	324.93	**1985**
371.37	382.86	350.67	360.77	359.57	349.33	**1986**
434.93	454.97	444.29	323.30	305.16	330.47	**1987**
387.33	376.55	387.71	382.46	371.45	381.38	**1988**
453.84	469.33	472.92	455.63	456.09	454.82	**1989**
438.24	381.21	344.51	329.84	359.06	373.84	**1990**
502.04	525.68	526.88	542.98	523.90	586.34	**1991**
580.83	563.12	583.27	605.17	652.73	676.95	**1992**
704.70	742.84	762.78	779.26	754.39	776.80	**1993**
722.16	765.62	764.29	777.49	750.32	751.96	**1994**
1001.21	1020.11	1043.54	1036.06	1059.20	1052.13	**1995**
1080.59	1141.50	1226.92	1221.51	1292.61	1291.03	**1996**
1593.81	1587.32	1685.69	1593.61	1600.55	1570.35	**1997**
1872.39	1499.25	1693.84	1771.39	1949.54	2192.69	**1998**
2638.49	2739.35	2746.16	2966.43	3336.16	4069.31	**1999**
3766.99	4206.35	3672.82	3369.63	2597.93	2470.52	**2000**
2027.13	1805.43	1498.80	1690.20	1930.58	1950.40	**2001**
1328.26	1314.85	1172.06	1329.75	1478.78	1335.51	**2002**
1735.02	1810.45	1786.94	1932.21	1960.26	2003.37	**2003**
						2004

BEST & WORST <u>DOW</u> DAYS SINCE 1901
BY POINTS AND PERCENT

BEST TWENTY DAYS SINCE 1901 BY POINTS

Day	DJIA Close	Points Change	% Change
3/16/2000	10630.60	499.19	4.9
7/24/2002	8191.29	488.95	6.3
7/29/2002	8711.88	447.49	5.4
4/5/2001	9918.05	402.63	4.2
4/18/2001	10615.83	399.10	3.9
9/8/1998	8020.78	380.53	5.0
10/15/2002	8255.68	378.28	4.8
9/24/2001	8603.86	368.05	4.5
10/1/2002	7938.79	346.86	4.6
5/16/2001	11215.92	342.95	3.2
12/5/2000	10898.72	338.62	3.2
10/28/1997	7498.32	337.17	4.7
10/15/1998	8299.36	330.58	4.1
7/5/2002	9379.50	324.53	3.6
3/15/2000	10131.41	320.17	3.3
10/11/2002	7850.29	316.34	4.2
5/8/2002	10141.83	305.28	3.1
4/3/2000	11221.93	300.01	2.7
1/3/2001	10945.75	299.60	2.8
9/1/1998	7827.43	288.36	3.8

WORST TWENTY DAYS SINCE 1901 BY POINTS

Day	DJIA Close	Points Change	% Change
9/17/2001	8920.70	− 684.81	− 7.1
4/14/2000	10305.77	− 617.78	− 5.7
10/27/1997	7161.15	− 554.26	− 7.2
8/31/1998	7539.07	− 512.61	− 6.4
10/19/1987	1738.74	− 508.00	− 22.6
3/12/2001	10208.25	− 436.37	− 4.1
7/19/2002	8019.26	− 390.23	− 4.6
9/20/2001	8376.21	− 382.92	− 4.4
10/12/2000	10034.58	− 379.21	− 3.6
3/7/2000	9796.03	− 374.47	− 3.7
1/4/2000	10997.93	− 359.58	− 3.2
8/27/1998	8165.99	− 357.36	− 4.2
9/3/2002	8308.05	− 355.45	− 4.1
3/14/2001	9973.46	− 317.34	− 3.1
3/24/2003	8214.68	− 307.29	− 3.6
8/4/1998	8487.31	− 299.43	− 3.4
9/27/2002	7701.45	− 295.67	− 3.7
2/18/2000	10219.52	− 295.05	− 2.8
4/3/2001	9485.71	− 292.22	− 3.0
1/28/2000	10738.87	− 289.15	− 2.6

BEST TWENTY DAYS SINCE 1950 BY %

Day	DJIA Close	Points Change	% Change
10/21/1987	2027.85	186.84	10.1
7/24/2002	8191.29	488.95	6.3
10/20/1987	1841.01	102.27	5.9
7/29/2002	8711.88	447.49	5.4
5/27/1970	663.20	32.04	5.1
9/8/1998	8020.78	380.53	5.0
10/29/1987	1938.33	91.51	5.0
3/16/2000	10630.60	499.19	4.9
8/17/1982	831.24	38.81	4.9
10/15/2002	8255.68	378.28	4.8
10/9/1974	631.02	28.39	4.7
10/28/1997	7498.32	337.17	4.7
5/29/1962	603.96	27.03	4.7
10/1/2002	7938.79	346.86	4.6
1/17/1991	2623.51	114.60	4.6
11/26/1963	743.52	32.03	4.5
9/24/2001	8603.86	368.05	4.5
11/1/1978	827.79	35.34	4.5
11/3/1982	1065.49	43.41	4.2

WORST TWENTY DAYS SINCE 1950 BY %

Day	DJIA Close	Points Change	% Change
10/19/1987	1738.74	− 508.00	− 22.6
10/26/1987	1793.93	− 156.83	− 8.0
10/27/1997	7161.15	− 554.26	− 7.2
9/17/2001	8920.70	− 684.81	− 7.1
10/13/1989	2569.26	− 190.58	− 6.9
1/8/1988	1911.31	− 140.58	− 6.9
9/26/1955	455.56	− 31.89	− 6.5
8/31/1998	7539.07	− 512.61	− 6.4
5/28/1962	576.93	− 34.95	− 5.7
4/14/2000	10305.77	− 617.78	− 5.7
4/14/1988	2005.64	− 101.46	− 4.8
6/26/1950	213.91	− 10.44	− 4.7
7/19/2002	8019.26	− 390.23	− 4.6
9/11/1986	1792.89	− 86.61	− 4.6
10/16/1987	2246.74	− 108.35	− 4.6
9/20/2001	8376.21	− 382.92	− 4.4
8/27/1998	8165.99	− 357.36	− 4.2
9/3/2002	8308.05	− 355.45	− 4.1
3/12/2001	10208.25	− 436.37	− 4.1
11/30/1987	1833.55	− 76.93	− 4.0

BEST FIFTEEN DAYS 1901-1949 BY %

Day	DJIA Close	Points Change	% Change
3/15/1933	62.10	8.26	15.3
10/6/1931	99.34	12.86	14.9
10/30/1929	258.47	28.40	12.3
9/21/1932	75.16	7.67	11.4
8/3/1932	58.22	5.06	9.5
2/11/1932	78.60	6.80	9.5
11/14/1929	217.28	18.59	9.4
12/18/1931	80.69	6.90	9.4
2/13/1932	85.82	7.22	9.2
5/6/1932	59.01	4.91	9.1
4/19/1933	68.31	5.66	9.0
10/8/1931	105.79	8.47	8.7
6/10/1932	48.94	3.62	8.0
9/5/1939	148.12	10.03	7.3
6/3/1931	130.37	8.67	7.1

WORST FIFTEEN DAYS 1901-1949 BY %

Day	DJIA Close	Points Change	% Change
10/28/1929	260.64	− 38.33	− 12.8
10/29/1929	230.07	− 30.57	− 11.7
11/6/1929	232.13	− 25.55	− 9.9
8/12/1932	63.11	− 5.79	− 8.4
3/14/1907	55.84	− 5.05	− 8.3
7/21/1933	88.71	− 7.55	− 7.8
10/18/1937	125.73	− 10.57	− 7.8
2/1/1917	88.52	− 6.91	− 7.2
10/5/1932	66.07	− 5.09	− 7.2
9/24/1931	107.79	− 8.20	− 7.1
7/20/1933	96.26	− 7.32	− 7.1
7/30/1914	52.32	− 3.88	− 6.9
11/11/1929	220.39	− 16.14	− 6.8
5/14/1940	128.27	− 9.36	− 6.8
10/5/1931	86.48	− 6.29	− 6.8

BEST TWENTY DAYS SINCE 1971 BY POINTS					WORST TWENTY DAYS SINCE 1971 BY POINTS			
Day	NASDAQ Close	Points Change	% Change		Day	NASDAQ Close	Points Change	% Change
1/3/2001	2616.69	324.83	14.2		4/14/2000	3321.29	− 355.49	− 9.7
12/5/2000	2889.80	274.05	10.5		4/3/2000	4223.68	− 349.15	− 7.6
4/18/2000	3793.57	254.41	7.2		4/12/2000	3769.63	− 286.27	− 7.1
5/30/2000	3459.48	254.37	7.9		4/10/2000	4188.20	− 258.25	− 5.8
10/19/2000	3418.60	247.04	7.8		1/4/2000	3901.69	− 229.46	− 5.6
10/13/2000	3316.77	242.09	7.9		3/14/2000	4706.63	− 200.61	− 4.1
6/2/2000	3813.38	230.88	6.4		5/10/2000	3384.73	− 200.28	− 5.6
4/25/2000	3711.23	228.75	6.6		5/23/2000	3164.55	− 199.66	− 5.9
4/17/2000	3539.16	217.87	6.6		10/25/2000	3229.57	− 190.22	− 5.6
6/1/2000	3582.50	181.59	5.3		3/29/2000	4644.67	− 189.22	− 3.9
4/7/2000	4446.45	178.89	4.2		3/20/2000	4610.00	− 188.13	− 3.9
10/31/2000	3369.63	178.23	5.6		3/30/2000	4457.89	− 186.78	− 4.0
12/22/2000	2517.02	176.90	7.6		11/8/2000	3231.70	− 184.09	− 5.4
11/14/2000	3138.27	171.55	5.8		7/28/2000	3663.00	− 179.23	− 4.7
2/23/2000	4550.33	168.21	3.8		12/20/2000	2332.78	− 178.93	− 7.1
1/10/2000	4049.67	167.05	4.3		1/2/2001	2291.86	− 178.66	− 7.2
12/8/2000	2917.43	164.77	6.0		5/2/2000	3785.45	− 172.63	− 4.4
3/3/2000	4914.79	160.28	3.4		11/10/2000	3028.99	− 171.36	− 5.4
4/18/2001	2079.44	156.22	8.1		4/24/2000	3482.48	− 161.40	− 4.4
1/7/2000	3882.62	155.49	4.2		1/5/2001	2407.65	− 159.18	− 6.2

BEST TWENTY DAYS SINCE 1971 BY %					WORST TWENTY DAYS SINCE 1971 BY %			
Day	NASDAQ Close	Points Change	% Change		Day	NASDAQ Close	Points Change	% Change
1/3/2001	2616.69	324.83	14.2		10/19/1987	360.21	− 46.12	−11.4
12/5/2000	2889.80	274.05	10.5		4/14/2000	3321.29	− 355.49	− 9.7
4/5/2001	1785.00	146.20	8.9		10/20/1987	327.79	− 32.42	− 9.0
4/18/2001	2079.44	156.22	8.1		10/26/1987	298.90	− 29.55	− 9.0
5/30/2000	3459.48	254.37	7.9		8/31/1998	1499.25	− 140.43	− 8.6
10/13/2000	3316.77	242.09	7.9		4/3/2000	4223.68	− 349.15	− 7.6
10/19/2000	3418.60	247.04	7.8		1/2/2001	2291.86	− 178.66	− 7.2
5/8/2002	1696.29	122.47	7.8		12/20/2000	2332.78	− 178.93	− 7.1
12/22/2000	2517.02	176.90	7.6		4/12/2000	3769.63	− 286.27	− 7.1
10/21/1987	351.86	24.07	7.3		10/27/1997	1535.09	− 115.83	− 7.0
4/18/2000	3793.57	254.41	7.2		9/17/2001	1579.55	− 115.83	− 6.8
4/25/2000	3711.23	228.75	6.6		3/12/2001	1923.38	− 129.40	− 6.3
4/17/2000	3539.16	217.87	6.6		1/5/2001	2407.65	− 159.18	− 6.2
6/2/2000	3813.38	230.88	6.4		4/3/2001	1673.00	− 109.97	− 6.2
4/10/2001	1852.03	106.32	6.1		3/27/1980	124.09	− 8.13	− 6.1
9/8/1998	1660.86	94.34	6.0		3/28/2001	1854.13	− 118.13	− 6.0
12/8/2000	2917.43	164.77	6.0		5/23/2000	3164.55	− 199.66	− 5.9
10/3/2001	1580.81	88.48	5.9		4/10/2000	4188.20	− 258.25	− 5.8
7/29/2002	1335.25	73.13	5.8		5/10/2000	3384.73	− 200.28	− 5.6
11/14/2000	3138.27	171.55	5.8		4/19/1999	2345.61	− 138.43	− 5.6

Based on NASDAQ composite, prior to February 5, 1971, based on National Quotation Bureau indices

BEST & WORST DOW WEEKS
SINCE 1901 BY POINTS AND PERCENT

BEST TWENTY WEEKS SINCE 1901 BY POINTS

Week Ending	DJIA Close	Points Change	% Change
3/17/2000	10595.23	666.41	6.7
3/21/2003	8521.97	662.26	8.4
9/28/2001	8847.56	611.75	7.4
7/2/1999	11139.24	586.68	5.6
4/20/2000	10844.05	538.28	5.2
3/24/2000	11112.72	517.49	4.9
10/16/1998	8416.76	517.24	6.5
3/3/2000	10367.20	505.08	5.1
6/2/2000	10794.76	495.52	4.8
5/18/2001	11301.74	480.43	4.4
10/18/2002	8322.40	472.11	6.0
1/8/1999	9643.32	461.89	5.0
4/20/2001	10579.85	452.91	4.5
10/22/1999	10470.25	450.54	4.5
8/9/2002	8745.45	432.32	5.2
3/5/1999	9736.08	429.50	4.6
5/17/2002	10353.08	413.16	4.2
3/1/2002	10368.86	400.71	4.0
11/6/1998	8975.46	383.36	4.5
10/8/1999	10649.76	376.76	3.7

WORST TWENTY WEEKS SINCE 1901 BY POINTS

Week Ending	DJIA Close	Points Change	% Change
9/21/2001	8235.81	−1369.70	− 14.3
3/16/2001	9823.41	− 821.21	− 7.7
4/14/2000	10305.77	− 805.71	− 7.3
7/12/2002	8684.53	− 694.97	− 7.4
7/19/2002	8019.26	− 665.27	− 7.7
10/15/1999	10019.71	− 630.05	− 5.9
2/11/2000	10425.21	− 538.59	− 4.9
9/24/1999	10279.33	− 524.30	− 4.9
1/28/2000	10738.87	− 512.84	− 4.6
8/28/1998	8051.68	− 481.97	− 5.6
8/31/2001	9949.75	− 473.42	− 4.5
1/21/2000	11251.71	− 471.27	− 4.0
1/24/2003	8131.01	− 455.73	− 5.3
3/10/2000	9928.82	− 438.38	− 4.2
9/4/1998	7640.25	− 411.43	− 5.1
10/13/2000	10192.18	− 404.36	− 3.8
7/24/1998	8937.36	− 400.61	− 4.3
1/9/1998	7580.42	− 384.62	− 4.8
3/28/2003	8145.77	− 376.20	− 4.4
2/23/2001	10441.90	− 357.92	− 3.3

BEST TWENTY WEEKS SINCE 1950 BY %

Week Ending	DJIA Close	Points Change	% Change
10/11/1974	658.17	73.61	12.6
8/20/1982	869.29	81.24	10.3
10/8/1982	986.85	79.11	8.7
3/21/2003	8521.97	662.26	8.4
8/3/1984	1202.08	87.46	7.8
9/28/2001	8847.56	611.75	7.4
9/20/1974	670.76	43.57	6.9
3/17/2000	10595.23	666.41	6.7
10/16/1998	8416.76	517.24	6.5
6/7/1974	853.72	51.55	6.4
11/2/1962	604.58	35.56	6.2
1/9/1976	911.13	52.42	6.1
11/5/1982	1051.78	60.06	6.1
10/18/2002	8322.40	472.11	6.0
6/3/1988	2071.30	114.86	5.9
1/18/1991	2646.78	145.29	5.8
12/18/1987	1975.30	108.26	5.8
11/14/1980	986.35	53.93	5.8
5/29/1970	700.44	38.27	5.8
12/11/1987	1867.04	100.30	5.7

WORST TWENTY WEEKS SINCE 1950 BY %

Week Ending	DJIA Close	Points Change	% Change
9/21/2001	8235.81	−1369.70	− 14.3
10/23/1987	1950.76	− 295.98	− 13.2
10/16/1987	2246.74	− 235.47	− 9.5
10/13/1989	2569.26	− 216.26	− 7.8
3/16/2001	9823.41	− 821.21	− 7.7
7/19/2002	8019.26	− 665.27	− 7.7
12/4/1987	1766.74	− 143.74	− 7.5
9/13/1974	627.19	− 50.69	− 7.5
9/12/1986	1758.72	− 141.03	− 7.4
7/12/2002	8684.53	− 694.97	− 7.4
9/27/1974	621.95	− 48.81	− 7.3
4/14/2000	10305.77	− 805.71	− 7.3
6/30/1950	209.11	− 15.24	− 6.8
6/22/1962	539.19	− 38.99	− 6.7
12/6/1974	577.60	− 41.06	− 6.6
10/20/1978	838.01	− 59.08	− 6.6
10/12/1979	838.99	− 58.62	− 6.5
8/23/1974	686.80	− 44.74	− 6.1
10/9/1987	2482.21	− 158.78	− 6.0
10/4/1974	584.56	− 37.39	− 6.0

BEST TEN WEEKS 1901-1949 BY %

Week Ending	DJIA Close	Points Change	% Change
8/6/32	66.56	12.30	22.7
6/25/38	131.94	18.71	16.5
2/13/32	85.82	11.37	15.3
4/22/33	72.24	9.36	14.9
10/10/31	105.61	12.84	13.8
7/30/32	54.26	6.42	13.4
6/27/31	156.93	17.97	12.9
9/24/32	74.83	8.39	12.6
8/27/32	75.61	8.43	12.5
3/18/33	60.56	6.72	12.5

WORST TEN WEEKS 1901-1949 BY %

Week Ending	DJIA Close	Points Change	% Change
7/22/33	88.42	− 17.68	− 16.7
5/18/40	122.43	− 22.42	− 15.5
10/8/32	61.17	− 10.92	− 15.1
10/3/31	92.77	− 14.59	− 13.6
11/8/29	236.53	− 36.98	− 13.5
9/17/32	66.44	− 10.10	− 13.2
10/21/33	83.64	− 11.95	− 12.5
12/12/31	78.93	− 11.21	− 12.4
5/8/15	62.77	− 8.74	− 12.2
6/21/30	215.30	− 28.95	− 11.9

BEST & WORST NASDAQ WEEKS
SINCE 1971 BY POINTS AND PERCENT

BEST TWENTY WEEKS SINCE 1971 BY POINTS

Week Ending	NASDAQ Close	Points Change	% Change
6/2/2000	3813.38	608.27	19.0
2/4/2000	4244.14	357.07	9.2
3/3/2000	4914.79	324.29	7.1
4/20/2000	3643.88	322.59	9.7
12/8/2000	2917.43	272.14	10.3
4/12/2001	1961.43	241.07	14.0
7/14/2000	4246.18	222.98	5.5
1/12/2001	2626.50	218.85	9.1
4/28/2000	3860.66	216.78	5.9
2/23/1999	3969.44	216.38	5.8
4/20/2001	2163.41	201.98	10.3
9/1/2000	4234.33	191.65	4.7
7/2/1999	2741.02	188.37	7.4
1/14/2000	4064.27	181.65	4.7
2/25/2000	4590.50	178.76	4.1
11/3/2000	3451.58	173.22	5.3
1/21/2000	4235.40	171.13	4.2
1/29/1999	2505.89	167.01	7.1
10/20/2000	3483.14	166.37	5.0
3/24/2000	4963.03	164.90	3.4

WORST TWENTY WEEKS SINCE 1971 BY POINTS

Week Ending	NASDAQ Close	Points Change	% Change
4/14/00	3321.29	−1125.16	− 25.3
7/28/00	3663.00	− 431.45	− 10.5
11/10/00	3028.99	− 422.59	− 12.2
3/31/00	4572.83	− 390.20	− 7.9
1/28/00	3887.07	− 348.33	− 8.2
10/6/00	3361.01	− 311.81	− 8.5
5/12/00	3529.06	− 287.76	− 7.5
9/21/01	1423.19	− 272.19	− 16.1
12/15/00	2653.27	− 264.16	− 9.1
12/1/00	2645.29	− 259.09	− 8.9
9/8/00	3978.41	− 255.92	− 6.0
3/17/00	4798.13	− 250.49	− 5.0
10/27/00	3278.36	− 204.78	− 5.9
2/9/01	2470.97	− 189.53	− 7.1
1/7/00	3882.62	− 186.69	− 4.6
6/15/01	2028.43	− 186.67	− 8.4
5/26/00	3205.11	− 185.29	− 5.5
7/23/99	2692.40	− 172.08	− 6.0
2/23/01	2262.51	− 162.87	− 6.7
3/16/01	1890.91	− 161.87	− 7.9

BEST TWENTY WEEKS SINCE 1971 BY %

Week Ending	NASDAQ Close	Points Change	% Change
6/2/2000	3813.38	608.27	19.0
4/12/2001	1961.43	241.07	14.0
4/20/2001	2163.41	201.98	10.3
12/8/2000	2917.43	272.14	10.3
4/20/2000	3643.88	322.59	9.7
10/11/1974	60.42	5.26	9.5
2/4/2000	4244.14	357.07	9.2
1/12/2001	2626.50	218.85	9.1
5/17/2002	1741.39	140.54	8.8
10/16/1998	1620.95	128.46	8.6
12/18/1987	326.91	24.34	8.0
5/2/1997	1305.33	96.04	7.9
1/9/1987	380.65	27.39	7.8
8/3/1984	246.24	16.94	7.4
7/2/1999	2741.02	188.37	7.4
1/29/1999	2505.89	167.01	7.1
10/5/2001	1605.30	106.50	7.1
3/3/2000	4914.79	324.29	7.1
3/8/2002	1929.67	126.93	7.0
1/8/1999	2344.41	151.72	6.9

WORST TWENTY WEEKS SINCE 1971 BY %

Week Ending	NASDAQ Close	Points Change	% Change
4/14/00	3321.29	−1125.16	−25.3
10/23/87	328.45	− 77.88	−19.2
9/21/01	1423.19	− 272.19	−16.1
11/10/00	3028.99	− 422.59	−12.2
7/28/00	3663.00	− 431.45	−10.5
12/15/00	2653.27	− 264.16	− 9.1
12/1/00	2645.29	− 259.09	− 8.9
8/28/98	1639.68	− 157.93	− 8.8
10/20/78	123.82	− 11.76	− 8.7
10/6/00	3361.01	− 311.81	− 8.5
6/15/01	2028.43	− 186.67	− 8.4
9/12/86	346.78	− 31.58	− 8.3
1/28/00	3887.07	− 348.33	− 8.2
3/16/01	1890.91	− 161.87	− 7.9
3/31/00	4572.83	− 390.20	− 7.9
10/12/79	140.71	− 11.58	− 7.6
10/9/98	1492.49	− 122.49	− 7.6
5/12/00	3529.06	− 287.76	− 7.5
12/6/74	58.21	− 4.74	− 7.5
3/7/80	146.19	− 11.84	− 7.5

Based on NASDAQ composite, prior to February 5, 1971, based on National Quotation Bureau indices

BEST & WORST <u>DOW</u> MONTHS
SINCE 1901 BY POINTS AND PERCENT

BEST TWENTY MONTHS SINCE 1901 BY POINTS

Month	DJIA Close	Points Change	% Change
Apr-1999	10789.04	1002.88	10.2
Apr-2001	10734.97	856.19	8.7
Oct-2002	8397.03	805.10	10.6
Mar-2000	10921.92	793.61	7.8
Nov-2001	9851.56	776.42	8.6
Oct-1998	8592.10	749.48	9.6
Aug-2000	11215.10	693.12	6.6
Dec-2003	10453.92	671.46	6.9
Feb-1998	8545.72	639.22	8.1
Dec-1999	11497.12	619.31	5.7
Jul-1997	8222.61	549.82	7.2
Oct-2003	9801.12	526.06	5.7
Nov-1998	9116.55	524.45	6.1
Nov-2002	8896.09	499.06	5.9
Nov-1996	6521.70	492.32	8.2
Apr-2003	8480.09	487.96	6.1
Mar-1999	9786.16	479.58	5.2
Apr-1997	7008.99	425.51	6.5
Jun-1999	10970.80	411.06	3.9
Oct-1999	10729.86	392.91	3.8

WORST TWENTY MONTHS SINCE 1901 BY POINTS

Month	DJIA Close	Points Change	% Change
Aug-1998	7539.07	−1344.22	− 15.1
Sep-2001	8847.56	−1102.19	− 11.1
Sep-2002	7591.93	−1071.57	− 12.4
Feb-2000	10128.31	− 812.22	− 7.4
Jun-2002	9243.26	− 681.99	− 6.9
Mar-2001	9878.78	− 616.50	− 5.9
Oct-1987	1993.53	− 602.75	− 23.2
Aug-1997	7622.42	− 600.19	− 7.3
Aug-2001	9949.75	− 573.06	− 5.4
Sep-2000	10650.92	− 564.18	− 5.0
Nov-2000	10414.49	− 556.65	− 5.1
Jan-2000	10940.53	− 556.59	− 4.8
Dec-2002	8341.63	− 554.46	− 6.2
Jul-2002	8736.59	− 506.67	− 5.5
Oct-1997	7442.08	− 503.18	− 6.3
Sep-1999	10336.95	− 492.33	− 4.5
Apr-2002	9946.22	− 457.72	− 4.4
Jun-2001	10502.40	− 409.54	− 3.8
Feb-2001	10495.28	− 392.08	− 3.6
Jul-1999	10655.15	− 315.65	− 2.9

BEST TWENTY MONTHS SINCE 1950 BY %

Month	DJIA Close	Points Change	% Change
Jan-1976	975.28	122.87	14.4
Jan-1975	703.69	87.45	14.2
Jan-1987	2158.04	262.09	13.8
Aug-1982	901.31	92.71	11.5
Oct-1982	991.72	95.47	10.7
Oct-2002	8397.03	805.10	10.6
Apr-1978	837.32	79.96	10.6
Apr-1999	10789.04	1002.88	10.2
Nov-1962	649.30	59.53	10.1
Nov-1954	386.77	34.63	9.8
Aug-1984	1224.38	109.10	9.8
Oct-1998	8592.10	749.48	9.6
Oct-1974	665.52	57.65	9.5
Dec-1991	3168.83	274.15	9.5
Jul-1989	2660.66	220.60	9.0
Feb-1986	1709.06	138.07	8.8
Apr-2001	10734.97	856.19	8.7
Nov-2001	9851.56	776.42	8.6
Apr-1968	912.22	71.55	8.5
Apr-1983	1226.20	96.17	8.5

WORST TWENTY MONTHS SINCE 1950 BY %

Month	DJIA Close	Points Change	% Change
Oct-1987	1993.53	− 602.75	− 23.2
Aug-1998	7539.07	−1344.22	− 15.1
Nov-1973	822.25	− 134.33	− 14.0
Sep-2002	7591.93	−1071.57	− 12.4
Sep-2001	8847.56	−1102.19	− 11.1
Sep-1974	607.87	− 70.71	− 10.4
Aug-1974	678.58	− 78.85	− 10.4
Aug-1990	2614.36	− 290.84	− 10.0
Mar-1980	785.75	− 77.39	− 9.0
Jun-1962	561.28	− 52.08	− 8.5
Oct-1978	792.45	− 73.37	− 8.5
Jan-1960	622.62	− 56.74	− 8.4
Nov-1987	1833.55	− 159.98	− 8.0
May-1962	613.36	− 51.97	− 7.8
Aug-1981	881.47	− 70.87	− 7.4
Feb-2000	10128.31	− 812.22	− 7.4
May-1956	478.05	− 38.07	− 7.4
Jan-1978	769.92	− 61.25	− 7.4
Sep-1960	580.14	− 45.85	− 7.3
Aug-1997	7622.42	− 600.19	− 7.3

BEST TEN MONTHS 1901-1949 BY %

Month	DJIA Close	Points Change	% Change
Apr-1933	77.66	22.26	40.2
Aug-1932	73.16	18.90	34.8
Jul-1932	54.26	11.42	26.7
Jun-1938	133.88	26.14	24.3
Apr-1915	71.78	10.95	18.0
Jun-1931	150.18	21.72	16.9
Nov-1928	293.38	41.22	16.3
Nov-1904	52.76	6.59	14.3
May-1919	105.50	12.62	13.6
Sep-1939	152.54	18.13	13.5

WORST TEN MONTHS 1901-1949 BY %

Month	DJIA Close	Points Change	% Change
Sep-1931	96.61	− 42.80	− 30.7
Mar-1938	98.95	− 30.69	− 23.7
Apr-1932	56.11	− 17.17	− 23.4
May-1940	116.22	− 32.21	− 21.7
Oct-1929	273.51	− 69.94	− 20.4
May-1932	44.74	− 11.37	− 20.3
Jun-1930	226.34	− 48.73	− 17.7
Dec-1931	77.90	− 15.97	− 17.0
Feb-1933	51.39	− 9.51	− 15.6
May-1931	128.46	− 22.73	− 15.0

BEST TWENTY MONTHS SINCE 1971 BY POINTS

Month	NASDAQ Close	Points Change	% Change
Feb-2000	4696.69	756.34	19.2
Dec-1999	4069.31	733.15	22.0
Jun-2000	3966.11	565.20	16.6
Aug-2000	4206.35	439.36	11.7
Nov-1999	3336.16	369.73	12.5
Jan-1999	2505.89	313.20	14.3
Jan-2001	2772.73	302.21	12.2
Apr-2001	2116.24	275.98	15.0
Dec-1998	2192.69	243.15	12.5
Nov-2001	1930.58	240.38	14.2
Oct-1999	2966.43	220.27	8.0
Jun-1999	2686.12	215.60	8.7
Sep-1998	1693.84	194.59	13.0
Oct-2001	1690.20	191.40	12.8
Nov-1998	1949.54	178.15	10.1
Mar-1999	2461.40	173.37	7.6
Oct-2002	1329.75	157.69	13.5
Jul-1997	1593.81	151.74	10.5
Feb-1998	1770.51	151.15	9.3
Nov-2002	1478.78	149.03	11.2

WORST TWENTY MONTHS SINCE 1971 BY POINTS

Month	NASDAQ Close	Points Change	% Change
Nov-2000	2597.93	− 771.70	− 22.9
Apr-2000	3860.66	− 712.17	− 15.6
Feb-2001	2151.83	− 620.90	− 22.4
Sep-2000	3672.82	− 533.53	− 12.7
May-2000	3400.91	− 459.75	− 11.9
Aug-1998	1499.25	− 373.14	− 19.9
Mar-2001	1840.26	− 311.57	− 14.5
Sep-2001	1498.80	− 306.63	− 17.0
Oct-2000	3369.63	− 303.19	− 8.3
Aug-2001	1805.43	− 221.70	− 10.9
Feb-1999	2288.03	− 217.86	− 8.7
Feb-2002	1731.49	− 202.54	− 10.5
Jul-2000	3766.99	− 199.12	− 5.0
Apr-2002	1688.23	− 157.12	− 8.5
Jun-2002	1463.21	− 152.52	− 9.4
Dec-2002	1335.51	− 143.27	− 9.7
Sep-2002	1172.06	− 142.79	− 10.9
Jul-2002	1328.26	− 134.95	− 9.2
Jul-2001	2027.13	− 133.41	− 6.2
Jan-2000	3940.35	− 128.96	− 3.2

BEST TWENTY MONTHS SINCE 1971 BY %

Month	NASDAQ Close	Points Change	% Change
Dec-1999	4069.31	733.15	22.0
Feb-2000	4696.69	756.34	19.2
Oct-1974	65.23	9.56	17.2
Jan-1975	69.78	9.96	16.6
Jun-2000	3966.11	565.20	16.6
Apr-2001	2116.24	275.98	15.0
Jan-1999	2505.89	313.20	14.3
Nov-2001	1930.58	240.38	14.2
Oct-2002	1329.75	157.69	13.5
Oct-1982	212.63	24.98	13.3
Sep-1998	1693.84	194.59	13.0
Oct-2001	1690.20	191.40	12.8
Jan-1985	278.70	31.35	12.7
Dec-1998	2192.69	243.15	12.5
Nov-1999	3336.16	369.73	12.5
Jan-2001	2772.73	302.21	12.2
Jan-1987	392.06	42.73	12.2
Jan-1976	87.05	9.43	12.1
Dec-1991	586.34	62.44	11.9
Aug-2000	4206.35	439.36	11.7

WORST TWENTY MONTHS SINCE 1971 BY %

Month	NASDAQ Close	Points Change	% Change
Oct-1987	323.30	− 120.99	− 27.2
Nov-2000	2597.93	− 771.70	− 22.9
Feb-2001	2151.83	− 620.90	− 22.4
Aug-1998	1499.25	− 373.14	− 19.9
Mar-1980	131.00	− 27.03	− 17.1
Sep-2001	1498.80	− 306.63	− 17.0
Oct-1978	111.12	− 21.77	− 16.4
Apr-2000	3860.66	− 712.17	− 15.6
Nov-1973	93.51	− 16.66	− 15.1
Mar-2001	1840.26	− 311.57	− 14.5
Aug-1990	381.21	− 57.03	− 13.0
Sep-2000	3672.82	− 533.53	− 12.7
May-2000	3400.91	− 459.75	− 11.9
Aug-2001	1805.43	− 221.70	− 10.9
Aug-1974	62.37	− 7.62	− 10.9
Sep-2002	1172.06	− 142.79	− 10.9
Sep-1974	55.67	− 6.70	− 10.7
Feb-2002	1731.49	− 202.54	− 10.5
Dec-2002	1335.51	− 143.27	− 9.7
Oct-1979	135.53	− 14.45	− 9.6

Based on NASDAQ composite, prior to February 5, 1971, based on National Quotation Bureau indices

BEST & WORST <u>DOW</u> AND <u>NASDAQ</u> YEARS

<u>DOW</u> SINCE 1901 BY POINTS AND PERCENT

BEST FIFTEEN YEARS SINCE 1901 BY POINTS

Year	DJIA Close	Points Change	% Change
1999	11497.12	2315.69	25.2
2003	10453.92	2112.29	25.3
1997	7908.25	1459.98	22.6
1996	6448.27	1331.15	26.0
1995	5117.12	1282.68	33.5
1998	9181.43	1273.18	16.1
1989	2753.20	584.63	27.0
1991	3168.83	535.17	20.3
1993	3754.09	452.98	13.7
1986	1895.95	349.28	22.6
1985	1546.67	335.10	27.7
1975	852.41	236.17	38.3
1988	2168.57	229.74	11.8
1983	1258.64	212.10	20.3
1982	1046.54	171.54	19.6

WORST FIFTEEN YEARS SINCE 1901 BY POINTS

Year	DJIA Close	Points Change	% Change
2002	8341.63	−1679.87	− 16.8
2001	10021.50	− 765.35	− 7.1
2000	10786.85	− 710.27	− 6.2
1974	616.24	− 234.62	− 27.6
1966	785.69	− 183.57	− 18.9
1977	831.17	− 173.48	− 17.3
1973	850.86	− 169.16	− 16.6
1969	800.36	− 143.39	− 15.2
1990	2633.66	− 119.54	− 4.3
1981	875.00	− 88.99	− 9.2
1931	77.90	− 86.68	− 52.7
1930	164.58	− 83.90	− 33.8
1962	652.10	− 79.04	− 10.8
1957	435.69	− 63.78	− 12.8
1960	615.89	− 63.47	− 9.3

BEST FIFTEEN YEARS SINCE 1901 BY %

Year	DJIA Close	Points Change	% Change
1915	99.15	44.57	81.7
1933	99.90	39.97	66.7
1928	300.00	97.60	48.2
1908	63.11	20.07	46.6
1954	404.39	123.49	44.0
1904	50.99	15.01	41.7
1935	144.13	40.09	38.5
1975	852.41	236.17	38.3
1905	70.47	19.48	38.2
1958	583.65	147.96	34.0
1995	5117.12	1282.68	33.5
1919	107.23	25.03	30.5
1925	156.66	36.15	30.0
1927	202.40	45.20	28.8
1938	154.76	33.91	28.1

WORST FIFTEEN YEARS SINCE 1901 BY %

Year	DJIA Close	Points Change	% Change
1931	77.90	− 86.68	− 52.7
1907	43.04	− 26.08	− 37.7
1930	164.58	− 83.90	− 33.8
1920	71.95	− 35.28	− 32.9
1937	120.85	− 59.05	− 32.8
1974	616.24	− 234.62	− 27.6
1903	35.98	− 11.12	− 23.6
1932	59.93	− 17.97	− 23.1
1917	74.38	− 20.62	− 21.7
1966	785.69	− 183.57	− 18.9
1910	59.60	− 12.96	− 17.9
1977	831.17	− 173.48	− 17.3
1929	248.48	− 51.52	− 17.2
2002	8341.63	−1679.87	− 16.8
1973	850.86	− 169.16	− 16.6

<u>NASDAQ</u> SINCE 1971 BY POINTS AND PERCENT

BEST TEN YEARS SINCE 1971 BY POINTS

Year	NASDAQ Close	Points Change	% Change
1999	4069.31	1876.62	85.6
2003	2003.37	667.86	50.0
1998	2192.69	622.34	39.6
1995	1052.13	300.17	39.9
1997	1570.35	279.32	21.6
1996	1291.03	238.90	22.7
1991	586.34	212.50	56.8
1993	776.80	99.85	14.7
1992	676.95	90.61	15.5
1985	324.93	77.58	31.4

WORST TEN YEARS SINCE 1971 BY POINTS

Year	NASDAQ Close	Points Change	% Change
2000	2470.52	−1598.79	− 39.3
2002	1335.51	− 614.89	− 31.5
2001	1950.40	− 520.12	− 21.1
1990	373.84	− 80.98	− 17.8
1973	92.19	− 41.54	− 31.1
1974	59.82	− 32.37	− 35.1
1984	247.35	− 31.25	− 11.2
1994	751.96	− 24.84	− 3.2
1987	330.47	− 18.86	− 5.4
1981	195.84	− 6.50	− 3.2

BEST TEN YEARS SINCE 1971 BY %

Year	NASDAQ Close	Points Change	% Change
1999	4069.31	1876.62	85.6
1991	586.34	212.50	56.8
2003	2003.37	667.86	50.0
1995	1052.13	300.17	39.9
1998	2192.69	622.34	39.6
1980	202.34	51.20	33.9
1985	324.93	77.58	31.4
1975	77.62	17.80	29.8
1979	151.14	33.16	28.1
1971	114.12	24.51	27.4

WORST TEN YEARS SINCE 1971 BY %

Year	NASDAQ Close	Points Change	% Change
2000	2470.52	−1598.79	− 39.3
1974	59.82	− 32.37	− 35.1
2002	1335.51	− 614.89	− 31.5
1973	92.19	− 41.54	− 31.1
2001	1950.40	− 520.12	− 21.1
1990	373.84	− 80.98	− 17.8
1984	247.35	− 31.25	− 11.2
1987	330.47	− 18.86	− 5.4
1981	195.84	− 6.50	− 3.2
1994	751.96	− 24.84	− 3.2

Based on NASDAQ composite, prior to February 5, 1971, based on National Quotation Bureau indices

STRATEGY PLANNING & RECORD SECTION

CONTENTS

PORTFOLIO AT START OF 2005

DATE ACQUIRED	NO. OF SHARES	SECURITY	PRICE	TOTAL COST	PAPER PROFITS	PAPER LOSSES

PORTFOLIO AT START OF 2005

DATE ACQUIRED	NO. OF SHARES	SECURITY	PRICE	TOTAL COST	PAPER PROFITS	PAPER LOSSES

ADDITIONAL PURCHASES

DATE ACQUIRED	NO. OF SHARES	SECURITY	PRICE	TOTAL COST	REASON FOR PURCHASE PRIME OBJECTIVE, ETC.

ADDITIONAL PURCHASES

DATE ACQUIRED	NO. OF SHARES	SECURITY	PRICE	TOTAL COST	REASON FOR PURCHASE PRIME OBJECTIVE, ETC.

ADDITIONAL PURCHASES

DATE ACQUIRED	NO. OF SHARES	SECURITY	PRICE	TOTAL COST	REASON FOR PURCHASE PRIME OBJECTIVE, ETC.

HORT–TERM TRANSACTIONS

Pages 167–176 can accompany next year's income tax return (Schedule D). Enter transactions as completed to avoid last minute pressures.

NO. OF SHARES	SECURITY	DATE ACQUIRED	DATE SOLD	SALE PRICE	COST	LOSS	GAIN

TOTALS: Carry over to next page

167

SHORT–TERM TRANSACTIONS *(continued)*

NO. OF SHARES	SECURITY	DATE ACQUIRED	DATE SOLD	SALE PRICE	COST	LOSS	GAIN

TOTALS:

NO. OF SHARES	SECURITY	DATE ACQUIRED	DATE SOLD	SALE PRICE	COST	LOSS	GAIN

TOTALS:

Carry over to next page

SHORT–TERM TRANSACTIONS *(continued)*

NO. OF SHARES	SECURITY	DATE ACQUIRED	DATE SOLD	SALE PRICE	COST	LOSS	GAIN

TOTALS:

HORT–TERM TRANSACTIONS *(continued)*

NO. OF SHARES	SECURITY	DATE ACQUIRED	DATE SOLD	SALE PRICE	COST	LOSS	GAIN

TOTALS:
Carry over to next page

SHORT–TERM TRANSACTIONS *(continued)*

NO. OF SHARES	SECURITY	DATE ACQUIRED	DATE SOLD	SALE PRICE	COST	LOSS	GAIN

TOTALS:

ONG–TERM TRANSACTIONS

Pages 167–176 can accompany next year's income tax return (Schedule D). Enter transactions as completed to avoid last minute pressures.

NO. OF SHARES	SECURITY	DATE ACQUIRED	DATE SOLD	SALE PRICE	COST	LOSS	GAIN

TOTALS:
Carry over to next page

LONG–TERM TRANSACTIONS *(continued)*

NO. OF SHARES	SECURITY	DATE ACQUIRED	DATE SOLD	SALE PRICE	COST	LOSS	GAIN

TOTALS:

NO. OF SHARES	SECURITY	DATE ACQUIRED	DATE SOLD	SALE PRICE	COST	LOSS	GAIN

TOTALS:
Carry over to next page

LONG–TERM TRANSACTIONS *(continued)*

NO. OF SHARES	SECURITY	DATE ACQUIRED	DATE SOLD	SALE PRICE	COST	LOSS	GAIN

TOTALS:

NTEREST/DIVIDENDS RECEIVED DURING 2005

HARES	STOCK/BOND	FIRST QUARTER		SECOND QUARTER		THIRD QUARTER		FOURTH QUARTER	
		$		$		$		$	

BROKERAGE ACCOUNT DATA 2005

	MARGIN INTEREST	TRANSFER TAXES	CAPITAL ADDED	CAPITAL WITHDRAWN
JAN				
FEB				
MAR				
APR				
MAY				
JUN				
JUL				
AUG				
SEP				
OCT				
NOV				
DEC				

PORTFOLIO AT END OF 2005

DATE ACQUIRED	NO. OF SHARES	SECURITY	PRICE	TOTAL COST	PAPER PROFITS	PAPER LOSSES

PORTFOLIO AT END OF 2005

DATE ACQUIRED	NO. OF SHARES	SECURITY	PRICE	TOTAL COST	PAPER PROFITS	PAPER LOSSES

PORTFOLIO PRICE RECORD 2005 (FIRST HALF)

Place purchase price above stock name and weekly closes below

STOCKS Week Ending	1	2	3	4	5	6	7	8	9	10
JANUARY 7										
14										
21										
28										
FEBRUARY 4										
11										
18										
25										
MARCH 4										
11										
18										
25										
APRIL 1										
8										
15										
22										
29										
MAY 6										
13										
20										
27										
JUNE 3										
10										
17										
24										

PORTFOLIO PRICE RECORD 2005 (FIRST HALF)

Place purchase price above stock name and weekly closes below

STOCKS / Week Ending	11	12	13	14	15	16	17	18	Dow Jones Industrial Average	Net Change For Week
7										
14										
21										
28										
4										
11										
18										
25										
4										
11										
18										
25										
1										
8										
15										
22										
29										
6										
13										
20										
27										
3										
10										
17										
24										

PORTFOLIO PRICE RECORD 2005 (SECOND HALF)

Place purchase price above stock name and weekly closes below

	STOCKS									
Week Ending	1	2	3	4	5	6	7	8	9	10
JULY 1										
8										
15										
22										
29										
AUGUST 5										
12										
19										
26										
SEPTEMBER 2										
9										
16										
23										
30										
OCTOBER 7										
14										
21										
28										
NOVEMBER 4										
11										
18										
25										
DECEMBER 2										
9										
16										
23										
30										

PORTFOLIO PRICE RECORD 2005 (SECOND HALF)

Place purchase price above stock name and weekly closes below

STOCKS / Week Ending	11	12	13	14	15	16	17	18	Dow Jones Industrial Average	Net Change For Week
1										
8										
15										
22										
29										
5										
12										
19										
26										
2										
9										
16										
23										
30										
7										
14										
21										
28										
4										
11										
18										
25										
2										
9										
16										
23										
30										

SEPTEMBER

OCTOBER

NOVEMBER

DECEMBER

WEEKLY INDICATOR DATA 2005 (FIRST HALF)

	Week Ending	Dow Jones Industrial Average	Net Change For Week	Net Change On Friday	Net Change Next Monday	S&P Or NASDAQ	NYSE Ad-vances	NYSE De-clines	New Highs	New Lows	CBOE Put/Call Ratio	90-Day Treas. Rate	Mood AAA Rate
JANUARY	7												
	14												
	21												
	28												
FEBRUARY	4												
	11												
	18												
	25												
MARCH	4												
	11												
	18												
	25												
APRIL	1												
	8												
	15												
	22												
	29												
MAY	6												
	13												
	20												
	27												
JUNE	3												
	10												
	17												
	24												

WEEKLY INDICATOR DATA 2005 (SECOND HALF)

Week Ending	Dow Jones Industrial Average	Net Change For Week	Net Change On Friday	Net Change Next Monday	S&P Or NASDAQ	NYSE Ad-vances	NYSE De-clines	New Highs	New Lows	CBOE Put/Call Ratio	90-Day Treas. Rate	Moody's AAA Rate
1												
8												
15												
22												
29												
5												
12												
19												
26												
2												
9												
16												
23												
30												
7												
14												
21												
28												
4												
11												
18												
25												
2												
9												
16												
23												
30												

MONTHLY INDICATOR DATA 2005

	DJIA% Last 3 + 1st 2 Days	DJIA% 9th - 11th Trading Days	DJIA% Change Rest Of Month	DJIA% Change Whole Month	% Change Your Stocks	Gross Domestic Product	Prime Rate	Trade Deficit $ Billion	CPI % Change	% Unemployment Rate
JAN										
FEB										
MAR										
APR										
MAY										
JUN										
JUL										
AUG										
SEP										
OCT										
NOV										
DEC										

INSTRUCTIONS:

Weekly Indicator Data (pages 184-185). Keeping data on several indicators may give you a better feel of the market. In addition to the closing DJIA and its net change for the week, post the net change for Friday's Dow and also the following Monday's. A series of "down Fridays" followed by "down Mondays" often precedes a downswing. Tracking either the S&P or NASDAQ composite, and advances and declines, will help prevent the Dow from misleading you. New highs and lows and put/call ratios (www.cboe.com) are also useful indicators. All these weekly figures appear in weekend papers or *Barron's*. Data for 90-day Treasury Rate and Moody's AAA Bond Rate are quite important to track short- and long-term interest rates. These figures are available from:

Weekly U.S. Financial Data
Federal Reserve Bank of St. Louis
P.O. Box 442
St. Louis MO 63166
http://research.stlouisfed.org

Monthly Indicator Data. The purpose of the first three columns is to enable you to track the market's bullish bias near the end, beginning and middle of the month, which has been shifting lately (see pages 88, 136 & 137). Market direction, performance of your stocks, Gross Domestic Product, Prime Rate, Trade Deficit, Consumer Price Index, and Unemployment Rate are worthwhile indicators to follow. Or, readers may wish to gauge other data.

IF YOU DON'T PROFIT FROM YOUR
INVESTMENT MISTAKES, SOMEONE ELSE WILL

No matter how much we may deny it, almost every successful person in Wall Street pays a great deal of attention to trading suggestions—especially when they come from "the right sources."

One of the hardest things to learn is to distinguish between good tips and bad ones. Usually the best tips have a logical reason in back of them, which accompanies the tip. Poor tips usually have no reason to support them.

The important thing to remember is that the market discounts. It does not review, it does not reflect. The Street's real interest in "tips," inside information, buying and selling suggestions, and everything else of this kind emanates from a desire to find out just what the market has on hand to discount. The process of finding out involves separating the wheat from the chaff—and there is plenty of chaff.

HOW TO MAKE USE OF STOCK "TIPS"

- The source should be **reliable**. (By listing all "tips" and suggestions on a Performance Record of Recommendations, such as below, and then periodically evaluating the outcomes, you will soon know the "batting average" of your sources.)

- The story should make sense. Would the merger violate anti-trust laws? Are there too many computers on the market already? How many years will it take to become profitable?

- The stock should not have had a recent sharp run-up. Otherwise, the story may already be discounted and confirmation or denial in the press would most likely be accompanied by a sell-off in the stock.

PERFORMANCE RECORD OF RECOMMENDATIONS

STOCK RECOMMENDED	BY WHOM	DATE	PRICE	REASON FOR RECOMMENDATION	SUBSEQUENT ACTION OF STOCK

INDIVIDUAL RETIREMENT ACCOUNTS: MOST AWESOME INVESTMENT INCENTIVE EVER DEVISED

MAX IRA INVESTMENTS OF $3,000 A YEAR COMPOUNDING AT VARIOUS RATES OF RETURN FOR DIFFERENT PERIODS

Annual Rate	5 Yrs	10 Yrs	15 Yrs	20 Yrs	25 Yrs	30 Yrs	35 Yrs	40 Yrs	45 Yrs	50 Yrs
1%	$15,456	$31,701	$48,774	$66,718	$85,577	$105,398	$126,231	$148,126	$171,138	$195,323
2%	15,924	33,506	52,918	74,350	98,013	124,138	152,983	184,830	219,992	258,813
3%	16,405	35,423	57,471	83,029	112,659	147,008	186,828	232,990	286,504	348,542
4%	16,899	37,459	62,474	92,908	129,935	174,985	229,795	296,480	377,612	476,321
5%	17,406	39,620	67,972	104,158	150,340	209,282	284,509	380,519	503,055	659,446
6%	17,926	41,915	74,018	116,978	174,469	251,405	354,363	492,143	676,524	923,268
7%	18,460	44,351	80,664	131,596	203,029	303,219	443,740	640,829	917,255	1,304,958
8%	19,008	46,936	87,973	148,269	236,863	367,038	558,306	839,343	1,252,278	1,859,015
9%	19,570	49,681	96,010	167,294	276,972	445,726	705,374	1,104,876	1,719,558	2,665,323
10%	20,147	52,594	104,849	189,007	324,545	542,830	894,380	1,460,555	2,372,386	3,840,898
11%	20,739	55,684	114,570	213,795	380,996	662,740	1,137,493	1,937,481	3,285,506	5,557,008
12%	21,346	58,964	125,260	242,096	448,002	810,878	1,450,389	2,577,427	4,563,653	8,064,061
13%	21,968	62,443	137,015	274,410	527,550	993,945	1,853,248	3,436,457	6,353,418	11,727,729
14%	22,607	66,134	149,941	311,305	621,998	1,220,211	2,372,019	4,589,726	8,859,732	17,081,263
15%	23,261	70,048	164,152	353,430	734,136	1,499,871	3,040,037	6,137,862	12,368,693	24,901,121
16%	23,932	74,199	179,775	401,522	867,265	1,845,485	3,900,081	8,215,435	17,279,153	36,316,058
17%	24,621	78,600	196,947	456,416	1,025,288	2,272,511	5,006,983	11,002,172	24,146,310	52,964,151
18%	25,326	83,265	215,817	519,063	1,212,816	2,799,956	6,430,947	14,737,774	33,741,783	77,218,352
19%	26,049	88,211	236,551	590,542	1,435,292	3,451,162	8,261,743	19,741,489	47,136,224	112,509,751
20%	26,790	93,451	259,326	672,077	1,699,132	4,254,774	10,614,028	26,437,888	65,812,716	163,789,887

TOP 140 EXCHANGE TRADED FUNDS

(Traded on the American Stock Exchange. See page 118 for Sector Seasonalities.)

Ticker	Exchange Traded Fund	Ticker	Exchange Traded Fund
SPY	S&P 500 SPDRS	XLY	Select Sector SPDR-Consumer
DIA	Dow Jones Industrials DIAMONDS	XLP	Select Sector SPDR-Consumer Staples
MDY	MidCap SPDRS	XLE	Select Sector SPDR-Energy
QQQ	Nasdaq-100 Index	XLF	Select Sector SPDR-Financial
FFF	FORTUNE 500 Index	XLV	Select Sector SPDR-Health Care
RSP	Rydex S&P Equal Weight ETF	XLI	Select Sector SPDR-Industrial
OEF	iShares S&P 100 Index Fund	XLB	Select Sector SPDR-Materials
ISI	iShares S&P 1500 Index Fund	XLK	Select Sector SPDR-Technology
IVV	iShares S&P 500	XLU	Select Sector SPDR-Utilities
NEQ	Fidelity NASDAQ Composite*	DGT	streetTRACKS DJ Global Titans
PWC	PowerShares Dynamic Market Portfolio	ELG	streetTRACKS DJ US Large Cap Growth
PWO	PowerShares Dynamic OTC Portfolio	ELV	streetTRACKS DJ US Large Cap Value
BHH	B2B Internet HOLDRS	DSG	streetTRACKS DJ US Small Cap Growth
BBH	Biotech HOLDRS	DSV	streetTRACKS DJ US Small Cap Value
BDH	Broadband HOLDRS	MTK	streetTRACKS Morgan Stanley Technology
EKH	Europe 2001 HOLDRS	RWR	streetTRACKS Wilshire REIT
IAH	Internet Architecture HOLDRS	VCR	Vanguard Consumer Discretionary VIPERs
HHH	Internet HOLDRS	VDC	Vanguard Consumer Staples VIPERs
IIH	Internet Infrastructure HOLDRS	VXF	Vanguard Extended Market VIPERs
MKH	Market 2000+ HOLDRS	VFH	Vanguard Financials VIPERs
OIH	Oil Service HOLDRS	VUG	Vanguard Growth VIPERs
PPH	Pharmaceutical HOLDRS	VHT	Vanguard Health Care VIPERs
RKH	Regional Bank HOLDRS	VGT	Vanguard Information Technology VIPERs
RTH	Retail HOLDRS	VV	Vanguard Large-Cap VIPERs
SMH	Semiconductor HOLDRS	VAW	Vanguard Materials VIPERs
SWH	Software HOLDRS	VO	Vanguard Mid-Cap VIPERs
TTH	Telecom HOLDRS	VBK	Vanguard Small-Cap Growth VIPERs
UTH	Utilities HOLDRS	VBR	Vanguard Small-Cap Value VIPERs
WMH	Wireless HOLDRS	VB	Vanguard Small-Cap VIPERs
ICF	iShares Cohen & Steers Realty Majors	VTI	Vanguard Total Stock Market VIPERs
IYT	iShares DJ US Transportation	VPU	Vanguard Utilities VIPERs
IYM	iShares Dow Jones US Basic Materials	VTV	Vanguard Value VIPERs
IYK	iShares Dow Jones US Cons Non-Cyclical	LQD	iShares Goldman Sachs InvesTop Corp Bond
IYC	iShares Dow Jones US Consumer Cyclical	IGE	iShares Goldman Sachs Natural Resources
IYE	iShares Dow Jones US Energy	IGN	iShares Goldman Sachs Networking
IYF	iShares Dow Jones US Financial Sector	IGW	iShares Goldman Sachs Semiconductor
IYG	iShares Dow Jones US Financial Services	IGV	iShares Goldman Sachs Software
IYH	iShares Dow Jones US Healthcare	IGM	iShares Goldman Sachs Technology
IYJ	iShares Dow Jones US Industrial	SHY	iShares Lehman 1-3 Year Treasury Bond
IYR	iShares Dow Jones US Real Estate	TLT	iShares Lehman 20+ Year Treasury Bond
IYW	iShares Dow Jones US Technology	IEF	iShares Lehman 7-10 Year Treasury Bond
IYZ	iShares Dow Jones US Telecom	AGG	iShares Lehman Aggregate Bond Fund
IYY	iShares Dow Jones US Total Market	IWB	iShares Russell 1000
IDU	iShares Dow Jones US Utilities	IWF	iShares Russell 1000 Growth
EWA	iShares MSCI - Australia	IWD	iShares Russell 1000 Value
EWO	iShares MSCI - Austria	IWM	iShares Russell 2000
EWK	iShares MSCI - Belgium	IWO	iShares Russell 2000 Growth
EWZ	iShares MSCI - Brazil	IWN	iShares Russell 2000 Value
EWC	iShares MSCI - Canada	IWV	iShares Russell 3000
EFA	iShares MSCI - EAFE	IWZ	iShares Russell 3000 Growth
EEM	iShares MSCI - Emerging Markets	IWW	iShares Russell 3000 Value
EZU	iShares MSCI - EMU (European Union)	IWR	iShares Russell Midcap
EWQ	iShares MSCI - France	IWP	iShares Russell MidCap Growth
EWG	iShares MSCI - Germany	IWS	iShares Russell MidCap Value
EWH	iShares MSCI - Hong Kong	IVW	iShares S&P 500/BARRA Growth
EWI	iShares MSCI - Italy	IVE	iShares S&P 500/BARRA Value
EWJ	iShares MSCI - Japan	IEV	iShares S&P Europe 350
EWM	iShares MSCI - Malaysia	IXC	iShares S&P Global Energy
EWW	iShares MSCI - Mexico	IXG	iShares S&P Global Financial
EWN	iShares MSCI - Netherlands	IXJ	iShares S&P Global Healthcare
EWS	iShares MSCI - Singapore	IXN	iShares S&P Global Info Technology
EZA	iShares MSCI - South Africa	IXP	iShares S&P Global Telecommunications
EWY	iShares MSCI - South Korea	ILF	iShares S&P Latin America 40
EWP	iShares MSCI - Spain	IJH	iShares S&P MidCap 400
EWD	iShares MSCI - Sweden	IJK	iShares S&P MidCap 400/BARRA Growth
EWL	iShares MSCI - Switzerland	IJJ	iShares S&P MidCap 400/BARRA Value
EWT	iShares MSCI - Taiwan	IJR	iShares S&P SmallCap 600
EWU	iShares MSCI - United Kingdom	IJT	iShares S&P SmallCap 600/BARRA Growth
EPP	iShares MSCI - Pacific Ex-Japan	IJS	iShares S&P SmallCap 600/BARRA Value
IBB	iShares Nasdaq Biotechnology	ITF	iShares S&P TOPIX 150

*Traded on NASDAQ

G.M. LOEB'S "BATTLE PLAN" FOR INVESTMENT SURVIVAL

LIFE IS CHANGE: Nothing can ever be the same a minute from now as it was minute ago. Everything you own is changing in price and value. You can find th last price of an active security on the stock ticker, but you cannot find the next pri anywhere. The value of your money is changing. Even the value of your home changing, though no one walks in front of it with a sandwich board consistent posting the changes.

RECOGNIZE CHANGE: Your basic objective should be to profit from chang The art of investing is being able to recognize change and to adjust investme goals accordingly.

WRITE THINGS DOWN: You will score more investment success and avo more investment failures if you write things down. Very few investors have the dri and inclination to do this.

KEEP A CHECKLIST: If you aim to improve your investment results, get into th habit of keeping a checklist on every issue you consider buying. Before making a con mitment, it will pay you to write down the answers to at least some of the basic que tions—How much am I investing in this company? How much do I think I can make How much do I have to risk? How long do I expect to take to reach my goal?

HAVE A SINGLE RULING REASON: Above all, writing things down is the best wa to find "the ruling reason." When all is said and done, there is invariably a single reaso that stands out above all others why a particular security transaction can be expected t show a profit. All too often many relatively unimportant statistics are allowed to obscur this single important point.

Any one of a dozen factors may be the point of a particular purchase or sale. It coul be a technical reason—an increase in earnings or dividend not yet discounted in th market price—a change of management—a promising new product—an expecte improvement in the market's valuation of earnings—or many others. But, in an given case, one of these factors will almost certainly be more important than all th rest put together.

CLOSING OUT A COMMITMENT: If you have a loss, the solution is automatic provided you decide what to do at the time you buy. Otherwise, the question divide itself into two parts. Are we in a bull or bear market? Few of us really know unti it is too late. For the sake of the record, if you think it is a bear market, just pu that consideration first and sell as much as your conviction suggests and you nature allows.

If you think it is a bull market, or at least a market where some stocks move up, some mark time and only a few decline, do not sell unless:

✓ You see a bear market ahead.

✓ You see trouble for a particular company in which you own shares.

✓ Time and circumstances have turned up a new and seemingly far better buy than the issue you like least in your list.

✓ Your shares stop going up and start going down.

A subsidiary question is, which stock to sell first? Two further observations may help:

✓ Do not sell solely because you think a stock is "overvalued."

✓ If you want to sell some of your stocks and not all, in most cases it is better to go against your emotional inclinations and sell first the issues with losses, small profits or none at all, the weakest, the most disappointing, etc.

Mr. Loeb is the author of *The Battle for Investment Survival*, John Wiley & Sons.

G.M. LOEB'S INVESTMENT SURVIVAL CHECKLIST

OBJECTIVES AND RISKS

Security	Price	Shares	Date

"Ruling reason" for commitment	Amount of commitment $_____
	% of my investment capital _____%

Price objective	Est. time to achieve it	I will risk _____ points	Which would be $_____

TECHNICAL POSITION

Price action of stock:

☐ hitting new highs   ☐ in a trading range

☐ pausing in an uptrend   ☐ moving up from low ground

☐ acting stronger than market   ☐ _____

Dow Jones Industrial Average

Trend of Market

SELECTED YARDSTICKS

	Price Range		Earnings Per Share Actual or Projected	Price/Earnings Ratio Actual or Projected
	High	Low		
Current Year				
Previous Year				

Merger Possibilities	Years for earnings to double in past
Comment on Future	Years for market price to double in past

PERIODIC RE-CHECKS

Date	Stock Price	D.J.I.A.	Comment	Action taken, if any

COMPLETED TRANSACTIONS

Date Closed	Period of time held	Profit or loss

Reason for profit or loss

IMPORTANT CONTACTS

NAME	TELEPHONE	E-MAIL